Director 8®
Primer

ISBN 0-13-090970-X

90000

9 780130 909701

Prentice Hall PTR
The Primer Series

Director 8® Primer

DENNIS CHOMINSKY

Prentice Hall PTR
Upper Saddle River, NJ 07458
www.phptr.com

Library of Congress Cataloging-in-Publication Data

Chominsky, Dennis.
    Director 8 primer / Dennis Chominsky
       p. cm.
    Includes index.
    ISBN 0-13-090970-X
     1. Interactive multimedia. 2. Director (Computer file). I. Title

QA76.76.I59 2001
006.7'869--dc21

00-053762

Production Editor: Wil Mara
Acquisitions Editor: Tim Moore
Editorial Assistant: Allyson Kloss
Marketing Manager: Debby van Dijk
Manufacturing Manager: Alexis R. Heydt
Cover Designer: Anthony Gemmellaro
Cover Design Direction: Jerry Votta
Art Director: Gail Cocker-Bogusz
Composition: Ronnie Bucci

 © 2001 Prentice Hall PTR
Prentice-Hall, Inc.
Upper Saddle River, NJ 07458

The publisher offers discounts on this book when ordered in bulk quantities. For more information contact: Corporate Sales Department, Prentice Hall PTR, One Lake Street, Upper Saddle River, NJ 07458. Phone: 800-382-3419; Fax: 201-236-7141; E-mail: corpsales@prenhall.com

Printed in the United States of America

10 9 8 7 6 5 4 3 2 1

ISBN 0-13-090970-X

Prentice-Hall International (UK) Limited, *London*
Prentice-Hall of Australia Pty. Limited, *Sydney*
Prentice-Hall Canada Inc., *Toronto*
Prentice-Hall Hispanoamericana, S.A., *Mexico*
Prentice-Hall of India Private Limited, *New Delhi*
Prentice-Hall of Japan, Inc., *Tokyo*
Pearson Education Asia Pte. Ltd.
Editora Prentice-Hall do Brasil, Ltda., *Rio de Janeiro*

This book is dedicated to

Mom and Dad.

Thanks for all of your love and support.

CONTENTS

CHAPTER 2

CHAPTER 3

NAVIGATIONAL CONTROLS FOR INTERACTIVE APPLICATIONS

CHAPTER 4

CHAPTER 5

IMAGING AND ANIMATION: THE KEYS TO DIRECTOR ..107

CHAPTER 6

CHAPTER 7

CHAPTER 8

CHAPTER 9

ADVANCING TECHNIQUES WITH BEHAVIORS AND LINGO 257

CHAPTER 10

CHAPTER 11

INTRODUCTION

In the past few years, I have seen interactive presentations that have ranged from simple slide shows to the most unbelievable interactive programs. Some have been run from CD-ROMs, others have streamed over the Internet. Director has truly become the industry standard among programs for creating and distributing interactive applications with its award-winning power, performance, and productivity.

This book will benefit you if you have worked in Director before and want to improve your knowledge of how the program works. Each chapter breaks down areas where most Director users either stumble into problems and need work-arounds or hit creative roadblocks and are looking for ideas that other developers have used in their programs. I think if you read this book with the intention of pulling out the concepts of what can be done, you will position yourself ahead of the pack. The wonderful thing about multimedia is that there are several ways to accomplish the same goals. Some ways may be better than others, depending on the circumstances, but as long as you get the results you were looking for, you did fine.

Due to the vast capabilities of Director, I will only be able to touch on a small amount of the true flexibility and power of this program. I will cover some of the more advanced features and real-life examples for those users who know the basics of Director and are looking to increase their knowledge of the program. Once you have conquered the basics and have a good handle on how Director works, let your imagination run wild with whatever you want to create. This book is written to demonstrate just how easy it is to begin putting together high-powered presentations and interactive multimedia movies. Take the time to experiment on your own. Use the examples presented in this book as just that ... *examples*. What you should get out of each situation presented in this book are ideas that will get you started in the right direction for putting together your own creative programs and the know-how to build the types of projects you used to just admire. Remember, be patient. Miracles may happen overnight, but programming complex interactive applications does not. This book tries to cut through the fluff and focus on the essentials.

WHO SHOULD READ THIS BOOK

This book is written for people who are already designing multimedia applications and want to continue developing their interactive programming abilities to bring their skills up to the next level. This book is intended toward users who:

◆ Are in a hurry—Programmers who want and need information fast.

◆ Already know the basics—This is not an introduction to Director book.

◆ Expect real insight—The examples are from real projects. The Notes, Tips, and Warnings will really give you the perspective you are looking for in a book.

◆ Want to improve the quality of their work—Serious individuals who take pride in developing new applications while learning every step of the way.

Throughout the course of this book, I will introduce different features programmers have been integrating into their applications today. It would be great to fill up a book with the best and wildest programming scripts that have ever been developed, but if they don't warrant any practical use, then I have wasted your time.

HOW THIS BOOK IS WRITTEN

This book is laid out in a way that focuses on some very specific topics within Director. You can use this book as a quick reference, jump-right-in-and-get-the-answer-you need type of book. There are a few sections that do apply a bit more of a basic overtone. The reason for this is that with a program as powerful and dynamic as Director, with the ability to incorporate so many different media types, you need to understand how to put together and use the examples presented throughout the course of this book and look at the bigger picture. By analyzing the examples in this book and formulating your own versions when creating your projects, you will begin to expand the capabilities you can offer to your clients and pick from a multitude of tools to incorporate in your next Director piece.

Each chapter contains a variety of icons, indicating points of interest that will help you while developing your applications. These icons include:

Notes contain information that will make understanding the point being discussed more clear and include any related information that fulfills the topic being discussed.

Tips are suggestions that can save you time and energy while developing your program. Some tips contain recommendations about other topics that will help develop your skills.

These are cautions. I highly recommend you read them to make yourself aware of possible problems or pitfalls you may encounter while programming.

WHAT YOU WILL NEED

I will assume that if you are flipping through the pages of this book, you are interested in using Director or are already a Director programmer. My recommendation to get the best bang from this book is to own or have access to Director so that you can walk through the procedures step by step while working in front of your computer.

The next, and most obvious, thing you will need is a computer. Whether you work on Macintosh or Windows, just about all of the features apply to both platforms. Keep in mind that your original Director movies are cross-platform. Read Chapters 2 and 10 to learn more about working with cross-platform issues. Whichever system you choose, load it up with as much memory as possible. This will make your authoring time more enjoyable, leaving you more time to be creative and not waiting for your computer to process information.

The last thing you will need is Director (the full Studio package will be most beneficial). I also recommend having other third-party programs available, such as Photoshop. These are not necessarily required, but will be essential when building your multimedia applications. You can use just about any type of graphics, animation, audio, or video software to create files that you can import into Director so that you can begin developing your next Director movie.

GOING BEYOND THE BOOK

One thing that makes this book unique is that you can take it beyond the text and images printed on this page. If you need to contact me regarding the topics covered in this book or have suggestions and ideas that you would like to see in the next edition, let me know. I have learned while writing this book that the more you learn about a program, the more you still have to go. If you want to ask a question or show off some of the neat things you have created using Director, email me at **dennis@pfsnewmedia.com.** If you prefer snail mail, send a letter or CD with samples of your work to:

Dennis Chominsky
c/o PFS Marketwyse
409 Minnisink Road
Totowa, NJ 07512

OUTLOOK

Technology is moving faster than some of us can keep up with. Or is it that people today are pushing manufacturers for more features and greater performance out of their software? Whatever the case may be, software developers are constantly striving to improve on the current versions of software in distribution.

I asked a number of my friends and colleagues for their opinion regarding the future of multimedia and the role Director will play in it. A friend and fellow multimedia developer, Eric Mueller, summed up the majority of responses I received with his comments, "The future of Director and the interactive industry as a whole is very bright indeed. New, rich forms of media are continually being developed, allowing developers freedom never before experienced. Through support from these new types of media, developers will finally be free to focus more on content, rather than code ... Additionally, Director has and continues to become highly extensible, allowing developers to not only build their own authoring tools, but extend Director's own environment in ways undoubtedly never imagined by even Director's original authors."

I must agree. I think the information age is going to grow even more than we can imagine. People want more value, more content, an more excitement out of the information around them. I think Director will be one route people will use to provide that information in a more dynamic way. Take a look at the Internet and how it has developed so far. At first, people used it only to transfer files, pass along basic information (usually in text format), and it was accessed only by a select few. Today, I see more sites containing useful information while presenting it in a much more interesting way. Director has the ability to provide the end-user with the interactive capabilities desired for personalizing how that information is found while providing all the flare that catches people's attention. Video, audio, and animation are becoming more commonplace on the Web. The future indeed looks very bright for developers who can take advantage of this need for content-rich information and provide it in a way that will leave the user wanting more.

EXPANDING THE APPLICATIONS

As Director makes programming easier, more people will begin adopting its power and performance. Its flexibility allows for a wide array of users to begin programming whatever type of application they need. There will definitely be more:

◆ Complete Web sites—Including Director's animation, interactivity, and high-performance digital media capabilities.

◆ Corporate presentations—A shift from the over-indulged PowerPoint presentation to something with more impact.

◆ DVD home movies—Adding the extra features and interactive controls that make DVDs a better product than their linear cronies.

◆ Enhanced CDs—All music CDs released from the record companies will have interactive games, bios, and possibly even concert footage clips to go along with the music tracks.

◆ Kiosks—The trend for information kiosks will be popping up everywhere, in schools, in restaurants, and maybe even on sidewalk corners.

All of these things exists right now in some fashion, but will continue to increase at a rapid growth rate as Macromedia introduces more features and easier ways for developers to put these types of applications together.

TO SUM IT UP

This book tells it like it is with real-life examples and real-life applications. With the way technology is changing daily, more people will be using Director because of its flexibility to develop applications to suit specific needs. The great thing about Director is its versatility. It's hard to stop at the basics. More and more, developers are pushing the limits of technology and creativity, putting together some of the most amazing multimedia applications. Once again, I encourage you to read this book, use it as a stepping stone, and then let your creativity take it one step further. Remember, your only limitations are the ones you let stand in your way. Happy programming!

ACKNOWLEDGEMENTS

I think writing this book has pushed me to better understand the makings of this program and has opened my eyes on how the applications I create can expand and benefit the people around me. This book goes out to all the people who, throughout my life, believed in me and gave me the opportunity to fulfill my dreams. Thanks to everyone who has helped me get to where I am. To all my family and friends, I could not have done it without your support. Special thanks to the PFS crew, since these are our projects, ideas and creations that have come to put PFS on the map. Thanks to Joseph Graiff for all of his input with Online Boardwalk.com.

I would like to thank some other people who have, in some way, contributed directly or indirectly to this book, including Phil Pfisterer, Darlene Pepper, Eric Mueller, Trevor Crafts, and Jay Thompson.

To the people who put up with me while writing these books, I owe a great deal of thanks—Mom, Dad, JP, Diana, Tara, Sean, and Kim. To all of my friends: Brad, Joe, Jen, Ruben, Dinger, Andrea, Dave, Jen Rack, Todd, Karen, Ed, Andy, Richelle, and the rest of my friends, I'm available for that beer now. To everyone else who has influenced me and helped me achieve my goals…thanks for your insiration.

chapter 1

WHAT'S NEW IN

DIRECTOR 8

I always have mixed emotions anytime a company releases a new version of its software. On one hand, it involves taking the time to learn the new features and try to adjust to a new way of working with the program. On the other hand, there are usually a number of cool features to add into your repertoire. When I opened Director 8 and installed it on my system, I was excited. At first glance, the interface didn't look that much different. Then, the more I looked around, the more I noticed the new features that will truly make working in Director a breeze. This chapter will highlight many of the new features added into Director 8. I will go into much greater detail with many of them by showing how they are used throughout the course of this book.

PROPERTY INSPECTOR: A NEW WINDOW

The first addition to Director 8 that you should notice is a new window that appears on your screen when you launch Director 8 for the first time. This new (and very useful) window is called the Property Inspector (Figure 1–1). Without a doubt, this window will change the way you work. It doesn't perform any magic tricks and it won't revolutionize the multimedia industry, but instead, it just makes performing all of your daily authoring tasks simpler.

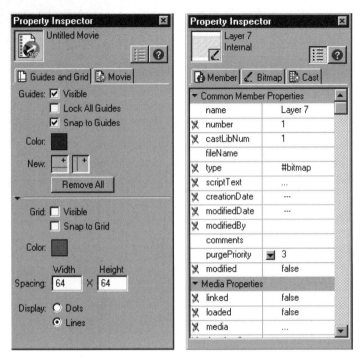

Figure 1–1 The Property Inspector window. You can view it in graphic view (left) or list view (right).

The Property Inspector window provides an easy-to-use, straightforward tool that contains all of the most often used features and functions right in one window. Select one of the tabs to access different attributes of the object you have selected. The Property Inspector adjusts its available categories depending upon what you have selected. Notice how the options change if you select a cast member or a sprite (Figure 1–2).

 If you select multiple items, the Property Inspector only displays the information that is common to all the selected items.

Basically, you will rely on the Property Inspector as command central. This is where you will control most of the attributes for your sprites and cast members. They are all neatly bundled into one area so you can quickly and easily access these options and make changes without having to search all over the place. It gives you one convenient location to adjust:

◆ Starting frames and ending frames.

◆ Inks.

◆ Position.

◆ Size.

◆ Rotation and skew.

◆ Behaviors.

This window will be helpful throughout the course of your programming. Just in the time spent jumping around from window to window to menu to whatever, you'll see how beneficial it is to have all of the most common attribute controls right in one location.

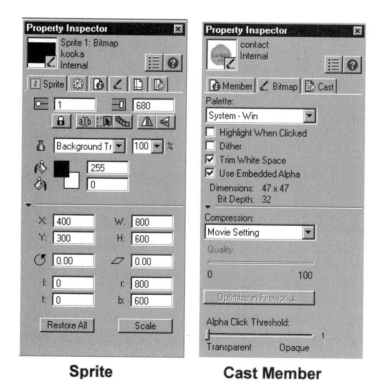

Sprite   **Cast Member**

Figure 1–2 The Property Inspector offers different attributes depending upon what has been selected (sprite vs. cast member).

SEEING IS BELIEVING: A ZOOMABLE STAGE

How many times have you caught yourself squinting at the monitor to see if you've placed an object in the right area or have too many windows open at once that you're constantly opening, closing, and reshuffling around just to see the stage? Well, no more. Now Director 8 offers a zoomable stage. For you Photoshop users, Macromedia has utilized the same commands. Hold the Control key (Windows) or the Command key (Macintosh) and press the plus key (+) to zoom into the stage, magnifying the area you are currently viewing. Hold the Control key (Windows) or the Command key (Macintosh) and press the minus key (-) to zoom out (Figure 1–3, also found in the color section).

If you're not a keyboard person and want to use your mouse to alter the view of your stage:

1. Select Zoom from the View menu.
2. Select Zoom Stage In or Zoom Stage Out on the popup menu or select from one of the predefined percentage settings.

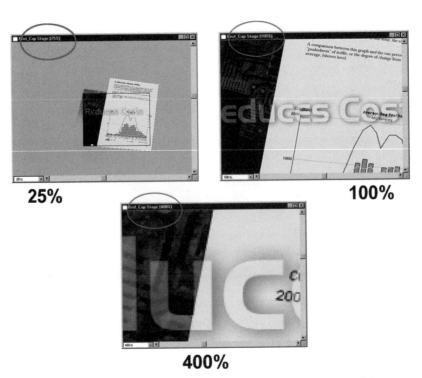

25%   **100%**

400%

Figure 1–3 Director now allows you to increase or decrease your view of the stage.

By decreasing the viewable stage size, you can now see and work in the off-stage canvas area. This helps when trying to adjust the exact placement of sprites that enter the viewable area from off-screen. Changing your view by zooming in and out does not change the placement of any sprites you have added to the stage. It simply works as a magnifying tool, allowing you to look at your stage real close up from a further distance without altering the true physical stage size of your movie.

One of the great things about Director is that there are many different ways to accomplish the same task. You don't need to remember them all, just the ones you use most frequently. The bottom left of the Stage window contains a popup box that allows you to quickly adjust the viewing size of your stage (Figure 1–4, also found in the color section).

If you can afford it, I highly recommend working with two monitors on your computer system. It involves having an additional video card installed into your system and a second monitor. This will eliminate the majority of hassles in trying to shuffle windows. Keep tools and palettes on one side and the stage open on the other.

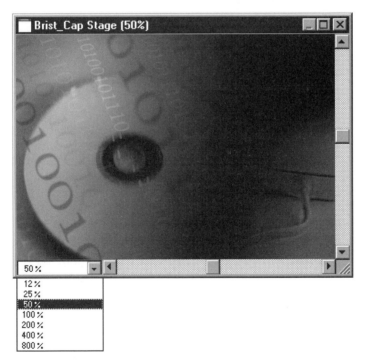

Figure 1–4 Use the Zoom Menu pulldown box to select one of the present viewable stage areas.

A NEW LOOK FOR THE CAST WINDOW

One thing that I find very helpful in any program is the ability to customize what I see and how I am able to work. Director has added the ability to change the way you view your cast. Traditionally, Director displayed cast members as a single image frame or thumbnail view (Figure 1–5). Now you can click the Cast View Style button at the top left corner of the Cast window. This button acts as a toggle between standard thumbnail view and the new list view (Figure 1–6).

There are several added benefits when working in list view. For one thing, you can see more information about each cast member right away. These rows and columns of information are referred to as Asset Management fields. The default settings include useful information such as:

◆   An icon to identify each type of cast member.

◆   The name of the cast member.

◆   The number assigned to that individual cast member.

Figure 1–5 The cast was traditionally displayed in thumbnail view.

◆   An asterisk indicating that the cast member has changed since the last time it was saved.

◆   Script information on whether the cast member is (or contains) a script or behavior.

◆   The type of cast member.

◆   The latest date and time the cast member was modified.

◆   A comments field (type in any useful information).

◆   The file size of the cast member*.

◆   The creation date of the cast member (when it was initially created or imported into Director)*.

◆   Who modified the cast member*.

◆   The full pathname for linked files*.

The asterisk (*) indicates the four optional informational fields that you can add to the list view.

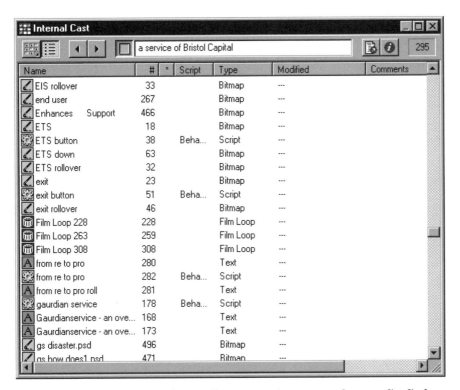

Figure 1–6 The Cast View Style button allows you to view cast members as a list display.

The order of the columns that the Asset Management fields are displayed in can be easily customized to your liking. If comments are the most vital piece of information, simply click and drag that heading where you would like it to appear. Rearrange the columns in any order to help speed up and improve your workflow within your next project. You can even turn any of these column settings on or off when viewing your cast members in the list display mode. To customize which columns are displayed in list mode:

1. Select Preferences from the File menu.
2. Select Cast from the popup menu.
3. Place a check mark before any of the options in the List Column section of the Cast Window Preferences window (Figure 1–7).
4. Click OK.

Click and drag the edge of any column heading to resize the display area. Director may automatically truncate the width of the column, hiding valuable information.

Lists of information become more useful if you can sort them and adjust the order in which they appear. For instance, you may want to view the cast members in order

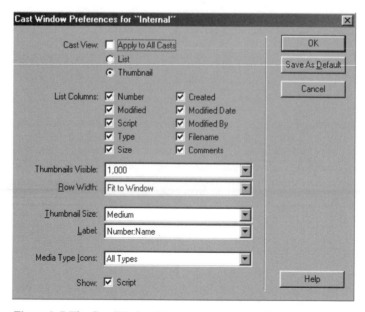

Figure 1–7 The Cast Window Preferences window allows you to customize the information columns in the cast member list display mode.

from the ones most recently modified to quickly fix a problem. Whatever the case, you can sort on each and every column in the cast when in list display mode. Simply click on a column heading to sort the information by that column. Click on it again to reverse the order of how the information is displayed.

LINKED SCRIPTS

There may be situations where you feel it is better to edit your Lingo scripts in an application outside of Director. Now you can link to external text files. Working with externally linked text file scripts is very similar to importing linked images and digital video files. The advantages to using externally linked text scripts include:

◆ Multiple people can work on one project at the same time (for instance, one works on the images, while another writes the scripts).

◆ A library of useful scripts is written once and used in any project.

To link to external script files:

1. Select Import from the File menu.
2. Select Script under the Files of type pull-down menu (Figure 1–8).
3. Click on the text file you want to be linked. Add as many files as desired.
4. Select Link to External File from the Media pull-down menu.
5. Click Import.

Director recognizes .TXT and .LS file extensions. (The .LS file extension is Director's own link script extension.)

Once an external text file has been imported as Linked to External File, you can then make basic adjustments to the script right inside of Director's Script window. Once you save your Director movie, the changes you made are updated into your external text file. Director will not allow you to make changes to a script if the externally linked file is locked. You can just as easily create a script inside of Director and then save a copy of it externally for other uses. To change an internal script into an externally linked file:

1. Select the internal script cast member.
2. Select the Script tab in the Property Inspector (Figure 1–9).
3. Click the Link Script As button.
4. Type in a name and select a destination where you want to save the script file.
5. Click Save.

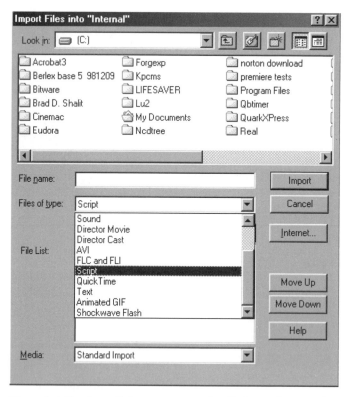

Figure 1–8 Use the pull-down menu to select Script as the type of file you want to import.

If you make changes externally to a linked script, you will need to unload that member in your Director movie and then reload it with the most recently updated version. You will need to update the movie using your Message window (see Chapter 4, "Lingo Basics: An Introduction," for more details on the Message window). Use the following Lingo script to unload then reload a script with updated changes (substitute "NameOfScript" with the name of your script):

```
unloadMember member "NameOfScript"
```

BITMAPPED COMPRESSION

Director now offers you the ability to use JPEG compression on bitmap cast members in a .DCR file. You can either apply compression to individual bitmaps or all bitmaps contained in your movie. This is a great feature, especially for those of you who distribute

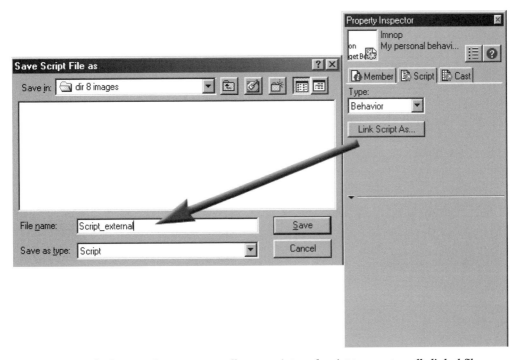

Figure 1–9 Use the Property Inspector to reallocate an internal script to an externally linked file.

your movies over the Internet. Compression allows you to optimize your bitmapped images to maintain as much of the quality as possible while dramatically reducing the size of the file. This, in turn, provides shorter download times for your movies.

 Applying bitmap compression at the individual cast member level will take precedence over compression applied at the movie level.

I highly recommend compressing individual cast members even if you are not publishing your movie for the Web. Any application that you develop will always run smoother when trying to open and play smaller file sizes. Today, my company is getting more requests to develop sales and promotional applications on Cyber Card, a business card-shaped CD-ROM that can hold up to 40MB of information (Figure 1–10, also found in the color section). These work great for promotional pieces and presentations. Forty megabytes is not a lot of room to put graphics, animation, text, audio narration, music, and sound effects, so anything you can do to reduce file size is helpful. But be careful not to over-compress your images. You don't want to jeopardize image quality (Figure 1–11, also found in the color section).

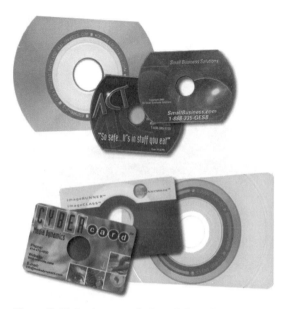

Figure 1–10 Business card-shaped CD-ROM that contains up to 40MB per disc.

To apply JPEG compression to individual cast members:

1. Select the bitmapped image of your cast or sprite in your score.
2. Click on the Bitmap tab in the Property Inspector.
3. Click on the triangle to display the Compression window (if not already open).
4. Select JPEG from the Compression pull-down menu (Figure 1–12).
5. Adjust the Quality slider as desired. The lower the value you select, the more compression you are applying. The higher the value, the less compression. A value of 100 means no compression.

To apply JPEG compression to an entire movie:

1. Select Publish Settings from the File menu. The Publish Settings window will appear (Figure 1–13).
2. Select the Compression tab on the top of the Publish Settings window.
3. Select JPEG for the Image Compression setting.
4. Adjust the Quality slider as desired. The lower the value you select, the more compression you are applying. The higher the value, the less compression. A value of 100 means no compression.
5. Click OK.

(a)

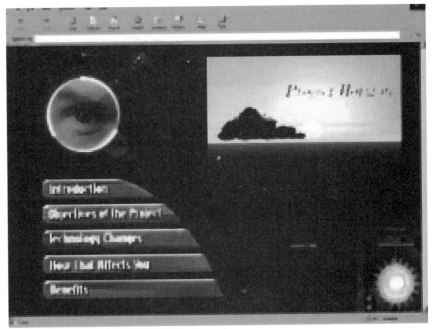

(b)

Figure 1–11 a & b Notice the difference between quality settings. Images quickly degrade with the more compression you apply.

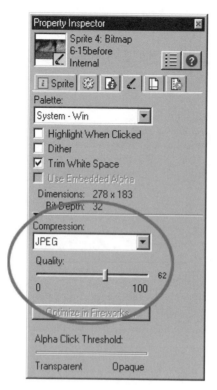

Figure 1–12 Use JPEG compression settings to optimize the file size of any bitmapped sprite.

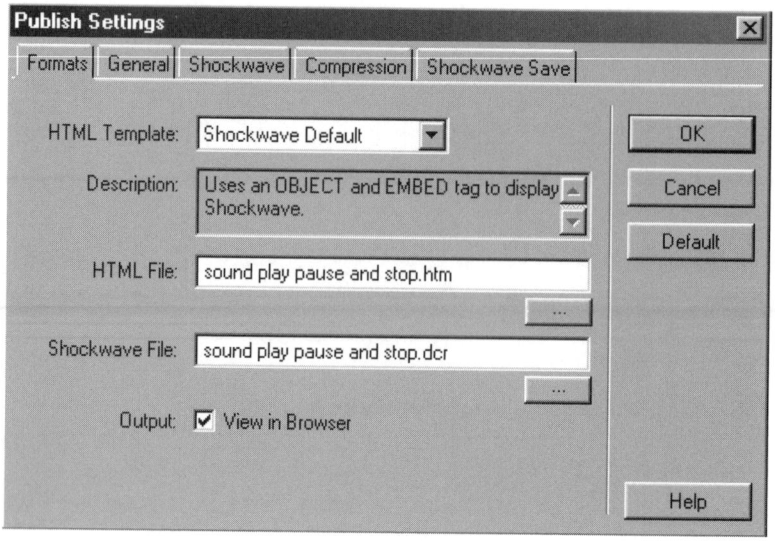

Figure 1–13 The Publish Settings window.

You will not notice the results of your compression adjustments in real time. Therefore, you must publish your file to see the results. To view your results:

1. Set the compression (and other) settings in the Publish Settings window.
2. Save your movie.
3. Select Publish from the File menu. The Compacting File progress bar will appear (Figure 1–14). Your movie will automatically open as a Shockwave file in your default browser (Figure 1–15, also found in the color section).

 Keep in mind that you must always save your work before Director will allow you to publish your movie. Therefore, I recommend saving a backup copy before applying compression just in case you accidentally save your project with images that get ruined by applying too much compression.

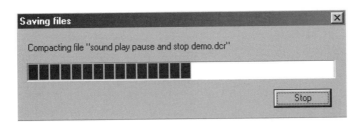

Figure 1–14 The Compacting files progress bar.

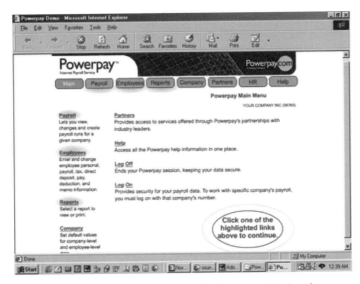

Figure 1–15 Publishing your movie defaults to opening in a browser to display your new Shockwave movie.

SAVE AS SHOCKWAVE HAS A NEW NAME

That's right. Macromedia has changed the name Save As Shockwave to Publish. This feature still saves your movies for the Web by converting them into Shockwave movies, but now it gives you even more control. Saving your movie, or now publishing your movie as a Shockwave movie, still produces a .DCR file (Figure 1–16). Shockwave movies play back in any Shockwave-enabled Web browser. If you do not have an updated version of the Shockwave plug-in, you can download it from www.macromedia.com.

Saving your movie as a Shockwave file creates a closed version and protects your movie from being altered, even by people who own Director.

The Publish command's default settings allow you to quickly and easily create Shockwave movies ready for distribution over the Internet. To publish your movie as a Shockwave file:

1. Open the Director movie you want to shock.
2. Select Publish from the File menu.

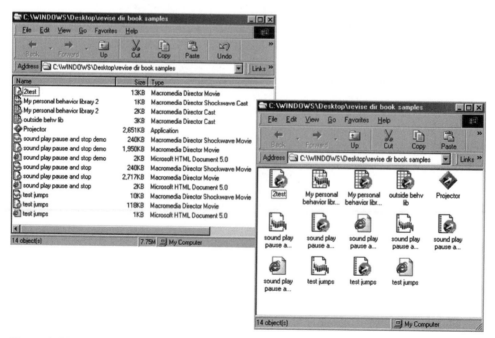

Figure 1–16 Director identifies each type of movie and file with unique icons and file extensions.

Director begins to compact the file. As part of the default settings, Director automatically converts your movie into a Shockwave file (.DCR) without changing the original Director file (.DIR). You should also notice that an HTML file is created in the same directory as your Shockwave movie. It has the same filename with the appropriate file extension applied to it. This is the file that holds the "setup" characteristics of your Shockwave movie.

 For more information on creating movies for distribution on the Internet, check out Chapter 11, "Shock It for the Web."

SCALABLE SHOCKWAVE MOVIES

Because more and more people are developing content to be distributed on the Web and every end-user has a slightly different setup (monitor size, preferred browser, etc.), Macromedia knew they had to introduce a way to make Shockwave movies look their best no matter what the circumstances were on the end-user's side. Director now contains setting options that will let Shockwave movies stretch to fit in the browser window. You can even set it to maintain the movie's original aspect ratio, to keep your movie looking its best during playback. Chapter 11, "Shock It for the Web," has a complete description of how to set your Shockwave movies for optimal playback in a browser.

KEEP SPRITES UNDER LOCK AND KEY

This feature is great for everyone—those new to Director and even some of the veterans. Director now offers the ability to lock sprites, preventing unwanted changes or deletions of sprites during your authoring session. I've heard many stories, especially on larger projects, where someone thought that a certain sprite was for something else, and you guessed it … it wasn't. If you catch it in time, you can simply undo your last step. But what happens if it altered your movie enough that you had to go back and rebuild half of it?

Locking sprites is especially good when you have multiple programmers working on a single project. The last thing you need is someone else unintentionally changing what you worked so hard to build. You can lock as many sprites as you feel necessary. If you select a group of sprites during an authoring session, some locked and some unlocked, Director will prompt you that alterations will only be made to the unlocked sprites.

 Locking sprites is not supported during playback.

Select the sprite or sprites that you want to lock either in the stage or in the score. Once selected, there are several different ways to lock a sprite or group of sprites:

♦ Select Lock Sprite from the Modify menu.

♦ Right mouse click (Windows) or Option-click (Macintosh) on a sprite and select Lock Sprite from the popup menu (Figure 1–17).

♦ Click on the padlock icon under the Sprite tab of the Property Inspector. Notice how all of the setting controls become grayed out once the sprite is locked (Figure 1–18).

In authoring mode, you cannot simply select a sprite on the stage once it has become locked. This prevents you from accidentally shifting its position or deleting it altogether. To select a locked sprite directly from the stage, you must first hold down the L key to activate it. Notice the bounding box does not have any corner or side markers that normally allow you to adjust, resize, or reposition a sprite on the stage. In addition, Director puts a padlock icon in front of the name of the locked sprite in the score (Figure 1–19). Locked sprites in the score are also represented with a lighter shading for easier distinction.

To unlock a sprite, simply apply one of the reverse techniques used to lock it:

♦ Select Unlock Sprite from the Modify menu.

♦ Right mouse click (Windows) or Option-click (Macintosh) on a sprite and select Unlock Sprite from the popup menu.

Figure 1–17 Select Lock Sprite from the Sprite popup menu.

◆   Click on the padlock icon under the Sprite tab of the Property Inspector. All of the
    feature settings should become active again.

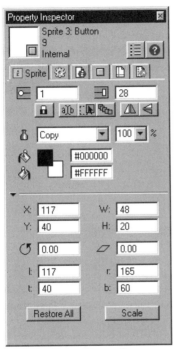 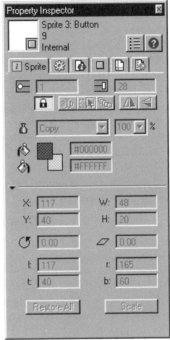

Unlocked   **Locked**

*Figure 1–18 You cannot alter a sprite once it has been locked. You must
first unlock the sprite to change any settings.*

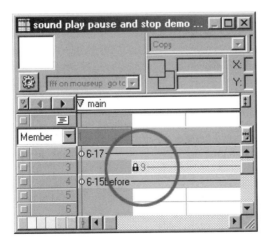

*Figure 1–19 A padlock icon appears
on the sprite to indicate that it has
been locked.*

POSITION WITH GUIDES

In addition to the normal grid that you have become accustomed to using for lining up your sprites on the stage, Director now includes a much better way to work with sprites when trying to position them in just the right place. Guides allow a much more accurate way of positioning your sprites anywhere on the stage without cluttering up the entire screen the way the grid does (Figure 1–20, also found in the color section).

For those of you who have worked in programs such as Photoshop, Illustrator, and Quark, you know how valuable tool guidelines can be for positioning your images accurately every time. Add Director to the list because you can now add any number of horizontal and vertical guidelines as necessary. You even have controls to hide guides, lock them in position, custom-select their color for easier visibility, and even snap your sprites to a guideline for exact positioning.

Setting up and using guides is very simple. You need to activate the guides before you can start adding them to your stage:

1. Open the Property Inspector (if not already open).
2. Click on the stage or score to select it.
3. Select the Guides and Grid tab at the top of the Property Inspector (Figure 1–21).
4. Activate guides by either selecting the Visible checkbox in the Guides portion of the Property Inspector.

    OR

    Select Guides and Grid from the View menu. Then select Show Guides from the popup menu.

    OR

    Use the keyboard shortcut Control-Shift-Alt-D (Windows) or Command-Shift-Option-D (Macintosh) to toggle guides off and on.

Once you have turned guides on, you can begin to add them to your stage and customize their functionality. To add guides to your stage:

1. Click and hold your mouse on either the New Horizontal Guide box or New Vertical Guide box in the Property Inspector (Figure 1–22).
2. While continuing to hold the mouse button down, drag your cursor onto the stage and release wherever you want to add a new guideline.
3. If you need to adjust the position of a guideline, roll your cursor slowly over the line. Your cursor should change to show two little lines with arrows pointing in either direction. Now you can click and drag the line to a new position.
4. To remove a single guide, click and drag it off the stage's viewable area.

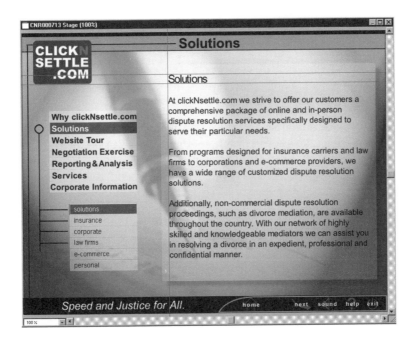

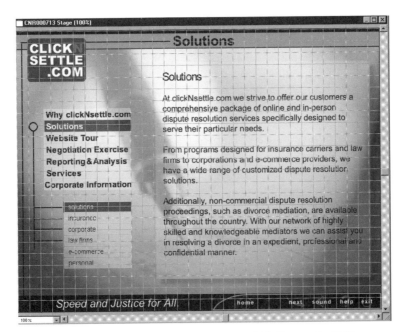

Figure 1–20 A comparison between working with Guides vs. the Grid.
Notice the clean and accurate results with Guides.

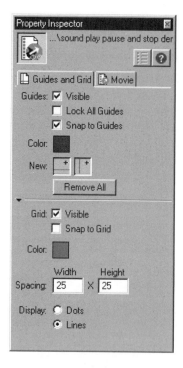

Figure 1–21 Use the Guides and Grid section of the Property Inspector to add and customize guidelines and grid patterns.

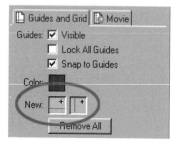

Figure 1–22 Click the New Horizontal Guide or New Vertical Guide buttons and drag onto the stage to add new positioning guidelines.

If your cursor does not change as you roll over the Guides, make sure that you do not have Lock All Guides marked in the Property Inspector. This will prevent you from repositioning any of the guidelines.

Other aspects you might find beneficial when working with guides:

◆ Change the color of the guides for easier visibility using the guide's color swatch in the Property Inspector. Depending upon the color scheme of your sprites, you can change the color of the guides at anytime throughout the authoring process.

◆ Click the Remove All button to clear all of the guides. Once you remove them, they are gone forever.

◆ Click the Visible checkbox to hide and then redisplay guides. This is extremely helpful if you want to view the stage without the guides, but don't want to remove them completely.

◆ Click the Lock Guides checkbox to hold all guides in their current position. Once this box is checked, you will not be able to reposition any of the guidelines. You can also lock the guides by selecting Guides and Grids from the View menu, then selecting Lock Guides from the popup menu.

◆ Turn on Snap To Guides. This will force the corner edges of your sprite's bounding box to "snap" up against the guides for easy and accurate placement of your sprites. You can turn on Snap To Guides by selecting Guides and Grids from the View menu, then selecting Snap To Guides from the popup menu, or by using the keyboard shortcut Shift-Control-G (Windows) or Shift-Command-G (Macintosh) to toggle this feature on and off.

MULTIPLE CURVE VECTORS

You probably know the benefits of working with vector graphics—reduced file size, scalability, and custom shapes. Now, Director allows you to control multiple vertices at the same time. This is helpful because it gives you complete control of customizing and tweaking shapes and curves any way you want (Figure 1–23). The handles that appear allow you to manipulate the degree of curvature applied to the image between two vertices. These curves are known as Bézier curves. You can simply adjust the curves by grabbing one of the handles and dragging it around until you get the desired look of the curve. Check out the chapter, "Creating Killer Visual Effects," to learn more about working with vector graphics.

ENHANCED LINGO PERFORMANCE

The power of Director keeps growing with every version Macromedia releases. That's also true in Director 8. Lingo, Director's internal programming language, allows you to build and control just about anything you can imagine. Programming in Director is becoming easier than ever. The use of parent scripts utilizes the advantages of object-oriented programming, allowing you to save time and better understand what is taking place without skimping on functionality.

Director has improved the relationship between parent scripts and child objects, making it easier to organize the basic programming functionality behind your movie. Child objects are generally used when you need the same type of logic or functionality to occur several times concurrently, each with slightly different parameters. Director refers to these individual object instances as "children" since they are all slight variations of

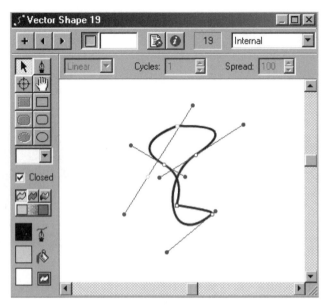

Figure 1–23 Apply Bézier curves to multiple vertices at the same time.

the same "Parent" script. Check out Chapter 9, "Advancing Techniques with Behaviors and Lingo," for more detailed information on enhanced Lingo functionality.

CONTROL BITMAPS WITH LINGO

Lingo also allows you to control bitmapped images. There are two basic ways that Lingo affects bitmaps inside of Director:

◆ You can perform simple controls that affect an entire cast (i.e., changing foreground color, background color, or switching cast members around).

◆ You can perform more complex adjustments and detailed manipulations, allowing for more flexibility and control of your bitmapped images.

SUMMARY

As you can see, Macromedia has added a number of new features and controls to really improve the speed at which you work and the quality of your final movie. Take your time and go through as many of the new features and functions of Director 8 that you can. Whether you are new to Director or have used it for years, I think you will appreciate how easy it is to get started building interactive applications.

chapter 2

PLANNING A
PROJECT FROM
THE START

A client calls you and wants to talk about putting together an interactive CD-ROM or Web site for his company. Before you can begin building the project, you need to have some questions answered first. Otherwise, you will find yourself revising everything halfway through the project or completely changing things that could have been avoided from the beginning. Even worse, you might lose future work from that client (or the client altogether) if you miss the direction of the project, who the client's audience is, and what he is trying to achieve with this project. Once you begin designing interactive applications for other people, you really need to get down to the details and find out exactly how they intend to use the program. Some of the questions in this chapter should help make your multimedia programming a more pleasurable and profitable experience. Use these suggestions as guidelines to tailor your own list of questions for developing interactive programs.

 Many of these questions are applicable beyond the scope of Director. They might expand into other types of multimedia projects, but nonetheless hold true for designing Director movies.

DEFINE THE PROJECT

Question #1: What type of project is this? (Make sure Director is the right application for your client's needs.)

Getting the best possible insight into the project will help in your approach to putting this thing together in the best possible way. Is it for training? Promotional purposes? Sales? Does the client intend to run it on the Web? Or distribute it on CD? All these different questions can determine what type of features you may want to include or exclude. If the program is going to be used by a select group of people, then you can probably consider using some more advanced interactive features. These features may include hidden links, which are hotspots of which only the user knows the location. If the program you are going to be designing is to be used by novice computer users, you will most likely want to make the navigational system as simple and easy to follow as possible. Another consideration might be to offer an interactive help section accessible through a Help button, or a glossary section for projects that contain a number of technical terms. These sections should be made available from virtually every section of the program (Figure 2–1). Throughout the course of this book, we will demonstrate examples from real programs that incorporate many of these features. Make sure that the end result of what you produce is in line with the requirements set forth by the scope of the project.

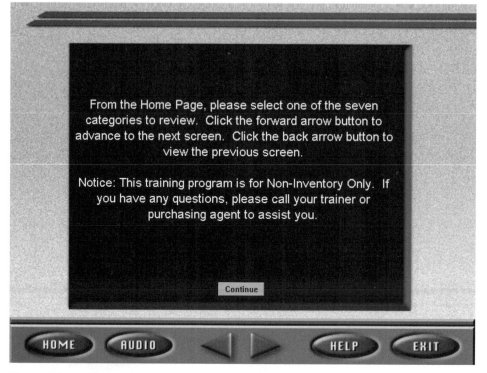

Figure 2–1 Provide easy-to-use and consistent navigational buttons/links available from every screen (especially the Help sections).

STRATEGY: HOW TO APPROACH THE PROJECT

Where should you begin? The first thing that you should do is sit down with the client and try to determine the overall content and focus of the program. This will help you to decide what types of media you will be working with, what content you will have to include, and how you can begin to lay this project out. One thing you must realize is that every multimedia project that comes your way is going to be different. Gather as much information as possible from the client. If the clients can, have them put together an outline of the general topics that the project will encompass. If they are supplying you with any types of artwork or other relevant files, try to get them as early as possible. Having these files in your possession will help you visualize the look of the project and start developing the layout. Once you have as many of the materials as they can provide (which 9 out of 10 times will either be not enough information or excessively too much), begin to sketch out a schematic or flowchart (Figure 2–2). You will begin to see what headings will be included, what topics you will need to expand on, and you will be able to see how the interactive navigational structure will function.

Depending on the nature of your project, the exact format shown in Figure 2–2 will not always apply, but the general concept should give you a good headstart. Begin by working

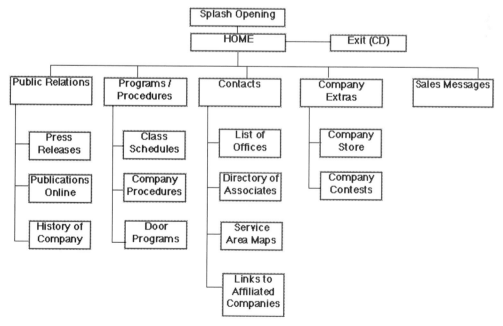

Figure 2–2 Schematic drawings and flowcharts help lay out the structure of a project.

from the top down, generally from some type of Main menu or Home page. Every section added will need a strong foundation and you can begin with the Home screen.

As you can see from the schematic drawing, having the Home screen as your foundation does not mean your actual program must begin with the Home screen. Splash screens or opening movie clips usually make for an interesting opening for your project.

Once you have all of the main topic headings and sub-sections mapped out on paper, you will quickly see the correlation between what you have sketched out and what you will begin to set up in Director. The score is where you will begin to compile all of your elements to bring life to your movie. Use markers in your score to signify where each topic section will be added to your Director movie. You will probably start with a marker (properly labeled) for each main topic area in your schematic (Figure 2–3).

Don't worry if a section is added later on or if the client changes the order of your movie. One of the most powerful features of Director is that the score works in a non-linear fashion. Figure 2–4 illustrates how you can set up your score. Notice how section 1 is not placed at the beginning of the score. You can begin to program your content in any order you wish. For example, you can have your ending be the second group of sprites in your score. For those programmers who tend to rush through projects,

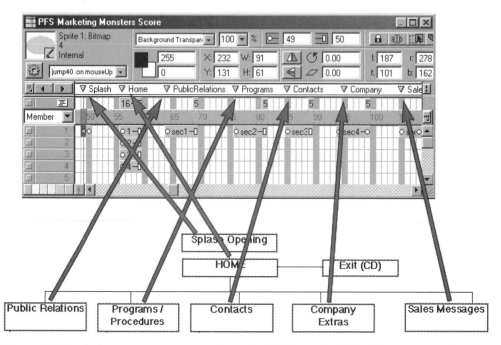

Figure 2–3 Developing an accurate paper schematic will help you build the infrastructure of your movie correctly.

Director's non-linear capabilities can be a drawback. Sound confused? That is exactly my point. The fact that your score does not have to be designed in a linear fashion means that, if you are not careful, you might accidentally link the wrong sections of your movie or spend a great deal of time hunting around for the section you need. Without that visual flowchart to look back and reference once in a while, all those sprites filling hundreds of frames across multiple channels intertwined and linking in every direction can be very cumbersome for even experienced programmers. You might wonder why then you wouldn't program in a purely linear manner. There are two reasons:

1. In real-life scenarios, clients tend to add things at the last minute and change their minds from time to time.

2. Non-linear capabilities allow you to build your program in any order you choose. You may not have all your materials together for the beginning sections, but can build other sections without wasting any time.

We will get into more specifics about actually building interactive presentations and using the navigational tools available through Director in later chapters.

A MIX OF MARKETING AND PRODUCTION

Question #2: Who are your clients and what are they trying to achieve?

One of the unique aspects at my company, PFS New Media, Inc., is the involvement of the marketing department in every project. One thing that we have found to speed up the process and deliver to the clients a piece that is specifically geared to what they are looking for is to understand the company you are working for. Know their style. Are they conservative or looking to push the envelope? Do they like hi-tech, vivid colors, or prefer a lot of white space? These things can make a big impact on how well a client likes a project.

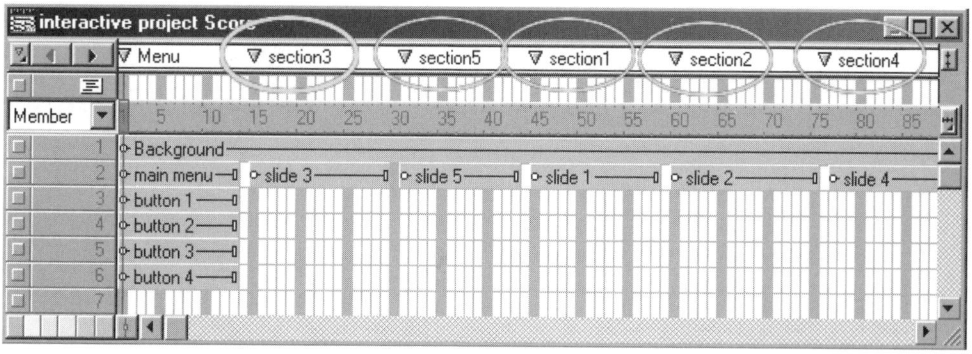

Figure 2–4 The order of sections in the score does not necessarily determine the playback order.

Our production department is filled with talented designers and programming tech-heads who can add practically any bells and whistles imaginable. The problem is that most of the projects we see do not need every frill and thrill thrown in just for the sake of throwing them in there. That's where our marketing department helps. When we sit down in our meeting room to review a project, we invite a team of people who will be involved in the project. It normally consists of:

◆   An account executive (who has reviewed the initial ideas with the client).

◆   A project manager.

◆   A senior programmer (fluent in Director and other applications).

◆   A graphic designer (fluent in Photoshop and other applications).

◆   A marketing director.

All of these people sit around discussing the various aspects of building the project, from content and analysis to interface design and distribution. The marketing person is the one who will do the research and analyze what the client needs and how best to ful-fill that requirement. You don't necessarily need a marketing department to build inter-active applications. Just keep in mind to employ *their* type of strategy … understanding *the clients'* needs; not just adding bells and whistles because you know how.

There are many aspects to consider. Understanding your clients and their needs does not always mean you have to develop along the same style that they have always used. Just because the client has a history of being traditionally conservative with simple lay-outs and a lot of white space doesn't mean they are not open to new, fresh ideas. After all, a new look may be just what they are looking for, and that's why they hired you.

DEFINE YOUR TARGET AUDIENCE

Question #3: Who will be using this program?

Your target audience is going to vary for just about every Director project you build. This is where Director really delivers. Its versatility and flexibility allow programmers to design just about any type of interactive application clients can dream up. Macromedia Director is continually upgrading and improving its capabilities to keep up with the grow-ing needs and demands of developers for more options and features. As technology changes, Director is there with new enhancements to help deliver the types of applica-tions you need, whether it's a stand-alone presentation or a shocked file for the Web.

How you develop your application will be dependent on how you classify the intended audience. If the users are computer-savvy, you will have the opportunity to work with more advanced features and interactions. If the target audience consists of novice computer users, you will have to concentrate on making the navigational con-trols and layout as clear and simple to use as possible. If the company you are pro-ducing the project for is conservative, bright flashy colors and animations probably won't appeal to them. Focus all aspects of the project on the clients' needs and demands while always keeping the end-user of the program in mind.

THE 3S'S: SCRIPTS, SCHEMATICS, AND STORYBOARDS

Question #4: What will be the content of the program?

The most beneficial tools for any programmer to develop and use are the script, storyboard, and schematic flowchart.

◆ The script basically tells the story of your program in a textual manner. Just like in the movies, a script is used to describe each section and list any audio or video files required, providing a basis for any text that will appear on-screen or be read by a voiceover talent (Figure 2–5).

◆ Storyboards are used when developing just about any type of visual image presentation that tells a story or flows from one section to another (whether it is for print or video). Each main screen, or change in scenery, is sketched out by the artist or designer to help other people involved in the project visualize the way each scene is going to look (Figure 2–6, also found in the color section). For multimedia, storyboards help you design the layout of each screen (placement of images and navigational elements, font styles, and color schemes).

◆ Schematics and flowcharts are the best ways to sketch out the navigational structure of a program and make sure that each section is properly connected. With this map sketched out on paper or in a computer document, you will be able to see if you are missing any sections or whether any links or connections will not work as initially planned.

 Always make navigational elements reversible. Too often, users tend to click around without realizing where they are going. Having either a Back button or at least a Return to Home button allows the users to quickly and safely get to where they belong.

 Use these three forms (and any other materials you create) for clients to look at, approve, and sign off on. This way, you will save yourself the trouble of redoing a lot of work if and when the clients change their minds. Once they sign off and approve the script and storyboard designs, any changes at that point can generally be billed at an additional fee.

Screen / Page	Text	Audio / Video
Home / Main Menu	Welcome to the Training Program. Please click you mouse on one of the buttons along the bottom of the screen to advance to the next section.	Custom Music V/O reading text SFX on Button Clicks
Screen 1	History. Our company was started over 5 years ago, with the dream of becoming a large production company.	Music Continues V/O reading text Video Clip 001
Screen 2	Today, with over 1,000 employees, XYZ Inc. has locations in over 24 countries world wide.	V/O reading text Video Clip 002
Screen 3	XYZ has become a leader in the industry for producing one of the industries leading widgets. With a record of 7 out of ten major awards under our belts, XYZ has been the choice of Fortune 500 companies for the past two years.	Awards Music Clip V/O reading text Video Clip 003
Screen 4	Closing Graphic. XYZ Inc. sees itself becoming one of the worlds most leading technology companies in the world. By expanding our markets into new territories, we can provide job opportunities to over 100 nations.	V/O reading text Visionary Music Video Clip 004

Figure 2–5 Typical Multimedia Script Format

WORK WITHIN THE BOUNDARIES OF SYSTEM REQUIREMENTS

Question #4: What type of system will this program be designed for?

Determining system requirement limitations is often referred to as trying to find the lowest common denominator. What this means is listing the minimum computer specifications (both hardware and software) that are required to run the application you are designing. The optimal scenario is to find out what types of computers your client or end-user plans to run these programs on. If they have a lot of Pentiums, fully loaded,

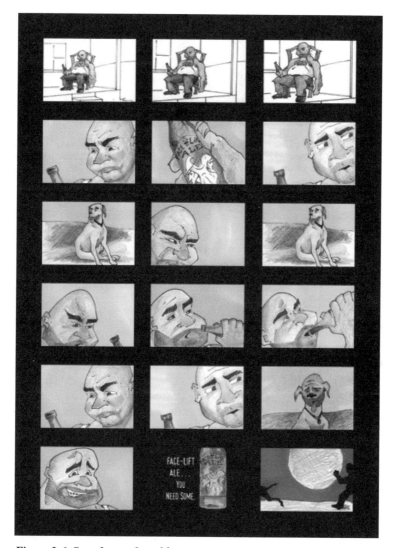

Figure 2-6 Sample storyboard layouts.

and only a few 486s with barely enough memory to remember that they are computers, you are faced with two choices:

1. Develop the program to meet the specs of the low-end systems.
2. Recommend to your client that you design the application for the high-end systems (for better performance and superior images) and not to run it on the slower systems.

As you program your Director movies, many factors will come into play as far as what types of media you can use and how they will play back:

♦ CPU (Central Processing Unit)—Clocked as the speed at which your computer can compute data and other types of information.

♦ RAM—The system's memory, which will play a vital role with how fast files load and how smoothly they run. This is especially true when it comes to digital video and audio files.

♦ Sound cards—Required for each computer to hear any sound files added to the movie.

♦ Graphic accelerator cards—Beneficial for better graphic and video display.

♦ Monitors—High-resolution monitors will be required to run applications set for resolutions of 800x600 or 1024x768. (See Chapter 5 for more detailed information regarding resolution and color depth.)

Generally, the more power (processor speed, memory, etc.) you have available, the fewer problems you will encounter when authoring with more complex features.

To go into a bit more detail on monitors, the screen resolution will have a significant impact on the color display, size, and overall look of your movie. The old standard for multimedia projects was to design your movies to run at 640 pixels (width) by 480 pixels (height). Today, with the advent of higher resolution monitors and LCD displays on laptops, it has become common to develop applications at much higher resolutions. All of these factors need to be determined before creating any images for your project. To change the screen resolution (Figure 2–7), follow the steps below.

For PC users:

1. Select Settings from the Start menu (Windows 95/98/NT).
2. Select Control Panel.
3. Double-click on Display.
4. Choose Settings in the Display Properties window.

For Mac users:

1. Select Control Panels from the Apple menu.
2. Choose Monitors and Sound.
3. From the Display window, select which resolution you want your system to display.

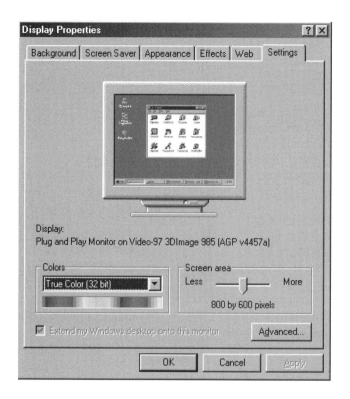

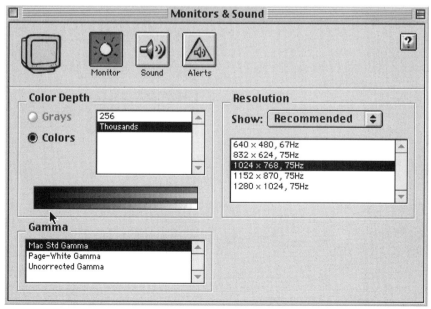

Figure 2–7 Windows and Macintosh screens for setting monitor displays.

The make and model of your computer monitor and the video card installed in your computer will determine the settings and resolutions available on your particular system.

PC, MAC, OR BOTH

Question #5: How would you like your project delivered?

To determine the types of files you will be able to author and design, you must figure out which platform the application will be created for. Macintosh? PC? Others? What type of operating system? If it is on a PC, is it for Windows 3.1, Windows 95/98, NT? Will it be for multiple operating systems? More importantly, will it be for cross-platform use? Do you want your end-users to have the ability to run the program on both a Macintosh- and PC-compatible system?

Designing a CD-ROM may seem easy at first. The biggest pitfall for developers is to overlook these basic questions or, even worse, assume that they know what the client wants. Perhaps after working with a client on several projects, these questions become irrelevant. Remember, each platform and operating system will determine a number of things, especially which types of files will work on which types of systems.

GATHER THE FILES

Question #6: Are files going to be provided by the client?

Many times, you will not be the only person working on a project from start to finish. There may have been design work done prior to this project that your clients would like to incorporate into this new Director piece. The clients might also have a logo that needs to be included (hopefully they can supply it to you in electronic format). Whatever the case may be, it is important to communicate with all parties involved to find out:

1. How they will be saving the files (PICT, TIFF, BMP).
2. What type of media will they be providing, containing all of these files (CD-R, Zip, Jaz).

WORK WITH PENCIL COMPS

Once you get a good understanding of the clients, what they are looking to accomplish, and an idea of who will be using the application, you can begin to start designing the interface. The best way to get off on the right track is to create pencil sketches of how you conceive the interface. I recommend (pending timeframe and budget, of course) developing three to four different versions. This way, the clients have something to help them make some decisions about what they want. There are many different directions to go in, so the real question is where to start. At PFS New Media, Inc., we try to develop several styles (Figure 2–8):

◆   The main concept (what most of the team feels will work best for this project based on the review of all materials and any direction offered by the client).

◆   An alternate version of that same concept (it may be as simple as changing the location of the navigation bar from the side to across the top of the screen).

◆   A scaled down version (more open space).

◆   A more creative, artsy design (a not-so-traditional layout).

Keep in mind that pencil comps are rarely exactly what the client is looking for, but that's okay. The idea is to narrow down to the best basic layout. Pick and choose the best

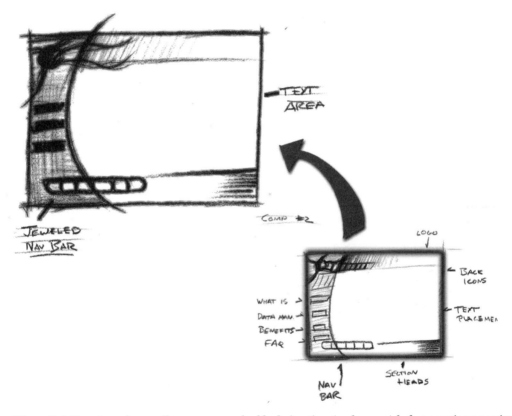

Figure 2–8 Easy-to-make pencil comps save valuable design time (and money) before creating a version on the computer. Clients can get a good sense of direction with pencil sketches.

elements from the various comps and discard any features that won't work for the scope of the current project. Once the best ideas have been selected, you can hit the computer and add life to the sketch, filling in all of the colors, textures, and transparencies that you were not able to see in the pencil drawings (Figure 2–9).

CREATE A FEW COLOR COMPS

After you have done a few pencil comps to get the preliminary layout for your interface, it's time to recreate that imagery on the computer using Director's internal Paint application or a graphics program like Photoshop. The detail of your pencil comps will dictate the number of computer renditions you make. I generally like to try a few versions, each version a slight variation of the other, based on the model that was selected from the pencil comps (Figure 2–10, also found in the color section).

You never quite know exactly how all the images will look once put together on the computer. Pencil comps are great for overall layout, shape, and size, but they really can't display color, texture, and transparency levels very well. Therefore, you'll find it beneficial to create your initial interface design and then try a few variations to fill in

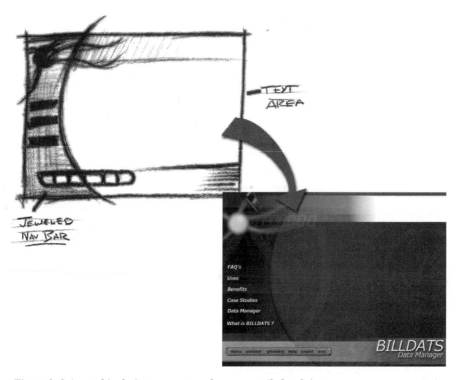

Figure 2–9 A graphic designer can transform a pencil sketch into a computer generated interface, ready for programming.

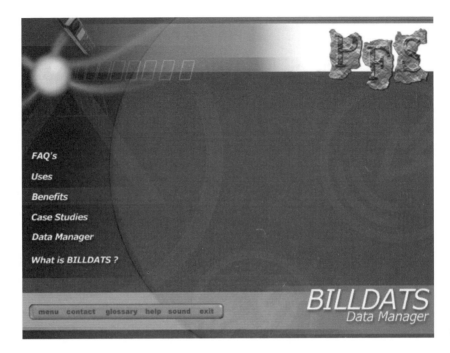

(a)

(b)

Figure 2–10 a, b, & c Clients generally like to see alternate versions of the same basic thematic design before selecting the final layout. (continued)

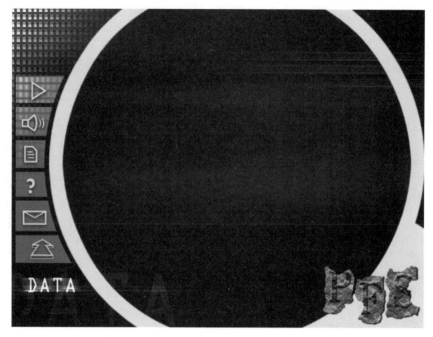

(c)

Figure 2–10 (continued)

the little details that can make all the difference in the world on which version of the selected layout (from the pencil comps) you choose to use as the final design.

 Always work with layers. Keep each element you create on its own layer. This way, you have complete control to add or remove aspects with very little effort (Figure 2–11).

 Build your computer comps in the exact size that you want your image to appear on your stage inside Director. Nothing is more frustrating than building something you like (at a different size) and then realizing it doesn't work inside Director.

CHOOSE YOUR WEAPON: SELECTING THE APPROPRIATE FILE TYPES

The thing that makes Director the number-one choice of developers is that it can develop for many different applications and situations. You can author one movie and then play it back on either a Macintosh or a PC computer. This is possible because

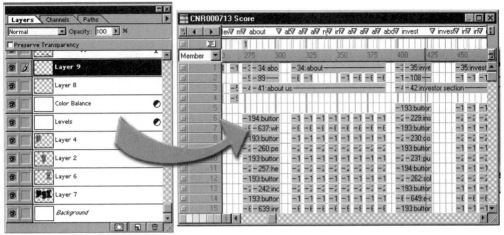

Photoshop   **Director**

Figure 2–11 Building all of your images with individual layers will help avoid tremendous headaches later if you need to change any aspect of your images.

Director handles so many different types of file formats. Whether you are using PICT, GIF, Targa, or TIFF files, you can import virtually any standard type of bitmapped or vector-based image into Director. Director also works with digital video and audio files, including AIFF, WAV, AVI, and QuickTime. If you want to add real high-quality illustrations and images, but want to reduce the file size of your movie, consider working with Flash movies, another one of Macromedia's powerful animation packages. With all these different types of files available, it is extremely important to know which files are cross-platform and which ones are system-specific.

File types supported by Director include:

◆ Animation and multimedia—Flash movies, animated GIFs, PowerPoint presentations, Director movies, Director external casts.

◆ Image—BMP, GIF, JPEG, LRG (xRes), Photoshop 3.0 or higher, MacPaint, PNG, TIFF, PICT, Targa.

◆ Multiple-image file—FLC, FLI (Windows), PICS, Scrapbook (Macintosh).

◆ Sound—AIFF, WAV, MP3, Shockwave Audio, Sun AU, uncompressed and IMA compressed, and System 7 Sound (Macintosh only).

◆ Video—QuickTime 2 and higher, AVI.

◆ Text—RFT, HTML, ASCII, Lingo scripts.

Use programs like Flash to create vector-based graphics and animations to import into Director (Figure 2–12, also found in the color section).

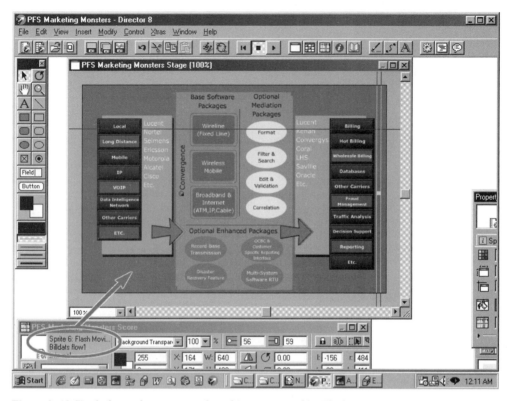

Figure 2–12 Single frame from a vector-based image created in Flash.

PREPARE TO TEST, TEST, AND RE-TEST

I cannot emphasize enough that you must get into the habit of testing early in the production process and testing often. This philosophy holds true even more so for those of you designing more complex programs. The higher the degree of complexity, the more often you need to test your program to ensure accurate results. No matter how good a programmer you think you are, it is never fun to assume that you have laid out all of your cards in the proper order, when … BAM! The program doesn't work. Every time you make a significant change to a portion of your Director movie is generally a good time to take a few moments and make sure that what you have designed is functioning the exact way you had intended it to play.

> **Give your program what I call the "Grandma test." Find a person who has little knowledge about computers and let them run through your application. If they can get through the majority of your application without struggling, then you know the average person will have no problem using your program.**

CUSTOMIZED SETTINGS

You will have to make some decisions when you set up your project from the very beginning. Depending upon the client's request, you will have to set your stage dimensions. Most stand-alone applications used to be set at 640 by 480 pixels. Today, with higher screen resolutions and more applications being developed for the Web, there really is no standard size. That is why it is so important to communicate with your client and establish these settings when you begin designing your program. To set the size of your movie's stage:

1. Select Movie from the Modify menu.
2. Select Properties from the popup menu.

   OR

   Select the Movie tab from the Property Inspector.
3. Enter numeric values in the Stage Size fields to set the dimensions for the current stage (Figure 2–13).

> **Tip!** Click on the triangle to view the popup menu of standard stage sizes for multimedia applications (Figure 2–14).

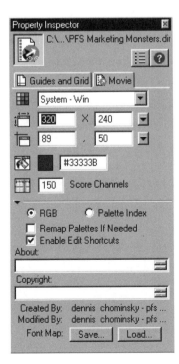

Figure 2–13 Use the Property Inspector to customize your movie's settings.

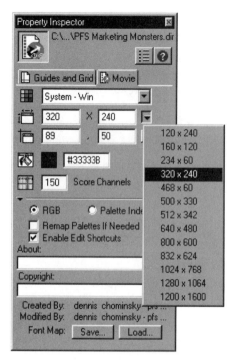

Figure 2–14 Use one of the default stage sizes or enter your own custom size (in pixels).

 You can change the size of your stage at a later time. However, changing the size may affect the placement of your sprites on the stage, and may even affect whether they are displayed at all.

The next set of field entries defines the stage's placement. Similar to the stage size, you can choose from one of the preset locations (Centered or Upper Left) or numerically enter your own custom setting. I highly recommend that if you do not need a custom screen location, set it to display in the Centered position. Depending on the stage size you set and the display settings of the end-user's system, you run the risk of having one or more of the edges hidden off-screen (Figure 2–15). By setting it for the Centered location, no matter what size monitor the user is watching your program on, the image will appear centered in the middle of his screen.

Color Palettes

The first setting in the Property Inspector under the Movie tab involves choosing a color palette that will be used to display your images (Figure 2–16).

Another important setting in this window that you will need is the Stage Fill Color. This is what determines the background color of the viewing area. To change the stage color:

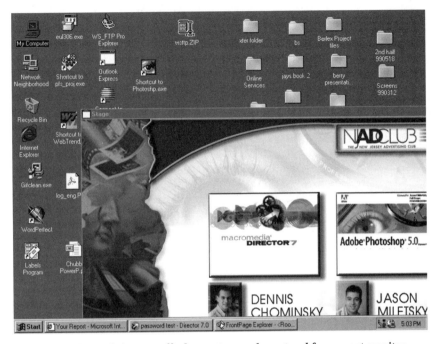

Figure 2–15 Image being cut off when not properly centered for current monitor settings.

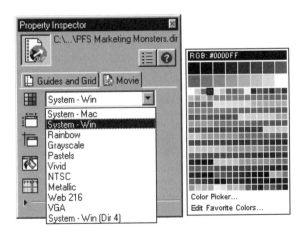

Figure 2–16 Director's default Movie Palette menu.

1. Click on the Stage Fill Color swatch located in the Property Inspector. A color palette will appear (Figure 2–17).

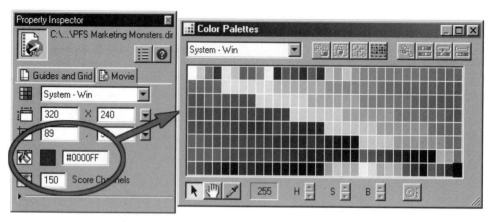

Figure 2–17 Select the background color from the popup Color Palette.

2. Select the color you wish to display in the background of your movie.

OR

Enter the RGB or hexidecimal number next to the color swatch. This value is used more often by Web developers (Figure 2–18).

For end-users who set their monitor resolution higher than that of the size of your movie's stage, you can select an option in Director to fill the outside of your application

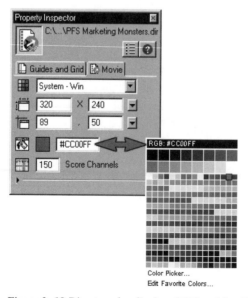

Figure 2–18 Director also displays RGB and hexidecimal color values for consistency with your HTML programming.

with the same color that you have chosen for the background color of the stage. This way, there is continuous color from the edge of your stage to the edge of the monitor. The viewer will not be distracted by any open desktop windows while viewing the movie (Figure 2–19). You can select this option to cover the desktop around the stage's viewing area when you are ready to finalize your movie and make a projector. To select this option:

1. Select Create Projector from the File menu. The Create Projector dialog box will appear.
2. Click the Options button. The Projector Options dialog box appears.
3. Click the Full Screen radio button under Options (Figure 2–20).
4. Click OK.

Once you save your project and create a projector, anytime you launch the executable projector file, your movie will play back fully covering the desktop screen (portions outside the outer boundaries of your stage). If the resolution of your monitor is the same as the program you made, your movie will play back filling up the entire screen. If the resolution of your monitor is set higher than the size of your Director application, your movie will play back in a window and the rest of the desktop will be filled with whatever color you selected as the stage color.

UTILIZE THIRD-PARTY PROGRAMS

What really makes Director a powerful authoring application is its ability to seamlessly integrate files from other programs. Even though Director 8 Shockwave Studio comes packaged with other applications, you may need to work with other professional design tools with features not included in the studio package's software. There are a few programs that no multimedia developer should live without.

 Keep one thing in mind before you go out and blow your whole budget on these software programs. Just because you buy the best programs doesn't mean you can create the best images and files.

Most multimedia software programs, including Director, take a little bit of talent and a whole lot of time before the user can become even remotely proficient with them. Some of the third-party software and hardware packages that I will be referencing throughout the course of this book include:

◆ Adobe Photoshop—For creating and editing bitmapped graphics and layered images.

◆ Macromedia Flash—For creating vector-based graphics and animations with extremely small file sizes.

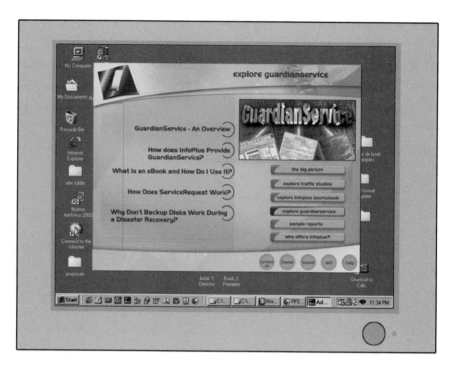

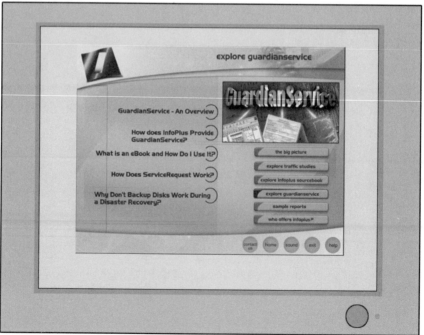

Figure 2–19 A comparison between filling the screen with background color and not fill-ing with background color when the stage size is smaller than the display resolution.

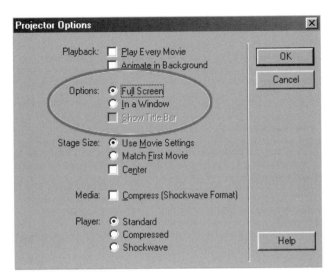

Figure 2–20 Full Screen setting for projectors.

◆ Adobe Premiere—For creating and editing digital audio and video clips.

◆ Terran Interactive Media Cleaner Pro—For compressing and formatting digital audio and video files.

◆ 3D Studio Max and Infini-D—For creating three-dimensional graphics and animations.

You can really use any combination of the various programs available on the market to create the elements you need to build your project. This again is what makes Director such a powerful and sophisticated authoring program.

BE A NEAT FREAK: MANAGE YOUR MOVIE

One of the best recommendations that I can make that will save you time and aggravation is to keep your cast members neat and organized from the beginning. Many developers waste time performing redundant steps or searching for a particular cast member through thousands of others because they did not break up and organize their project. Remember, each cast can hold up to 32,000 cast members. Do you have the time to constantly search and scroll through 32,000 cast members every time you need to find an image? Take the time in your pre-planning stage to organize the types of files you will be using and determine whether or not you will be able to use these files again in another project. Following are a few suggestions that you can employ so that you can devote more time toward building your movie rather than hunting for lost cast members:

◆   Name each cast member.

◆   Group similar cast members together.

◆   Group cast members for each section of your movie together.

◆   Work with multiple casts.

◆   Use the list view column headings to sort on various information.

◆   Build external casts of common images that can be used for other projects.

Do Not Name Files John Doe

If you follow only one of the above-mentioned organizational techniques, I suggest that you uniquely name each cast member. Do not just leave them numbered. Label each one with a name that identifies what image it relates to or what purpose the cast member fulfills. A proper naming convention might look like:

◆   Home button.

◆   FAQ button.

◆   Background image.

◆   Play loop script.

A not-so-effective method might be:

◆   Button.

◆   Button 2.

◆   Untitled.

◆   Script 1.

Developing an accurate naming convention will not only make finding cast members easier, but will ensure that you are working with the right sprites in the score (Figure 2–21).

Images to the Left, Behaviors to the Right

Another method to help organize your cast members is to group similar items together. If you import graphics that will be used as buttons for the interface, keep them all grouped together in-line. Keep all of your behaviors and scripts grouped together in another area of your cast (Figure 2–22). If you haphazardly place them all over throughout one cast, it takes time scrolling through the cast to find the one you are looking to use. In addition to placing similar cast members alongside each other, try to

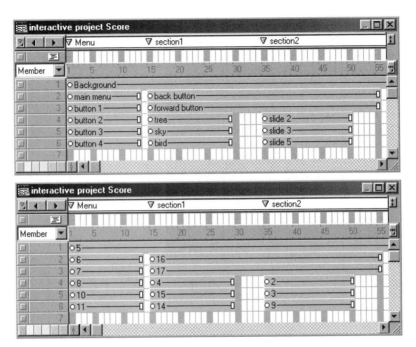

Figure 2–21 Naming sprites makes finding specific ones in the score much easier.

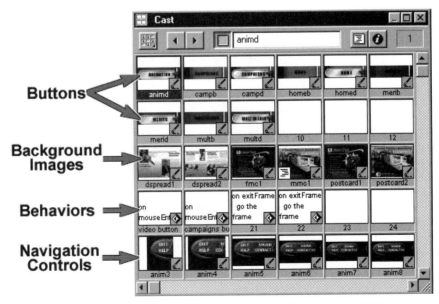

Figure 2–22 Organizing similar cast members in groups for easy accessibility.

group cast members used for each section of your movie in their own distinctive area of the cast. For instance, divide your cast up into distinctive areas for each part of your movie that is designated by a new marker (Figure 2–23). Cast members used within the same section of your movie should be grouped together in the cast.

You can leave empty cast member cells to space out your groups for easier visibility while in frame view.

Add a text cast member before each grouping of cast members to easily identify the name of each section (Figure 2–24).

Save Time with Multiple Casts

Setting up multiple casts may seem to be overkill at first, but once you start working on large multimedia projects with thousands of files, you will really appreciate how easy searching for the right files can be without the hassle of combing through unnecessary cast members. There is no need to try scrolling through hundreds of cast members trying to find a digital video clip among all the other graphics, behaviors, scripts, sound files, and text fields. By separating cast members into categories, it becomes very easy to find a particular file (Figure 2–25).

There are many other reasons to divide your elements into separate casts. One of the biggest advantages is that you can create and save these external casts as virtual libraries for use in other projects. If there are certain elements that you seem to use over

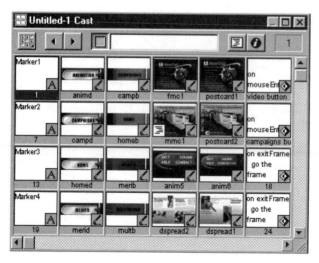

Figure 2–23 Organizing cast members by the section in which they appear in the movie.

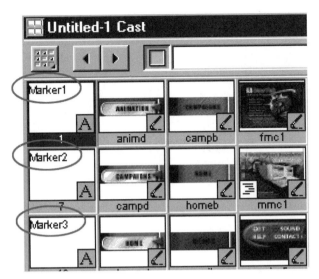

Figure 2–24 Using a text cast member to identify the sections or groupings of the cast members.

and over again in other projects, you can save yourself the hassle of importing these elements for every project. Depending on the types of projects you create, you may want to save separate casts for the following categories:

◆ Logos and images.

◆ Customized behaviors and scripts.

◆ Buttons and navigational elements.

◆ Sound clips.

◆ Digital video files.

◆ Transitions and effects.

 External cast members work just like other types of external files; they are just linked files. This means that you must keep the external cast with the Director movie (whether in .DIR, .DCR, or projector format).

Use Linked External Casts

Is this a project for a client that may have different applications for this material in the future? Are there certain files that you seem to use over and over in different projects? If so, you may be wasting time by constantly searching for and importing these files

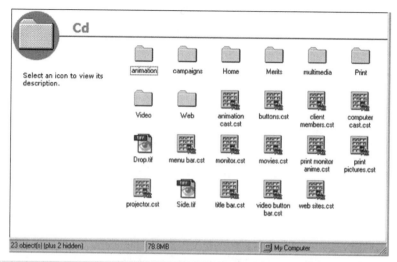

Figure 2–25 Dividing cast members into distinct multiple casts.

into new casts for every project. If you plan on using cast members across several Director movies, you might opt for linking an external cast to each individual movie. To link an external cast to the current movie:

1. Select Movie from the Modify menu.

2. Select Cast from the popup menu. A Movie Cast window appears, showing a list of all the casts associated with this particular movie.

3. Click the Link button at the bottom of the window to link an external cast to the current movie (Figure 2–26).

4. Use the standard filesystem to find your external cast and select it. Now your external cast has been added to the Movie Cast window.

5. Click OK.

To see which casts are available for your current movie, click the Choose Cast button on the current Cast window (Figure 2–27).

Using Unlinked External Casts

When you bring an unlinked external cast into a movie and try to drag a cast member to the score or stage, you will be prompted with a dialog box asking if you would

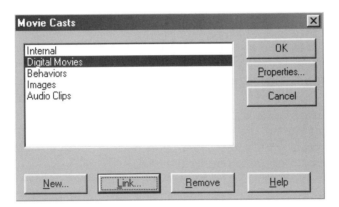

Figure 2–26 Link to external cast.

Figure 2–27 A pull-down menu displays a list of all casts linked to the current movie.

like to link this cast to the current movie. If you prefer not to link the entire external cast to the movie, you must then copy the cast member(s) that you wish to use into an internal cast.

Use Unlinked External Casts as Libraries

Not every cast needs to link to a particular movie. One great example is to consider creating your own cast library. To create an external cast to be used as a library, simply type the word "library" as the last word when you name and save your cast. Director will interpret this cast as a library (just like Director's internal libraries). Director will automatically copy a cast member to an internal cast in your current movie when you drag a cast member out from an external cast library to the stage or score. Basically, you can use this "library" of cast members as a pool or holding area for items such as buttons and behaviors that you will use on a regular basis in other movies.

Remember when distributing and packaging your movie either on a disk, CD, or the Internet, you must include the external cast file. For more information on packaging your movies, see Chapter 10.

LEAVE A PAPER TRAIL

No one likes to do paperwork. However, keeping a notebook on hand to document any important procedures or scripts that you produce will come in handy the next time you need to recreate the same situation. Nothing is more frustrating than trying to replicate or figure out how and why you did something a certain way. This will become your own personal database of information, full of tips and tricks you have learned and utilized. This personalized reference guide will come in handy the next time you are trying to troubleshoot a situation that you previously worked out in a project several months ago.

Have documentation to back up what steps were taken to perform certain programming tasks, especially when working with a team of people on a project. This way, if you or another team member is unable to continue, someone else can easily figure out where to pick up.

REPURPOSE FILES FOR MULTIMEDIA PROJECTS

If you are working on a project where the client may want to use the images and designs you create in a broader campaign of other media types (print, video, Web), you should consider developing your images so that they can be repurposed for more than one medium. Designing your images to be used for various media purposes from the beginning is more efficient than creating new content for each phase of a project. It is easy to design an image at 300 dpi (usual print resolution) and scale it down to 72 dpi (standard video and CD-ROM resolution). It is quite impossible to convert an image in the other direction. Therefore, planning ahead and asking the client before you start could save you the trouble of doing the work twice. Plus, you may even increase your budget and get more work out of the client. You will come out looking like a hero, producing a multi-product campaign with a consistent look and feel, all by doing the initial work once.

SUMMARY

This chapter discussed a number of techniques you can use to help manage a new multimedia project. The best steps when pre-planning any project are to ask a lot of questions in the beginning and continue to ask questions throughout the entire process of your development. No one likes to work with someone watching over her shoulder, but periodic progress and approval phases will keep your project on target. Taking the time to prepare all of your materials instead of trying to rush into things can save you an enormous amount of time in the long run. Get organized. Ask questions. Be patient.

chapter 3

NAVIGATIONAL CONTROLS FOR INTERACTIVE APPLICATIONS

Technology fascinates us, especially when it comes to CD-ROMs, kiosks, and the Internet. Whether it's for educational or entertainment purposes, what makes these things so interesting is the ability for us to interact with them. The real strength of Director comes from its ability to make your movies interactive. No matter what style designs you create, no matter what type of content you include, developing applications with Director offers the user the choice of how, where, and when to maneuver around the program.

CONTROL THE SPEED OF YOUR MOVIE

Before you can begin setting interactive controls, you need to know how your movie will play. To control how your movie will play, you need to add commands for Director to acknowledge so that your movie will perform the way you intended. Tempo settings are primarily used to adjust the rate of how fast or slow sprites are displayed and animated during playback.

The type of system you have will also affect the playback performance of your movie. The amount of RAM you have, type of hard drive, and the speed of your processor will determine how smoothly your Director movies run. If your computer cannot play a movie at its intended rate, Director will automatically slow down the tempo during playback to play every frame. The opposite effect occurs when Director tries to play digital audio and video files, however. Since it cannot change the speed at which the digital media files were created, Director begins to randomly drop frames to complete the duration time of the file. For example, a five-second video clip created at 30 frames per second will inevitably drop a few frames on a slower machine so Director can play the movie in exactly five seconds. Therefore, the Tempo setting does not have any bearing on how digital audio and video files play. The playback rate for these files is determined when they are created. Check out Chapter 7, "Avoiding Audio and Video Nightmares," to find out more about working with digital audio and video files in Director.

USE THE WAIT FEATURE

Although the Wait option is not technically an interactive command, it is a useful feature that adds more control to the playback performance of your movie. To set up a Wait command:

1. Double-click the frame in the Tempo channel of your score where you want to adjust the playback speed of your movie.

2. The Frame Properties: Tempo dialog box appears (Figure 3–1).

3. Select Wait to have the playback head pause on that particular frame for the amount of time you choose. When the playback head enters that frame, it will hold on that frame for the set time, and then continue playing the rest of your movie.

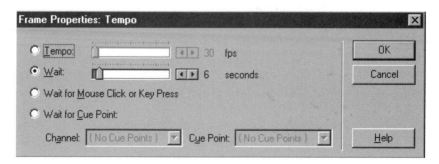

Figure 3–1 Frame Properties: Tempo dialog box.

ADD BASIC INTERACTION

The most basic type of user interaction you can add to your movie is the ability to continue on to the next section or screen with a click of the mouse or a keypress. This type of interactivity is useful when creating Director movies that will be used for presentations or when you want to allow the user to proceed at her own pace. Use the Wait for Mouse Click or Keypress feature to hold on a particular frame indefinitely until the user chooses to move on. There are two ways to set up this function:

Using Behaviors:

1. Open the Library Palette from the Window menu.
2. Select Navigation from the Library List popup menu.
3. Drag the Wait for Mouse Click or Keypress behavior into your score and place it in the frame of the Script channel (Figure 3–2).
4. The Parameters for "Wait for Mouse Click or Keypress" window appears. Select Wait for Click, Wait for Keypress, or both (Figure 3–3).
5. Click OK.

OR

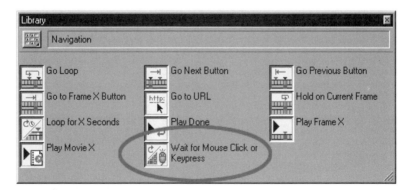

Figure 3–2 Some frame behaviors include all of the necessary scripting to add basic interactive features to your movie.

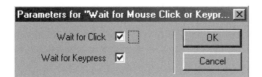

Figure 3–3 The Parameters for "Wait for Mouse Click or Keypress" window.

Using the Tempo channel:

1. Double-click the Tempo channel in the frame where you want to add this control. (Typically, add it to the last frame of a sprite before a new image appears or another event takes place.)

2. Click the Wait for Mouse Click or Keypress radio button in the Frame Properties: Tempo window to activate the command.

3. Click OK.

4. Rewind and play your movie.

The playback head will hold in the frame that you set in the Wait for Mouse Click or Keypress command. To signify that your movie is still in play mode, the cursor turns into a blinking arrow pointing down to let the user know that Director is waiting for a command to continue on with the program (Figure 3–4).

You are now *interacting* with your movie. If you want to add this control to every screen of a slideshow presentation, use copy and paste.

1. Create the first Wait for Mouse Click or Keypress command.

2. Single-click that frame to highlight it.

3. Use the Copy Sprite feature located under the Edit menu or use the keyboard shortcut Control-C for Windows or Command-C for Macintosh.

4. Click the frame where you want to add this command again.

5. Use the Paste Sprite feature under the Edit menu or use the keyboard shortcut Control-V for Windows or Command-V for Macintosh.

6. Repeat Steps 4 and 5 to add this command to any other frames.

DIRECTOR: A NON-LINEAR WORLD

The best way to approach any new Director project is to plan out your project before you begin programming. Don't panic, however, if you realize at the last minute that you forgot to include a section or need to change the order of the sequence. Depending on the complexity of your program, it may only involve changing a few commands as

Figure 3–4 The cursor changes to a blinking arrow while waiting for a mouse click.

opposed to completely renovating your entire score. Working in a non-linear fashion means that you do not have to build sections in your score next to each other for them to play sequentially. Director uses a combination of markers and script commands (behaviors and lingo) to allow the playback head to maneuver around the score to different sections of your movie.

MOVE AROUND WITH MARKERS

Markers are the key ingredients used for navigation to identify specific sections of your movie. Using Lingo scripts or behaviors, Director responds to these commands and brings the playback head to the area defined by these markers. To add a new marker, click in the Markers channel. To delete a marker, drag it out of the channel.

To set markers in the score and jump to different sections of the score:

1. Add the sprite(s) for the first section of your movie to the score starting in frame 1.
2. Add sprites to the score for additional sections starting in frames 30, 60, 90, etc.
3. Add a marker to frame 1 and name it "Menu".
4. Add a marker to frame 30 and name it "Section2".
5. Add a marker to the first frame of each sprite series that you added to the score and name each one appropriately (Figure 3–5).

These markers will designate the "jump to" areas for Director when you begin adding interactive commands to the movie using simple Lingo scripts. To leave one section and navigate with markers to a new area, add the following frame or sprite script:

Sprite script:

```
on mouseUp
      go to marker "NameOfMarker"
end
```

Frame script:

```
on exitFrame
      go to marker "NameOfMarker"
end
```

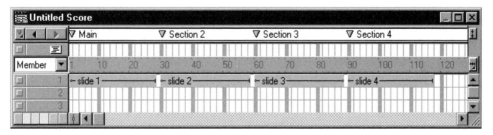

Figure 3–5 Naming each marker to identify a new section of the score.

When using Lingo, marker names must always be put in quotation marks.

You can also use behaviors to move around via markers you have added to your score:

1. Open the Library Palette from the Window menu.
2. Select Controls from the Library List pull-down menu.
3. Drag the Jump to Marker behavior from the Library Palette and place it onto a sprite. The Parameters for "Jump to Marker Button" window appears.
4. Select a marker by name or choose next, previous, or loop from the pull-down menu (Figure 3–6).
5. Optional: Check the Remember current marker for Back button? checkbox if you are using this behavior in conjunction with the Jump Back Button behavior.
6. Click OK.

NAME MARKERS

It is crucial that you take the time to name each marker you add to a score. Because Director uses markers as navigational reference points, they need to be labeled so that the playback head can locate the precise frame when a command is given. Things to keep in mind when naming markers:

◆ Keep the name limited to a one-word alphanumeric name with no spaces.
◆ Precise spelling counts.
◆ Markers are not case-sensitive (i.e., menu, MENU, Menu, mENU, and mEnU are all the same name).

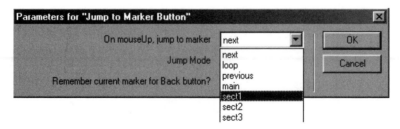

Figure 3–6 Choose from a complete list of user-created markers for this movie as well as relative markers to direct where the playback head should jump to on a mouseUp *command.*

ADD COMMENTS TO MARKERS

Since Director uses a one-word naming convention for markers, it can be limiting on how you name each section. Using the Marker window, you can add descriptive comments for each marker to remind you of the purpose and function of a marker. The Markers window is especially helpful when:

◆ Other programmers will be assisting you on a project. It will help them understand where these markers navigate to and from.

◆ You are working on multiple projects simultaneously.

◆ You need a refresher when updating a project that has not been worked on in some time.

To open the Markers window:

1. Add markers to your score and name them.

2. Select Markers from the Window menu or use the keyboard shortcut Control-Shift-M (Windows) or Command-Shift-M (Macintosh).

   OR

   Click the Markers Menu button in the score to open a menu with two choices. Select Markers to open the Markers window (Figure 3–7).

3. In the left-hand column, select from a list of markers already in your score.

4. Click in the right-hand column and press the Enter key (Windows) or the Return key (Macintosh) to start a new line.

5. Type in any useful text comment.

 Do not type over the marker name in the right-hand window as it will change the name of your marker. Make sure to press the Enter or Return key to move down to the next line.

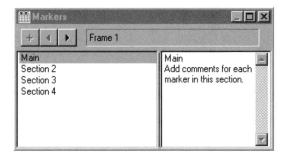

Figure 3–7 Markers window.

NEXT, PREVIOUS, AND REPEAT WITH MARKERS

In your Director movie, you will often find it helpful to have controls that move the user to the next section, return to the previous section, or loop within the same section (starting it over again from the beginning of that marker) (Figure 3–8, also found in the color section). Relative markers allow you to navigate forward or backward one section at a time in relationship to where the playback head is, without writing elaborate Lingo commands for each section (Figure 3–9). The user can jump from one section to the next in either direction by simply applying a command to a navigational sprite.

Figure 3–8 Previous, repeat, and next buttons for navigation.

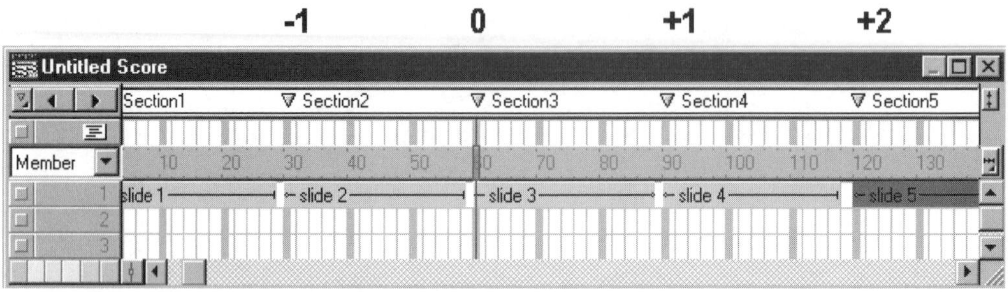

Figure 3–9 Relative markers illustrated for simplifying next and previous navigation.

To jump to the next section designated by a marker:

```
on mouseUp
    go to marker (1)
end
```

You can also use the Go Next Button behavior found under the Navigation section of the Library Palette. Simply drag it onto the sprite to cause the playback head to jump to the next marker in your score when the sprite is clicked.

To jump to the previous section designated by a marker:

```
on mouseUp
    go to marker (-1)
end
```

You can also use the Go Previous Button behavior. Simply drag it onto the sprite to cause the playback head to jump to the previous marker in your score when the sprite is clicked.

To jump back to the beginning of the same section designated by a marker:

```
on mouseUp
    go to marker (0)
end
```

You can also use the Go Loop behavior. Simply drag it onto the sprite to cause the playback head to jump to the marker at the beginning of the current section when the sprite is clicked. And for you Lingo fanatics:

```
on mouseUp
    go loop
end
```

The Return to Beginning of Current Section command, or Repeat button, is very useful in training-type applications where the user would benefit from repeating the information before continuing on to the next section (Figure 3–10).

THE BASICS OF BEHAVIORS

For those of you not already familiar with them, behaviors are templates of pre-written Lingo commands for those who wish to create interactive multimedia applications without having to learn how to write complex programming commands. Director has taken a great deal of the work out of manually typing lines of commands to implement

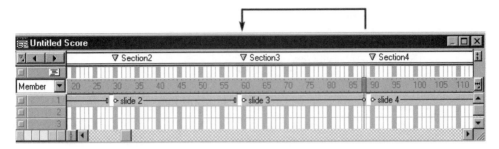

Figure 3–10 The Repeat button allows the viewer to replay the current section of the movie designated by the closest previous marker in the score.

common interactive events. Behaviors are simply a way to add functionality to your movie through a series of drag and drop icons that contain specific commands, applying all of the necessary Lingo scripts for you behind the scenes. All you have to do is enter the specific information you want the behavior to perform. When that specified event occurs, the behavior performs that certain function. After viewing this chapter, take a look at Chapter 9, "Advancing Techniques with Behaviors and Lingo," for more information on using behaviors to customize your movies.

 Behaviors can be attached to sprites or frames. Sprites can have as many behaviors as needed, whereas frames can only contain one behavior.

USE THE BEHAVIOR LIBRARY

Director has taken a number of the most often used commands and created behaviors for them. These behaviors reside in the Library Palette, ready to be applied to the sprites in your score.

To access the Library Palette:

1. Click the Window menu.
2. Select Library Palette (Figure 3–11). The Library Palette contains the default behaviors available in Director.
3. Click the Library List popup menu to select one of the different categories of behaviors (Figure 3–12).

Drag and drop the behavior onto the appropriate sprite or frame. It's basically that easy. The type of action you are trying to achieve will determine whether you apply the behavior to a sprite or place it on a frame in the Script channel. Director automatically adds a copy of that behavior to the current cast so you can customize its specific function without changing the original template. To apply a behavior from the Library Palette:

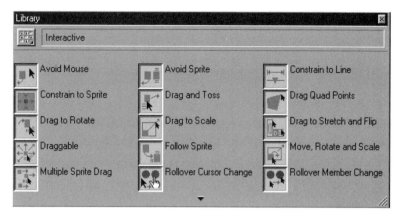

Figure 3–11 Library Palette.

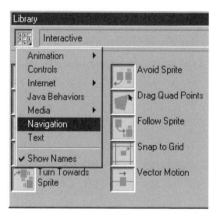

Figure 3–12 Library List category menu.

1. Select Library Palette from the Window menu.
2. Drag a behavior to the appropriate sprite or frame in your score.
3. Enter the desired parameters for the dialog box that appears (Figure 3–13).

Each dialog box contains a different set of parameters depending upon which behavior is selected.

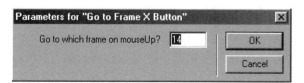

Figure 3–13 Example of a Parameters window for a behavior.

CUSTOMIZE BEHAVIORS

The default behaviors are a great time-saver for basic interactive programming. However, most of the time you will want to modify the commands. Use the Behavior Inspector to create your own or modify existing behaviors for interactive commands.

1. Click the Behavior Inspector icon (gear-shaped button) in the score (Figure 3–14).

   OR

   Click the Behavior Inspector icon (gear-shaped button) on the toolbar along the top of your screen (Figure 3–15).

   OR

   Select Inspectors from the Window menu. Choose Behavior from the submenu. The Behavior Inspector will appear (Figure 3–16).

2. Click the Behavior popup button (plus sign) at the top of the Behavior Inspector window. Click New Behavior to create a new behavior or select from one of the existing behaviors in your movie.

3. Click the Events popup button (plus sign) at the middle left of the Behavior Inspector window. Select from one of the existing events in the list or click New Event. For existing behaviors, highlight the event that you want to alter by single-clicking it.

4. Click the Actions popup button (plus sign) at the middle right of the Behavior Inspector window. Select a new action or alter an existing one.

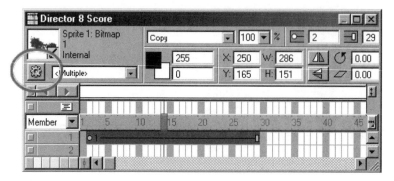

Figure 3–14 The Behavior Inspector icon located in the score.

Figure 3–15 The Behavior Inspector icon located on the toolbar.

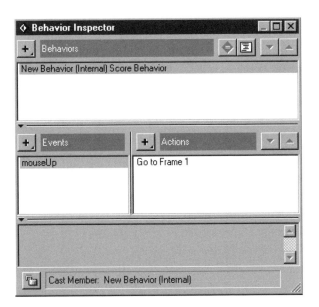

Figure 3–16 The Behavior Inspector.

 If you are using one of the included behaviors from the Library Palette, Director automatically places a copy of that behavior into your cast. This will prevent you from accidentally changing the characteristics of the template's behavior.

ADD COMMENTS TO BEHAVIORS

You can add comments to remind yourself or another developer about the purpose or function of a particular behavior. Type an on getBehaviorDescription handler in the script of the behavior to add a description in the bottom pane of the Behavior Inspector (Figure 3–17).

```
on getBehaviorDescription
        return "Type in the behavior comment here."
end
```

SAVE CUSTOM BEHAVIORS

The best time-saver of all comes when you only have to program functions once then reuse them over again in the same or a different project. There's no point in re-inventing the wheel every time you create a new project. To save your behaviors for later use, you

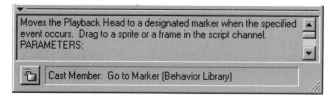

Figure 3–17 A description of a behavior at the bottom of the
Behavior Inspector window.

will need to create a new unlinked cast. This will act as a library where you store all of
your custom behaviors. To create a library in which to store custom behaviors:

1. Select New from the File menu.

2. Select Cast from the popup menu or use the keyboard shortcut Control-Alt-N
   (Windows) or Command-Option-N (Macintosh). The New Cast window appears
   (Figure 3–18).

3. Name the cast.

4. Select External as the Storage type.

5. Deselect the Use in Current Movie option.

6. With the new cast still highlighted, select Save from the File menu.

7. Save the movie in a location where you can access it (and remember where you
   put it).

 **Remember, you'll need to distribute the cast with your movie when
you use externally linked cast members.**

The next time you want to use that functionality, you can just drag it from your customized library cast of behaviors. Each one will maintain all of its events and action
characteristics you applied to it when creating it. All you have to do is supply Director
with the new specifications for the sprite or frame to which you are applying the custom behavior.

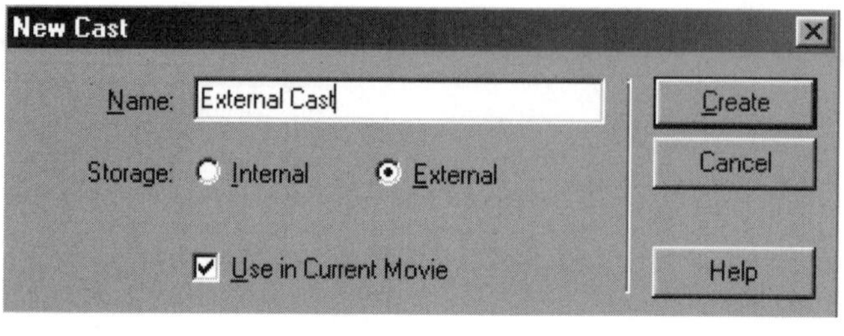

Figure 3–18 A New Cast window.

CHANGE THE DEFAULT EDITOR

The Behavior Inspector is the default window that appears when you want to make changes to an existing behavior. For those users who prefer to edit behaviors using Lingo, you can change the default setting to work in the Script window.

1. Choose Preferences from the File menu.
2. Select Editor. The Editors Preferences window appears (Figure 3–19).
3. Click Behavior.
4. Click the Edit button. A dialog box appears asking you to select the default editor for behaviors.
5. Click the radio button to select which method you would prefer to use to edit behaviors.
6. Click OK.

BUILD INTERACTIVE APPLICATIONS USING BEHAVIORS

Customizing behaviors allows you to create some pretty intricate functions, from interactive navigational links to controls for different media types. The following example

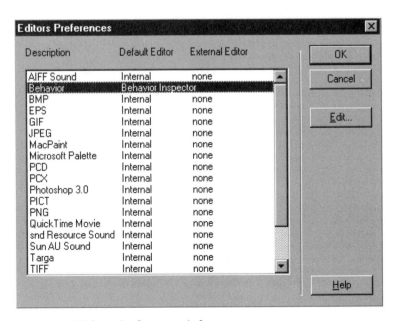

Figure 3–19 Editors Preferences window.

will show you how to apply behaviors to create an entire interactive project. Before you begin adding behaviors or scripts, build your timeline by placing all of the necessary sprites in their proper location in the score. Using various interactive screens as examples (Figure 3–20, also found in the color section), you will learn how to:

◆ Apply behaviors to create sprite rollover properties.

◆ Apply behaviors to create sprite navigational links.

◆ Apply behaviors to frame scripts.

◆ Duplicate behaviors to apply to different sprites.

◆ Customize and save behavior templates.

CONTROL PLAYBACK WITH BEHAVIORS

One of the most common commands used in Director is to hold the playback head on a particular frame, waiting for the user to choose an interactive selection available on the screen. To add this Hold on Current Frame behavior:

Figure 3–20 Various types of interactive multimedia interfaces.

1. Add a sprite to your score.
2. Select Library Palette from the Window menu.
3. Select Navigation from the Library List pull-down menu.
4. Drag the Hold on Current Frame behavior to the Script channel of your score and place it on the last frame of the sprite (Figure 3–21).
5. Rewind and play your movie. Notice how the playback head stops in the frame with the behavior script while the Director movie remains in play mode.

This type of command can be used on any frame where the user has navigation choices available. This command will keep the Director movie waiting in a frame until the user makes a choice of which step to take next. This command will be used more frequently as you add more interactive elements to your movie.

CREATE ROLLOVERS WITH THE BEHAVIOR INSPECTOR

Most multimedia applications that I've seen incorporate some type of user interaction to show responsiveness to the movements of the mouse. One of the most common is the basic rollover. That is, the program is set to change the characteristics of any button on the interface when the mouse moves into that area. Creating rollovers in Director is easy:

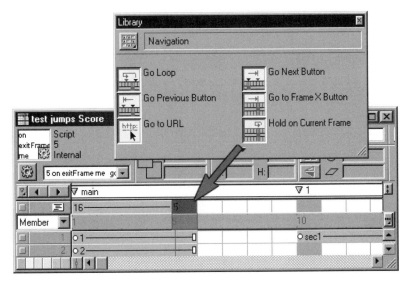

Figure 3–21 The Hold On Current Frame behavior is added to the score to hold the playback head in that frame while the movie remains in play mode.

1. Import all of the graphic elements you need (see Chapter 5 for more information on designing elements for interactive programs).

2. Select the sprite to which you want to apply rollover properties.

3. Open the Behavior Inspector.

4. Click the Behavior popup button (plus sign) at the top left corner of the window to add a new behavior.

5. Select New Behavior and name it (e.g., Rollover).

6. Click the Events popup button (plus sign) in the Events column. Select a command from the list of (most commonly used) events in the popup menu.

7. Choose mouseEnter. This command will tell Director to perform whichever action we set for this sprite when the mouse enters the proximity of the sprite. The bounding box area determines the proximity of the sprite (Figure 3–22).

8. Click the Actions popup button (plus sign) in the Actions column.

9. Select Sprite from the popup menu.

10. Choose Change Cast Member from the Sprite submenu.

11. Select the cast member that you want to display when your mouse enters the area of the original sprite.

12. Rewind and play back your movie.

 Note * Notice a new behavior named "Rollover" was automatically added to your cast.

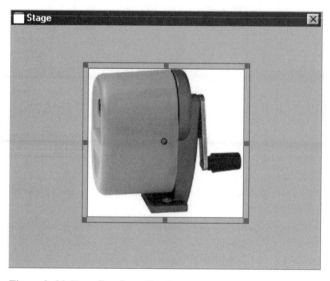

Figure 3–22 Bounding box of sprite.

Now when you play the movie, the original sprite will change to the new sprite you selected when the mouse rolls over the area of the original sprite. Since we only set a command to change the sprite when the mouse enters the area, the new sprite will remain displayed for the remainder of the movie. You must set the commands for the second part of a rollover, which is to change back to the original cast member as the mouse leaves the vicinity of the sprite. To set the reverse command:

1. With the original sprite still selected, open the Behavior Inspector.
2. Make sure "Rollover" is the behavior listed in the top of the dialog box.
3. In the Events column, select mouseLeave from the popup menu.
4. In the Actions column, select Sprite from the popup menu.
5. Choose Change Cast Member from the Sprite submenu.
6. Select the original cast member to be displayed when your mouse leaves the area of the rolled-over sprite.
7. Rewind and play your movie. Notice how the sprite changes when you move the mouse in and out of the area set for the original sprite (Figure 3–23).

SPRITE NAVIGATION WITH BEHAVIORS

Adding a navigational function when the user clicks an active button or link is the most basic yet important aspect of an interactive application. Using behaviors minimizes the time needed to add this functionality and eliminates most of the typographical errors common with writing Lingo scripts manually. To make sprites have navigational characteristics using behaviors:

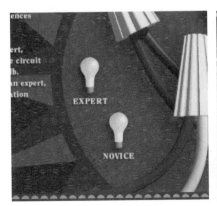 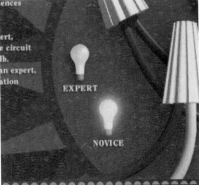

Figure 3–23 The sprite changes appearance as the mouse "rolls over" it.

1. Select the sprite you want to use as a navigational control element (Figure 3–24).
2. Open the Behavior Inspector.
3. Select New Behavior from the Behavior popup menu and name it.
4. Select mouseUp from the Events popup menu.
5. Select Navigation from the Actions popup menu.
6. Choose Go to Frame from the Navigation submenu.
7. Specify the frame number where you want the playback head to go when the mouse button is clicked and released (Figure 3–25).

REUSE BEHAVIOR TEMPLATES

Now that you have created an interactive link with behaviors, use that as a template to add navigational functionality to all of the other sprites in your movie that require the same type of command. Use the behavior that you created for the first button and apply it to the rest of the navigational buttons.

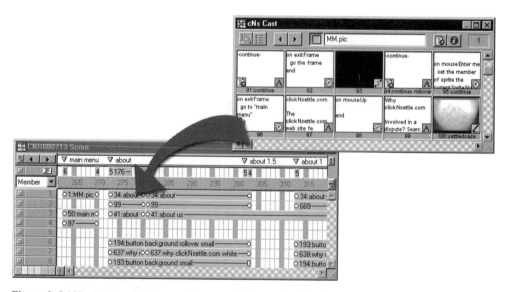

Figure 3–24 Navigational behavior being applied to a selected sprite.

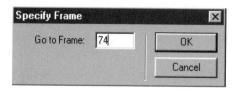

Figure 3–25 Specify a frame in the Go to Frame field.

Hold the Alt key (Windows) or the Option key (Macintosh) and drag a cast member to an open panel in the cast to make an exact copy of the cast member.

1. Select the behavior cast member you just created in the previous section and copy it.
2. Duplicate the behavior in your cast as many times as you need to assign one to each button on the interface (Figure 3–26).
3. Rename the behaviors according to the links to which they will be applied (Figure 3–27).
4. Drag each new behavior cast member to its respective sprite.
5. Single-click on one of the new sprites to select it.
6. Click one of the Script window buttons to open the Script window or use the keyboard shortcut Control-0 (Windows) or Command-0 (Macintosh).
7. Change the frame number variable in the Specify Frame dialog box to where you want that sprite to jump (Figure 3–28).

If you are using any type of interactivity, you will want to use a Wait command or a Hold on Current Frame script so that the user has ample time to make a selection without having the playback head leave that section. This way, the user gets a chance to make a selection.

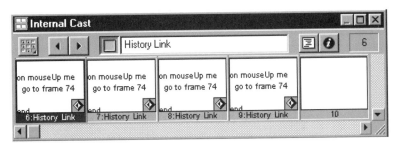

Figure 3–26 A cast with multiple copies of a behavior.

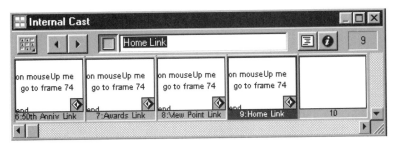

Figure 3–27 Renaming behaviors for specific tasks.

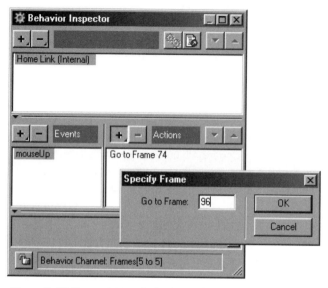

Figure 3–28 Customizing a behavior to link to a new frame number.

I QUIT

The most important navigational element you can include in your movie is a Quit or Exit feature. Unless your projector is set to automatically quit, the user will be stuck eternally inside your application without some type of Exit command. Even with an auto-exit, the user may want or need to stop your movie before the end. The only alternative would be to force-quit or reboot the system. The Quit command is the shortest and simplest command. Enter the following text depending on the type of script being applied:

For a frame script:

```
on exitFrame
      quit
end
```

For a sprite script:

```
on mouseUp
      quit
end
```

You can add different handlers to perform an action with any event you choose (on keyDown, **on** mouseEnter, **etc).**

SUMMARY

The examples listed in this chapter cover just some of the basic navigational controls that you can, and probably will, apply to every project you create. You can see how working with behaviors makes programming your Director movies fast, easy, and clean. There are obviously many more examples I could cover. Scan through the other chapters in this book to see how to use some of the other behaviors for different types of scenarios. If this has been your first experience working with behaviors, I'll bet you love it. Build a library of your own custom behaviors to save you the time and hassle of doing the work all over again. I hope these shortcuts help.

chapter 4

LINGO BASICS:
AN INTRODUCTION

To add more powerful features to your interactive multimedia applications, you will need to use Lingo, Director's scripting language. For those of you who have gotten by without experimenting with Lingo, don't wait any longer. Lingo is the magic behind your movie, allowing you to create interactive buttons, text fields, menus, and other movie controls. It can determine how your movie will function as the user interacts with the program. Without Lingo, you probably would not have the ability to set up any type of complex interactive features in your movie. As you will see, Lingo allows you to program choices for the end-users to determine how and where they proceed through the program. As you learn the capabilities involved with programming in Lingo, you will begin to see the sheer power and flexibility available to you when designing multimedia applications in Director. This chapter will highlight the basics of this powerful scripting language. Chapter 9 will cover some more advanced topics and give specific examples of how to incorporate Lingo into your projects.

HOW DOES LINGO WORK?

Lingo is written as a set of phrases called scripts (yet another theatrical metaphor) in the Script window. These scripts provide you with the ability to control the playback and interactivity of your movie in many ways, including:

◆ Keeping the playback head in position on a particular frame.
◆ Jumping to a different section of the score.

◆   Changing the properties of any sprite.

◆   Responding to the user's interactions with the program.

To open a new Script window:

◆   Select Script from the Window menu or use the keyboard shortcut Control-0 (Windows) or Command-0 (Macintosh).

OR

◆   Click the Script Window icon in the toolbar across the top of your screen (Figure 4–1).

OR

◆   Click the Script Window icon under the Behavior tab in the Property Inspector (Figure 4–2).

I know I went a bit overboard showing every possibility, but that goes to show you how easy Director makes accessing certain features. The more comfortable you become with Director, the more you'll find yourself using Lingo.

Figure 4–1 The Script Window icon in the toolbar.

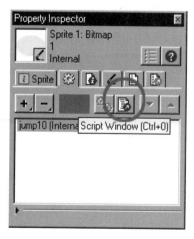

Figure 4–2 Open a Script window
from the Property Inspector.

TYPES OF LINGO SCRIPTS

All Director scripts can be categorized into four basic types:

◆ Behaviors.

◆ Movie scripts.

◆ Parent/child scripts.

◆ Scripts attached to cast members.

Behaviors are templates of functions or actions with the majority of the script commands already written. Behaviors are broken down into either frame behaviors or sprite behaviors. See Chapter 3 for more information on behaviors.

Movie scripts are used for controlling events that occur when a movie starts, stops, or pauses. These commands are usually triggered by mouse clicks or keypresses. Movie scripts are available only during the movie in which they were added. Therefore, if you link over to play another movie, movie scripts set in the original movie are not carried over to the new one.

Parent scripts add unique functionality to your application. Parent scripts provide similar advantages of object-oriented programming, now within Director. This means you have the ability to write fewer lines of code to accomplish the same advanced tasks in Lingo. You can use parent scripts to generate script objects that behave and respond similarly yet can still operate independently of each other. These scripts, written with Lingo, are referred to as child objects. Child objects are self-contained, independent occurrences of a parent script. The difference between the two is that child objects are created as slight variations (different parameters) of the basic parent script, and are used to perform a particular function using identical handlers (specific instances).

Other scripts can be attached to cast members directly and will therefore not appear in the cast. You can select the option to display the Cast Member Script icon so that you can see which cast members have scripts attached to them. To attach a script to a cast member, do one of the following:

◆ Right-click (Windows) or Control-click (Macintosh) on a cast member in the Cast window and choose Cast Member Script from the context menu.

◆ Select a cast member in the Cast window and then click the Cast Member Script button.

Child objects exist and function entirely in RAM. They do not get saved with the movie.

UNDERSTAND LINGO HANDLERS

The codes on exitFrame (or some variation) and end must appear in every script. The text that is added between these codes is part of a group of phrases that makes up an instructional phrase called a handler. Handlers give Director its ability to perform specific tasks. Every handler in Lingo must begin with an on command and end with an end command. Also note that handlers must be written in the exact structure that Lingo requires for Director to understand the command and perform the function.

If you are not sure of an exact Lingo code but have a good idea of the function you are trying to accomplish, Director provides a categorized list of Lingo commands in the Script window (Figure 4–3).

1. Open the Script window.
2. Click the Categorized Lingo button.

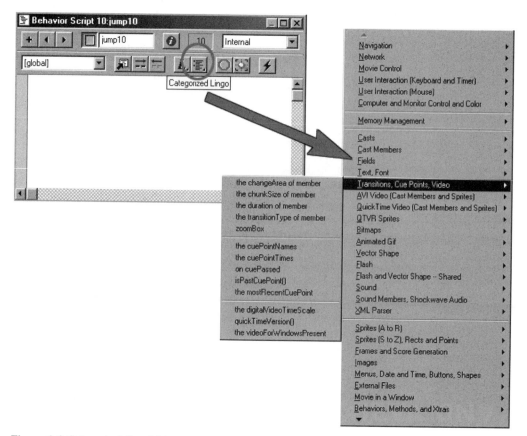

Figure 4–3 Categorized list of Lingo commands.

3. Roll your mouse down each category to display a submenu of Lingo commands.

4. Depending on which script command you select, Director adds the proper language to the Script window. Director will either highlight or give you instructions on what required information is needed to use the function correctly.

5. Type in the necessary information (Figure 4–4).

Lingo is not as complicated as it first appears. Break down each line and decipher what is being said. On exitFrame tells Director to perform the function as soon as the playback head exits the current frame. The on mouseUp command performs the same task as most other handlers, instructing Director to activate a function or perform a given task when the specified event occurs.

THE MOST COMMON SCRIPT

The go to the frame command tells the playback head to keep looping through the current frame. In essence, this command acts as a pause command, yet keeps all of the sprites located in the frame active. The playback head reads this instruction or script and continues to play the same frame over and over, thereby keeping the movie in play mode while waiting for some other type of user interaction. This script performs exactly like the Hold on Current Frame behavior that we applied in an earlier example. To use this script:

1. Double-click on a frame in the script channel where you want to place this function.

2. Type a string of commands as follows:

```
on exitFrame
    go to the frame
end
```

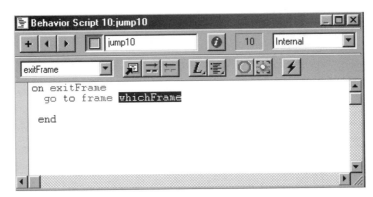

Figure 4–4 Director indicates where to type required information when using Lingo commands from the categorized list.

3. Close the Script window.

4. Rewind and play your movie. The playback head should stop when it reaches the frame where you placed the script.

Be very careful where you put this script. If you place it in a frame that also contains a transition, that transition will infinitely loop and you will have no way out. Unless you are looking for that particular effect in your Director movie (which I hope that no one will ever use), make sure not to place a transition on any frame that has a `go to the frame` script in the score.

Use the `go to the frame` command instead of entering a specific frame number so that if you slide the sprites around in the score, the function will still operate correctly. Having a specific frame number entered in a script will require you to make changes to that script every time you shift things around in the score in order for your movie to play back correctly.

GO TO ANOTHER LOCATION

The second most common Lingo commands used for navigation are `go to` (a specific frame number) and `go to` (a specific marker). These commands allow you to jump around to different sections of a movie to take advantage of Director being able to work in a non-linear environment. Apply these commands as either frame scripts or as sprite scripts. Set up the same type of navigational links that you did earlier using behaviors. To program the commands on the interactive menu screen using Lingo:

1. Add markers to the first frame of each section in your score and name them (Figure 4–5).

2. Select a sprite or frame on which to apply the navigational command.

3. Click the Script pull-down menu in the score.

4. Select New Script and name it.

5. In the Script window, enter one of the following scripts (Director automatically adds the beginning and end handlers):

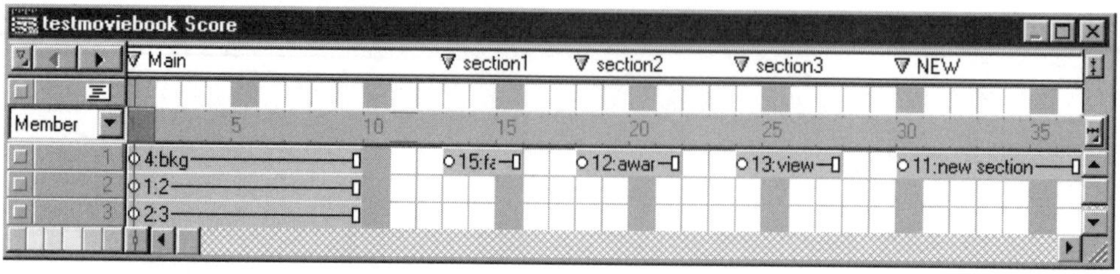

Figure 4–5 A score with markers that indicate the various sections of a movie.

```
on mouseUp
   go to "Section1"
   — goes to the marker name
end
```

OR

```
on mouseUp
   go to frame 2
   — goes to the frame number
end
```

6. Repeat Steps 2 through 5 for each button that you want to function as a button that links to a different portion of the score.

7. Rewind and play the movie.

When you click on the sprite containing the script, the playback head will automatically jump to the marker named Section1. You can also go to a specific frame by using the command go to frame #. This command will perform the same function as the go to Marker command, but with one disadvantage. During the course of developing your program, if you add and remove any frames, not to mention rearrange certain portions of your script, the command go to frame # will no longer take you to the same section (Figure 4–6).

By using the command go to marker, Director will always be able to jump to that exact frame location, no matter where you move that section to or how many frames you add to or delete from the score.

Marker names must be put in quotation marks and spelled exactly the same as they appear in the Marker channel.

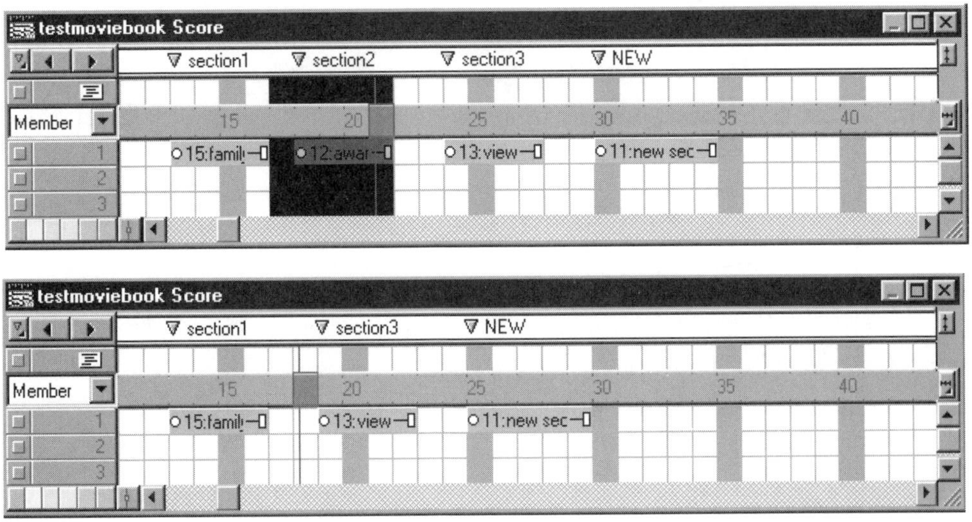

Figure 4–6 Comparison of scores—indicating how frame numbering is altered when deleting frames.

LOOP SECTIONS

There may be times when you want to keep the playback head within a particular section of your movie, waiting for the user to make a selection from one of the interactive elements on the screen. Normally you would add a `go to the frame` command. If the project required animations to be continuously playing, one way to do this while keeping the playback head within the current section would be to add a loop feature. The `go loop` command tells Director—when the playback head reaches this command (usually set as a script in the last frame of a given section)—to go back to the marker at the beginning of the current section and play it over again (Figure 4–7). The playback head will continuously loop until an interactive selection is made by the user. To add the `go loop` command:

1. Add a marker to the first frame of any given segment.
2. Add all necessary sprites and animate them as desired.
3. Double-click on the script channel in the last frame of the current section to open the Script window.
4. Type the command:

   ```
   on exitFrame
       go loop
   end
   ```

5. Rewind and play back your movie.

Notice how the playback head automatically returns to the frame with the marker and continues to play the current section over again.

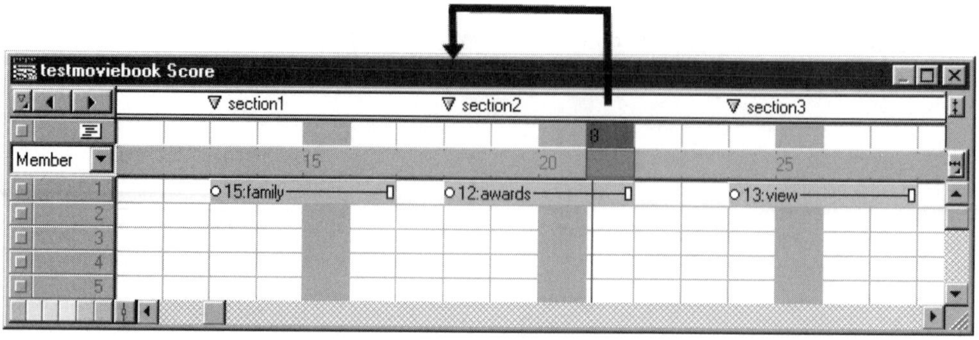

Figure 4–7 A `go loop` *script applied to a continuous loop section identified by markers.*

PLAY OTHER DIRECTOR MOVIES

Director has the ability to open other .DIR movies from your current movie. You can use this feature to make your movie function as if it were simply navigating to another section of the current movie. The advantages include:

♦ You can include complex programming that you designed in another application; you do not need to reprogram the entire movie.

♦ You can keep the file size of your current movie down, so that it will not over-load the system's memory.

♦ Each movie may have been built with different requirements, such as bit depth and color palettes. By calling up a separate movie entirely, it plays under its own custom parameters originally set when the program was developed. You may store the target movie anywhere on your system. The Open dialog box will prompt you to select a file, setting the path where the behavior can find this file on your system (Figure 4–8).

Linking other Director movies is a great way to design promotional products or compilation programs of past works. Advertising and marketing firms use this feature all the time, designing demo CDs to showcase their work on past projects. Students and independent developers can use this technique to create interactive resumes to high-light projects they have produced.

For this example, use image buttons to "link to" or open other Director movies. To open another movie from within Director:

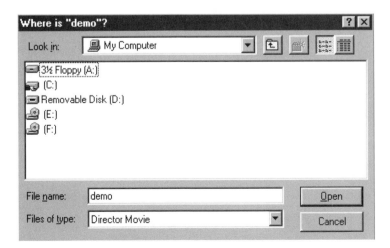

Figure 4–8 Open dialog box.

1. Open the main Director movie.

2. Determine the event that will play another Director movie. This can include most navigational sprite scripts or frame scripts, such as on mouseDown or on exitFrame.

3. Add the Lingo command to the sprite script for the event that you chose. For this example, type:

```
on mouseDown
    play movie "name of new movie"
end
```

This is the same as using the Jump to Movie Button or Play Movie X behaviors.

Use the behavior library:

    A. Open the Library Palette.

    B. Select Controls from the Library List popup menu (Figure 4–9).

    C. Drag the Jump to Movie Button behavior onto the desired sprite.

OR

    B. Select Navigation from the Library List popup menu.

    C. Drag the Play Movie X behavior onto the desired sprite.

    D. Select the filename from the Open dialog box.

OR

Use the Behavior Inspector:

    A. Open the Behavior Inspector.

    B. Select New Behavior and name it.

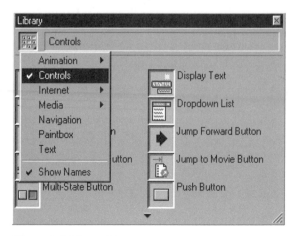

Figure 4–9 Library List popup menu.

C. Select mouseUp from the Events column.

D. Select Navigation from the Actions column.

E. Select Go To Movie… (Figure 4–10).

F. Enter the name or path of the Director movie you want to navigate to in the Specify Movie dialog box.

4. In the new movie, add a frame or sprite navigational link back to the original movie. Enter the same Lingo or use the same behavior, putting the original movie name in place of the new movie name.

5. Rewind and play back your movie.

AUTOMATICALLY RETURN TO A DIRECTOR MOVIE

A common feature when jumping to or playing another Director movie is to have it automatically return to the original movie. This feature is known as branching. To return to the original movie, use the Lingo movie script `play done`. This allows the user to automatically return to the original movie without adding any additional buttons. As long as the new movie does not contain any `mouseUp` handlers in any sprites, frames, or cast members, the user will be able to click the mouse anywhere on the screen to end the current movie. To add this movie script:

1. Select Script from the Window menu or use the keyboard shortcut Control-0 (Windows) or Command-0 (Macintosh).

2. Enter the following Lingo code (Figure 4–11):

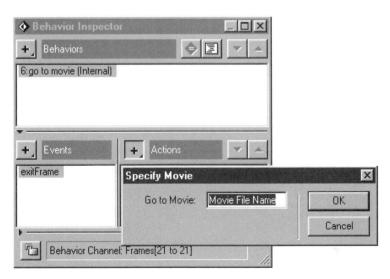

Figure 4–10 Go To Movie… action selected in the Behavior Inspector.

```
on mouseUp
    play done
end
```

3. Save the new movie.

4. Rewind and play the original Director movie. When you link to the new movie, click the mouse button to automatically return to the original movie.

Jump to movie, play movie, and branching are all techniques used to give the illusion that the playback head is instantaneously navigating to a different section of the score within the same movie as opposed to having the user close the current movie to play a new one. You can also branch to a specific frame of a new movie, instead of the default first frame (Figure 4–12), by entering the command:

```
on mouseUp
    play frame "section2" of movie "newmovie"
end
```

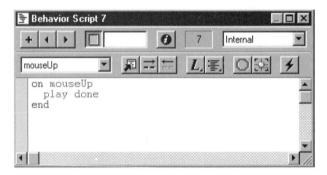

Figure 4–11 play done *Lingo script.*

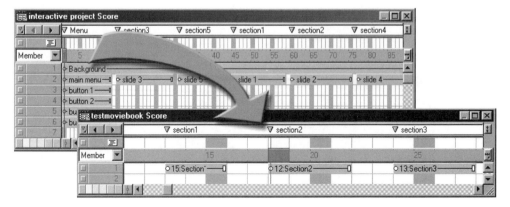

Figure 4–12 Branching to a specific section of a movie instead of the first frame.

LINGO CONDITIONS: TRUE OR FALSE

As you start adding more complex features to your Director movies, you will need to start relying on Lingo commands for more functionality. One common feature is to have Director check to see if a certain condition exists at the current time. Director looks at this command and determines whether the condition exists or does not exist.

◆ To instruct Director that a particular condition exists, set the condition equal to True (value=1).

◆ To instruct Director that a particular condition does not exist, set the condition equal to False (value=0).

A value of 1 can be used instead of typing the word "True." A value of 0 indicates a False statement.

For example, to make a sprite invisible during a particular section, set the visibility to False, or 0 (Figure 4–13, also found in the color section):

```
on enterFrame
      set the visibility of sprite (which channel) = False
end
```

To give the user the ability to drag a sprite around the screen while playing a movie, set moveableSprite equal to True, or 1:

```
on startMovie
      set the moveableSprite of sprite 1 = 1
end
```

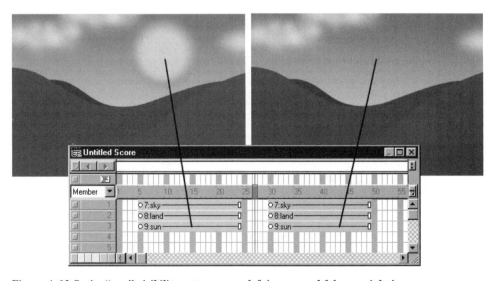

Figure 4–13 Sprite "sun" visibility set to true on left image, and false on right image.

ONE SPRITE, TWO FUNCTIONS

A feature that will be helpful in the development of your applications is to add the programming capability to use a single sprite as a toggle switch. A common example of this is to use a sprite to pause your movie. Click the sprite once to pause the movie; click the sprite again to resume playback from where you left off (Figure 4–14).

1. Select the sprite that will operate the pause/playback feature.
2. Open a Score's script and type:

```
on mouseDown
   if the pauseState = True then
       go to the frame + 1
   else
       pause
   end if
end
```

PauseState is a common Lingo command used to test the pause value of a movie. The value returns True when the movie is in pause mode. Otherwise, it returns a False value.

CAN SCRIPTS MAKE DECISIONS?

You can use a series of Lingo commands to allow your movie to interpret the conditions of a particular section of the movie and determine the appropriate action and response.

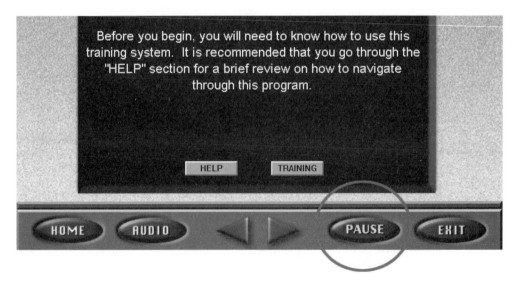

Figure 4–14 Interface showing a Pause/Play toggle button.

Use the `if`, `then`, and `else` statements to have Director check whether certain conditions are active or present for your movie at a given time. This is how they work:

1. Lingo checks to see whether the condition of the first statement exists by using the `if` command.
2. If that condition does indeed exist, Lingo responds with the proper action set in the `then` statement.
3. If the condition of that statement does not exist, then Lingo will execute the alternative action set by the `else` statement.

For example, you may want to add buttons to raise and lower the volume of your movie. This action is dependent on what the condition of the movie is at the current time (Figure 4–15). To raise the volume:

```
on mouseUp
        if soundLevel = 0 then
            set sound = 1
        else
        if soundLevel = 1 then
            set sound = 2
        end if
—Continue for each step of volume control you prefer.

—Use the opposite commands on the volume down sprite.
end
```

IF SHORTCUTS ARE NEEDED, THEN USE CASE

The `case` statement can be used as an alternative to `if...then` statements when you are incorporating many branches of Lingo. Instead of continuously entering the `then...else` portion of the command, use a `case` statement to list the possible responses to the actions of the statement. Lingo begins examining each possible condition until it comes across a statement that exists and then it executes that command. `case` statements can be used to create and implement many scenarios throughout your

Figure 4–15 Audio controls to adjust volume.

movie. A good example for using `case` statements is when setting up multiple-choice questions for your user to answer (Figure 4–16):

```
on keyDown
     case (the key) of
            "A": go to frame "Congratulations"
            "B", "C", "D", "E":
  alert "Incorrect. Please review the material again."
  beep
  go to frame "Question1"
     end case
end keyDown
```

This seemingly confusing script is actually fairly simple to understand if you break down its components. Basically, the command is checking the conditions as to which key on the keyboard was pressed. If the A key was pressed, Director jumps to the section labeled with the marker "`Congratulations`". If any of the other keys from the multiple-choice quiz were pressed (B, C, D, or E), Director puts up an alert window, beeps, and returns them to the question screen again.

This quiz method will not keep track of the number of questions a user got correct. It is merely used to check how well the user grasped the information.

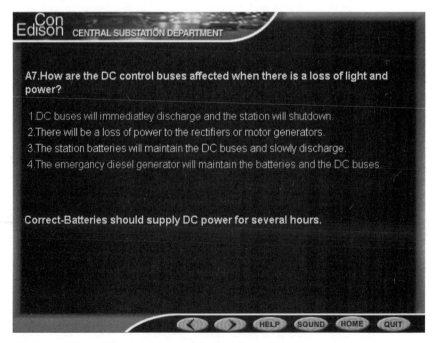

Figure 4–16 An application with a multiple-choice selection.

SET VALUES AND VARIABLES

A feature often needed in a multimedia application is to have the program calculate a value for something and continually update it as the movie plays. You can set just about any type of variable or equation in Director for this feature. By constantly changing the value of that variable, Director can keep track of items such as user input information, the score of a game, and whether or not a particular event occurred. Use the Lingo command `set x = y` to calculate the different values. To test commands before implementing them in your Director movie, use the Message window (Window menu > Message).

♦ The `set` phrase tells Director to make the first portion of the equation equal to the second portion of the equation.

♦ The `put` phrase tells Director to display the calculation in the Message window (Figure 4–17).

Director uses the internal components of the computer to calculate time, date, and mathematical equations.

Example 1:

1. Open the Message window.

2. Type:

```
set Score = 0
```

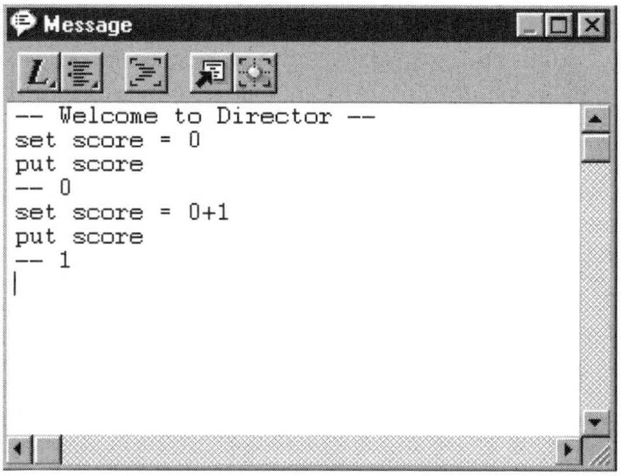

Figure 4–17 Message window demonstrating the set/put *commands.*

3. Type:

```
put Score
```

and press Return. Director should display "0".

4. Type:

```
set Score = 0 + 1
```

5. Type:

```
Put Score
```

and press Return. Director should now display "1" because you set the score equal to zero plus one.

Use a practical naming convention for all of your variables. As your program gets more complex, keeping track of variables with generic names is quite difficult. Use a descriptive term for the variable you are setting. For example, use set myName = Dennis instead of set x = Dennis.

GLOBAL VS. LOCAL VARIABLES

According to Director, a variable is created the first time you assign a value to it. Apply variables to different equations or change the value of a variable based on the frequency of an event. Global variables are set for the duration of a movie or until Director comes across a clearGlobals command. By declaring a variable as a global, it makes it available to every handler for the entire movie. A good example of when to use a global variable is during a program in which you want to display the user's name throughout the program (Figure 4–18, also found in the color section).

```
global gName
put "Dennis" into gName
```

This statement is telling Director to make the variable gName global and make it have the value Dennis. You can change the value of the variable later on in the movie without changing the global variable.

```
on nameChange
    global gName
    put "Jason" into gName
end
```

To help you quickly identify which items are global variables, put the letter "g" before each global variable.

You can also use global variables to keep track of whether a person has gone through a particular section of a movie already. This is the best way to have Director achieve this interactive record-keeping task during the course of a movie.

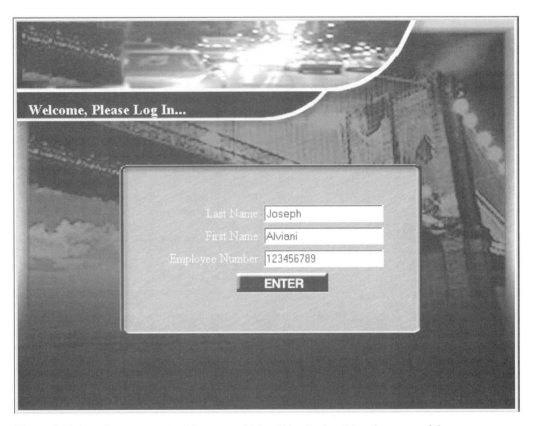

Figure 4–18 Area for user to enter his name, which will be displayed in other areas of the program.

This function will only work during one session of the program. If the user quits and restarts the program, the values are not saved from the previous session.

```
on startMovie
    global gSection1, gSection2, gSection3
    set gSection1 = False
    set gSection2 = False
    set gSection3 = False
end
```

Each of these statements tells Director to set the variable for each section equal to False, meaning that the user has not gone through any of these sections. To check whether or not a user has entered a screen, use an if...then statement to determine the conditions of the movie. If the user has entered a particular section, you can change the look of the button sprite for that section to let the user know that she has already gone through that section (Figure 4–19).

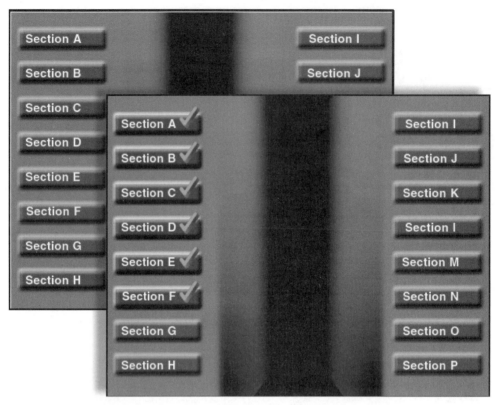

Figure 4–19 Check marks on buttons indicate which sections the user has completed.

```
on displayChecks
    - checking on main menu whether user entered a section
    global gSection1, gSection2, gSection3
    if gSection1 = True then set the visibility of sprite 7 to True
    if gSection2 = True then set the visibility of sprite 8 to True
    if gSection3 = True then set the visibility of sprite 9 to True
        —where sprites 7, 8, 9 are check marks that are
            positioned over the buttons to their respective sections.
    updateStage
end
```

On the first frame of each section (this script is for Section 1), add:

```
on enterFrame
    global gSection 1
    set gSection1 = True
end
```

When the user goes back to the Main menu, Director will look to see if any of the variables have changed, indicating that a user has entered that particular section:

```
on enterFrame
     displayChecks
end
```

As the user goes through each section of the program and returns to the Main menu, Director does a quick check through the Lingo commands to see if any sections have been visited. If any of the Lingo commands are set to True for a given section, Director is instructed to display a sprite of a check mark over the button linking to that section. This way, the user can quickly see which topics he has covered during this session of the program.

To effectively set global variables for an entire movie, assign your global variables before the actual movie begins by using the on prepareMovie handler.

Use global variables sparingly. They get loaded into the memory from the start of the movie and remain there until the end. Too many globals can greatly reduce the performance of your program.

Unless a handler contains the phrase "global," all other variables are automatically set as local variables. Local variables exist only while a specific handler is running and do not save their values. Once Lingo encounters an end command, the variable is no longer valid. Use local variables when you only want to set a variable for a short time, not the entire movie. The basic layout for local variables is:

```
set (variable) = (value)
set backgroundColor = Red
```

This type of command tells Director to replace any local variable with the value set in this equation.

CHECK A SPRITE'S BOUNDING BOX WITH LINGO

One important aspect to keep in mind when applying interactive commands to sprites is that the function of the sprite is determined by the entire sprite, or area within the bounding box of that sprite (Figure 4–20). This does not change if you add ink effects, such as Background Transparent. The entire bounding box area is used to interact with push button or rollover commands. To determine what the actual coordinates of a bounding box are, use the Message window to display the location coordinates of the box's corners. Director provides this information as a list of the left, top, right, and bottom coordinates of the sprite's bounding box (Figure 4–21). To access this information:

1. Open the Message window from the Window menu or use the keyboard shortcut Control-M (Windows) or Command-M (Macintosh).
2. Open the score and select the sprite you want to check.
3. Enter the following text in the Message window and press Enter:

```
put the rect of sprite (channelnumber)
```

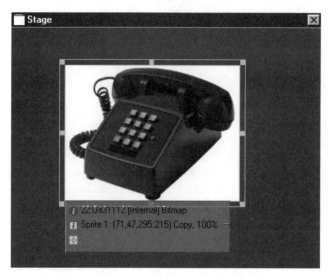

Figure 4–20 Wire framing outlines the bounding box area of the sprite.

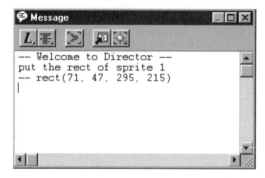

Figure 4–21 A message window displaying bounding box coordinates.

For instance, to check on the sprite in Frame 10, Channel 5, move the playback head to Frame 10 and enter the command put the rect of sprite 5. Director will display the coordinates for each corner of the bounding box as its location on the stage.

ANALYZE LINGO COMMANDS AND COMMENTS

The best way to learn how to write your own Lingo commands is to study the codes of someone who knows what they are doing. Who better to learn from than the creators of Lingo—Macromedia. After applying a behavior, open the Script window to analyze the precise codes used to perform the function. After all, behaviors are nothing more than shortcuts to actually writing Lingo codes. To analyze any behavior's Lingo script:

1. Select a behavior from a cast that has already had its parameters set (Figure 4–22).
2. Click the Cast Member Script icon at the top of the Cast window or use the keyboard shortcut Control-' (Windows) or Command-' (Macintosh). The pre-written Lingo script appears.
3. Try to break down what each handler is used for and what task each line of code is instructing Director to perform or evaluate.

Director 8 includes many helpful notes for developers written inside the actual codes to better explain the purpose of each line of a script.

SUMMARY

The examples in this chapter are just the tip of the iceberg of what types of interactive features you can incorporate into a Director movie. You can see how Lingo scripts add tremendous functionality to your program. Experiment with different combinations of applications, staying within the guidelines of the commands, to formulate your own custom applications

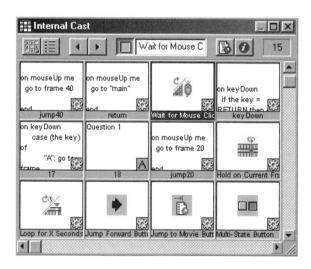

Figure 4–22 Customized behavior located in Cast window.

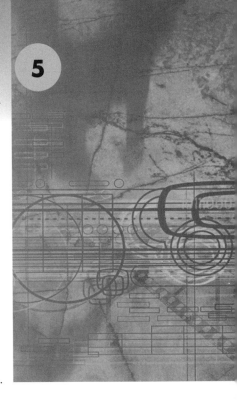

chapter 5

IMAGING AND ANIMATION: THE KEYS TO DIRECTOR

Despite all of its programming power, Director is still well-known for its imaging capabilities. One of Director's main specialties is offering multiple ways to create animations. Each technique offers various combinations that allow you to design your movie any way you want. You can bring all of your images to life by animating them across the stage, adding to the magic of your movie.

Using the analogy of how cartoons were drawn (before the use of computers), single frames of illustrations, each slightly different from the next, when played back at a certain speed, created the illusion of movement. This same principle is one way to utilize Director for creating animations. The playback head moves across the score, displaying images one frame at a time.

THE MAGIC OF INKS

Once you begin adding layers of images to your movie, you may find that some do not appear on-stage quite how you had imagined. Let's start off by getting your images to look their best once you place them on your stage. Applying one of the many different ink effects will change the appearance of your sprites. Each effect holds a certain characteristic that affects different sprites in different ways. Director's Help section has a great interactive movie that demonstrates how all the different ink effects work. I highly recommend checking it out to broaden that "I already know how inks work" mentality that we all seem to have until we learn something totally new that blows us away. You can apply inks to various images over different style backgrounds to get a better understanding of how inks affect the related images (Figure 5–1, also found in the color section).

In the score, select a sprite and hold the Control key while clicking the left mouse button (Windows) or hold the Option key while clicking the mouse (Macintosh) to see a complete list of inks.

Certain inks will look like they perform the same effect. Each one actually has its own unique characteristics. The results of an ink effect are dependent on both the foreground sprite that you apply the ink effect to and the image below it. One of the most common uses for ink effects is to drop out a region of an image to isolate only that portion of the sprite you need to display (Figure 5–2). For instance, the Mask ink effect works with a combination of two consecutive cast members to display only the portions of the sprite that you have masked (see "Masks" for more detail). Another common ink effect is to animate images with different ink effects intersecting with each other to achieve a cycling color effect. To demonstrate the way certain ink effects interact with one another, set up this quick animation:

1. Create three geometric shapes using the Paint tool.

2. Make each shape a different color. For best results, use bright, vivid colors.

3. Place each cast member at a different starting position on the stage. Leave Channel 1 open in the score at this point.

4. Using the tweening technique, animate these objects across the stage so that each sprite comes in contact with the others at some point during the animation (Figure 5–3).

(a)   *(b)*   *(c)*   *(d)*

Figure 5–1 a, b, c, & d Effects of different inks applied to the same images. (Shown: (a) lightest, (b) not copy, (c) not transparent, and (d) subtract).

Figure 5–2 Comparing images with and without the Background Transparent ink effect applied.

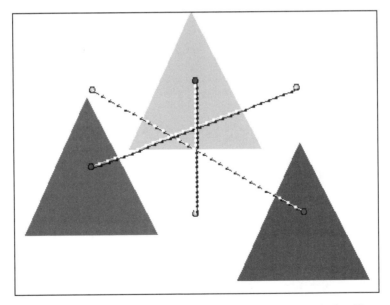

Figure 5–3 Animating colorful geometric shapes to demonstrate the effects of different inks and the interaction between the sprites as they intersect.

5. Apply one ink effect at a time and play back your movie. Take notice of how each sprite interacts with the other sprites due to the ink effect applied to it.

Give each sprite the reverse ink effect and watch how the colors mix together as the sprites intersect one another. Enhancing this type of effect can make for a great splash opening on your next Director project.

Try applying different inks to different sprites and see what kinds of results these changes create. After you have tested a few different variations, add a bitmapped image to Channel 1. You should see that some of these ink effects change the hue and brightness level of the background image.

WHEN TO ANTI-ALIAS OBJECTS

Aliasing is a term usually used to refer to the stair-stepping or jagged look of an object. Anti-aliasing is the computer's way of softening or blurring the edges of an object to make the image look like it has smoother edges (Figure 5–4). You will notice this effect in Director when you begin applying ink effects to drop out the background color of an object. Generally, if you use an ink effect, such as Background Transparent, you may notice a ghosting or outline effect happening around the image when placed over a different color background. This occurs when an object is created with anti-aliasing turned on (Figure 5–5). For images created over a different color background than the color they will be placed over, shut off anti-aliasing while creating these images. If you are placing an image over the same color background, you can turn on anti-aliasing to create cleaner-looking edges on your image.

Director's Paint utility does not default to anti-aliasing, thus giving you clean edges when applying inks. Photoshop users need to deselect the default anti-aliasing in Photoshop when creating objects, unless they will be placed over the same color background.

Figure 5–4 Comparison of aliased (top) and anti-aliased (bottom) text (magnified).

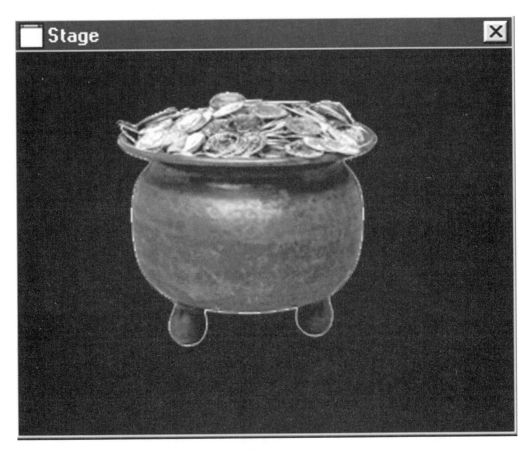

Figure 5–5 Ghosting effect with anti-aliased sprites.

MASKS

For those of you who have worked extensively with Photoshop or have a background in on-line video production, you are probably familiar with the term "alpha channel." For those of you who are not familiar with alpha channels, they are also referred to as masks in Director and are the best way to drop out unwanted portions of your image to display a clean cutout of the image when layering it on top of another image (Figure 5–6). If we apply the Background Transparent ink effect to the logo sprite, the white area inside the logo will be eliminated by the white area around the outside of the logo, which we want removed (Figure 5–7, also found in the color section). There is only one way to get a complex image such as this logo to be displayed where only the areas that you want to be displayed are shown and all other areas are eliminated. The proper method is to create a mask.

Figure 5–6 An example of a mask used to remove the unwanted background.

*Figure 5–7 a & b Background transparent ink does not always
work if the image contains the same color that you want to remove
from the background.*

A mask is commonly referred to as a hi-con in the video world, meaning an image containing two colors of high contrast. You generally set up these images with the exact detail and shape of your object as black and the areas you want to be transparent as white. In Photoshop, the channels for the mask show the reverse of this. Your object to keep is white and the area to be keyed out is black.

You can create a mask for any object, regardless of what software it was created in. This is where Director's Paint program really saves you time, allowing you to create the exact desired effect. Create a mask to make the logo appear correctly over the background image:

1. Set up your score with the background cast member on Channel 1 and the logo on Channel 2.

2. Double-click on the logo cast member to open it in Director Paint.

3. Choose Duplicate from the Edit menu so that you do not alter your original graphic. The Duplicate function automatically creates a new cast member and displays the cloned copy in the Paint window.

4. Click the Transform Bitmap option under the Modify menu. The Transform Bitmap dialog box will appear.

5. To change this colorful graphic into a black and white image, use the Color Depth pull-down menu to select 1-bit.

6. Click the Transform button.

   Create a mask or hi-con image, turning everything either black or white. The best way to achieve this effect is to convert the image into a 1-bit image that only displays black and white. This will also help reduce the file size. If you plan to use several masked images throughout your Director movie, having two versions for each of these images will take up a tremendous amount of space, increasing the size of your movie, especially if you are working with 24-bit images.

7. In the Paint window, use the paintbrush or other tools to clean up the image. Fill in the parts of the image that you want to be opaque (visible) with black. The areas that you leave white will become transparent.

8. Close the Paint window when you are finished.

9. Place the hi-con cast member immediately following the original cast member for the mask effect to work (Figure 5–8). There cannot be any other cast members or empty frames between the original image and the black and white image.

10. Select the logo sprite in your score on Channel 2.

11. Click the Ink Selector pull-down menu at the top of the score and choose Mask (Figure 5–9).

12. Rewind and play back your movie.

Notice how the effect allows for a clean cutout of your logo on the stage. Use the Mask ink effect and the technique described earlier when you need to separate a specific section of an image and layer that portion on top of another image.

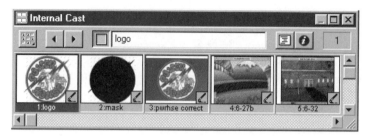

Figure 5–8 Cast with hi-con (mask) cast member directly following the regular cast member.

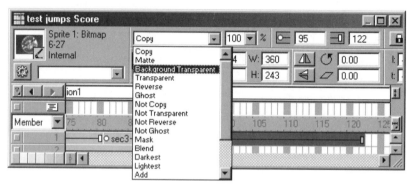

Figure 5–9 Ink Selector pull-down menu.

  The more intricate the design of your object, the more careful you will have to be when filling in the areas to be masked. Any areas that you paint outside the borders of your object might produce a pixilated or ghosting effect when you apply the mask to the sprite.

SEPARATE IMAGES FROM THE BACKGROUND

In a perfect world, you would be supplied with every image designed over a clean, white background that you could quickly and easily separate when you need to layer it over another image. WAKE UP! Unless you are creating every single element from scratch, I highly doubt that you will be provided with all the images in a clean and ready-to-use format.

To separate an image from the background of an image:

1. Import an image into Director.
2. Open the new cast member in the Paint window.

3. Choose Duplicate from the Edit menu so that you do not alter your original graphic. The Duplicate function automatically creates a new cast member and displays the cloned copy in the Paint window.

4. Paint out the shape of the object you want to separate from the background.

5. Rearrange the cast members so that the hi-con mask is in the Cast window directly following the original image.

6. Place a new background image in the score on Channel 1.

7. Place the cast member of the original image into the score on Channel 2.

8. Apply the Mask ink effect to your sprite in Channel 2.

This technique, even though masked perfectly, looks like the cutout image was just placed over the background image and was not really a part of the scene. To avoid this situation and create a more desirable effect, layer other portions of images above this sprite, concealing parts of the cutout image to give the illusion that it was a part of the scene (Figure 5–10).

ADVANCED LAYERING

If you animate several sprites across the stage without ever rearranging the channel order of the sprites, the sprite in Channel 1 will always appear below the sprite in Channel 2, and so on. Many projects involve altering the layers of sprites over time to create the effect of objects moving in front of one another. When dealing with rearranging sprite channels, spend time sketching out drawings to figure out when and where to place each sprite. Create a movie with race car sprites driving around a racetrack, constantly changing layers (Figure 5–11):

1. Sketch out on paper when and where each sprite will be in proximity to the other sprites (this will determine which channel to place the sprite in).

Figure 5–10 Before and after image with the key element displayed over a new background.

Figure 5–11 Example of layering sprites using a race car driving around a track.

2. Create the necessary graphics and import all the images into Director.
3. Following your notes taken during the planning stage, place each cast member into the sprite starting on Frame 1, leaving Channels 2 through 5 empty for now. This will allow you to keep the static layers on consistent channels throughout the movie (Figure 5–12).

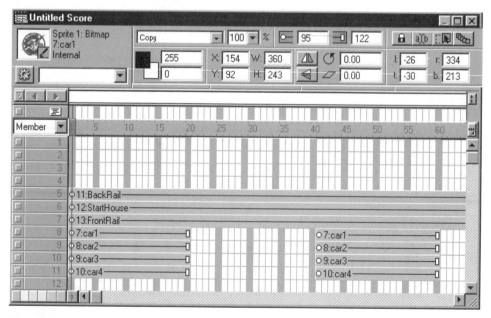

Figure 5–12 Score showing static images on higher channels with empty channels below to make layering easier.

4. Start with the back-most layered object (Back Rail cast member) in Channel 1.

5. Place the Watchtower cast member in Channel 6.

6. Place the Front Rail cast member in Channel 11.

7. Place each of the four Car cast members in Channels 7 through 10.

8. Color-code each sprite independently:

   A. Select a sprite.

   B. Click on one of the sprite color swatches in the lower left portion of the Score window.

   C. Repeat Steps 2 and 3 for each additional sprite, selecting a different color for each one.

9. Select all of the sprites (Control-A for Windows; Command-A for Macintosh).

10. Using the End Frame field in the score, enter 90. This will extend all of the cast members to span from Frame 1 to Frame 90.

11. Select Edit Sprite Frames from the Edit menu. This breaks up the long, single-object sprite into individual frame elements, resembling how Director 5 displayed the score.

   Now your score is ready to begin setting the animation aspect of your sprites. Use a combination of animation techniques, including adding keyframes, tweening, and creating film loops.

12. Animate the car sprites to turn on the right side of the screen using tweening.

13. Create a film loop for viewing the cars going around the turn.

14. Select the portion of the sprites that will be animated on the far side of the track and move them to Channels 2 through 5 (Figure 5–13).

15. Because the cars look like they are traveling in reverse, select these sprites and replace them with the appropriate cast members that show the cars facing the opposite direction. Click on the Exchange cast member button to replace an existing sprite with a different cast member.

16. Create a film loop for viewing the cars coming around the turn toward the front of the track.

17. Loop the movie to show a continuous cycle around the track.

Swapping many layers of sprites around in a score can get confusing quickly. Two techniques become useful for being able to work swiftly and accurately in a score of constantly changing cast members across several layers. Name each sprite to keep track of which sprite is on which channel. The other tip that makes life much easier is color-coding the sprites. This project could have easily taken twice as long without color-coding each sprite. Visually, you will be able to see where and when a sprite moves vertically in the channels (layers) as time goes on.

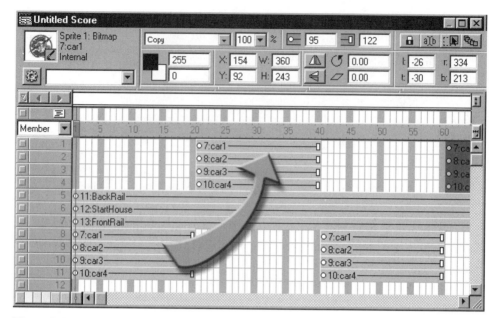

Figure 5–13 Moving portions of the sprites to the lower channels of a score to achieve the proper layering effect.

COMPARE THE BACKGROUND TRANSPARENT AND MASK INK EFFECTS

Sometimes certain ink effects will work and other times they will not. Going back to the car racing example, let's suppose that when you created the graphics of the cars, the only white portions of the car were the glass windows. When you used the Background Transparent ink effect for each of these sprites, you were able to see the images layered below each car as it animated across the screen. Now, change the design of the car graphics. Suppose you want to give each vehicle a number on the side door and you want these numbers to be white. Well, you already know that if you apply the Background Transparent ink effect to this sprite, the background images will show through the numbers just like they did for the windows on the car. How do you avoid this? This is a case where you would want to use the Mask ink effect and create that black and white cloned copy of your image. To keep the white portions of your object that you want to be displayed and key out all the other white areas, you need to create a mask of your object (Figure 5–14).

*Figure 5–14 Creating masks to display portions of the background
images through the windows of the cars.*

DO YOU LIKE TO WORK IN PHOTOSHOP?

Because we are discussing how to work with layers, I figured this was the appropriate
time to fill you in on a time-saving Xtra that you can use to make your design work much
cleaner and more accurate, while allowing you time to be creative. How great would it
be if you could build your interface once and not have to break it down to only piece it
back together in Director? Wouldn't it be great if you never had to flatten another
Photoshop graphic again? Well, would you believe me if I told you there is a way? There
is an Xtra that I would recommend to anyone who uses Photoshop to design images for
Director. It's an Xtra from Media Lab, Inc. called PhotoCaster. Check out their Web site
at www.medialab.com. This Xtra allows you to preserve all the layers of your Photoshop
file and import them directly into Director. What is really a huge time-saver is that they
create a new cast member for each layer of your Photoshop file (Figure 5–15). Best of all
with PhotoCaster, if your stage is set for the same dimensions as your Photoshop file,
each cast member will retain the same transparency, position, and registration points to
reproduce itself exactly as you had it in Photoshop.

**Unregistered versions of this application will display blue lines through
your image, requiring you to register it to use it in your productions.
Otherwise, you can download the plug-in for demonstration and
sample purposes from Media Lab's Web site.**

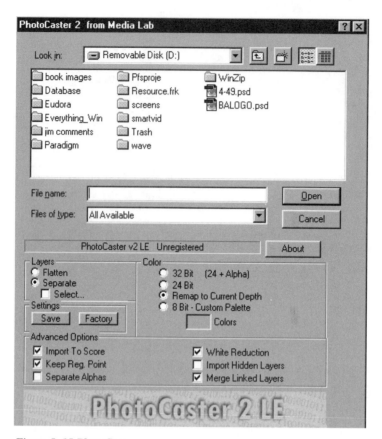

Figure 5–15 PhotoCaster screen.

 Set the dimensions of your Photoshop file to be the same as the stage size of your Director movie.

1. Create a layered image in Photoshop and save it as a .PSD file.
2. Open Director.
3. Under the Insert menu, select Media Lab Media.
4. Select PhotoCaster from the popup menu.
5. In the application's main screen, select the file that you want to bring into Director.
6. Set any other options you wish. (Media Lab's Set Effect Xtras contain a set of filters that you can apply to the layer with an alpha channel.)
7. Click OK.

Once you have selected the file you want to import, PhotoCaster does all the work. This application brings in every image layer and automatically aligns each one onto the stage in the exact layout that you created in Photoshop. What your image looks like in Photoshop is how it recreates itself in Director (Figure 5–16). Take a look in the color section of this book to see some of the filters applied to images using AlphaMania and Effector Sets.

APPLY FILTERS TO SPRITES

Just like high-end graphics programs such as Photoshop and After Effects, you can add third-party filters to Director that allow you to alter the appearance of your bitmapped images. Even if you design your graphics in Photoshop, there might be situations that will require applying these filters in Director instead. If you make any changes to a sprite that has already been saved with the filter effect applied to it from Photoshop, any changes to this filtered image may adversely affect the appearance of the new image. By having these filters available in Director, you can add the effect to the sprite after the changes have been made. To add a filter to Director:

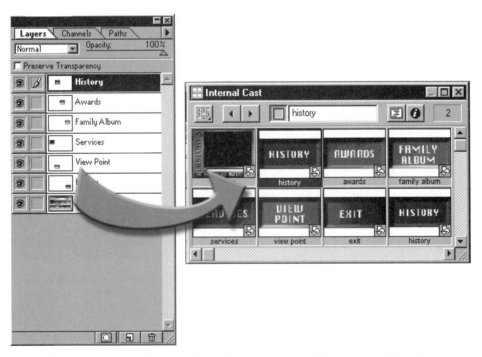

Figure 5–16 Comparison of layers in Photoshop and layers in Director using PhotoCaster.

1. Copy the filter(s) from the Filters folder of Photoshop, Kai Power Tools, or another program that contains bitmap image filters.

2. Paste the filter(s) into the Xtras folder in the Director Root file.

3. Re-launch Director.

You can apply filters to an entire cast member, portions of a cast member, or several cast members at once. However, not all filters work with Director. Check with each manufacturer for more information.

To apply a filter:

1. Double-click on a cast member to open it in the Paint window.

2. Select the Xtras menu from the top of the screen and choose Filter Bitmap. A Filter Bitmap dialog box will appear, displaying all of the filters installed in the Xtras folder for Director.

3. Select a category in the left column.

4. Select a filter in the right column.

5. Click the Filter button to apply that filter or bring up the Settings window for that filter.

ONION SKINNING

The best way to explain the onion skinning technique is to think back to your child-hood when you used tracing paper to redraw the objects underneath. Cartoon artists still use this technique for animation to monitor the amount of change from one frame to the next. This is the same theory applied in Director's Paint window. Onion skinning allows you to see several adjacent cast members so that you can slightly alter each one to create the illusion of movement (Figure 5–17).

For example, create the illusion of a triangle morphing into a thin line as it animates across the screen. Having the ability to monitor each frame and control the variations needed between these frames will make the effect flow more fluidly (Figure 5–18).

1. Open the Paint window.

2. Select Onion Skinning from the View menu.

3. Turn on the onion skinning feature (Figure 5–19).

4. Select the number of preceding cast members you wish to view underneath the one you are currently working on.

5. Using the line tool, draw a triangle.

6. Click the New Cast Member button to create the next image. The first image should now appear ghosted (Figure 5–20).

7. Repeat Steps 4 and 5, continuously manipulating the object from a triangle into a straight line.

8. When you are finished, close the Paint window.

9. In your cast, you should see a series of progressive cast members changing from a triangle into a straight line.

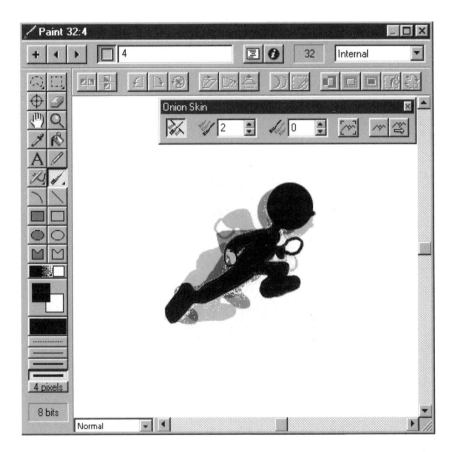

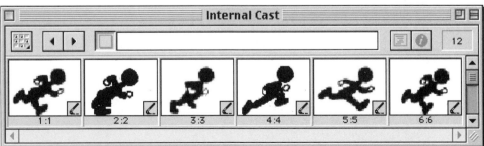

Figure 5–17 Viewing adjacent cast members using the onion skinning feature for proper placement.

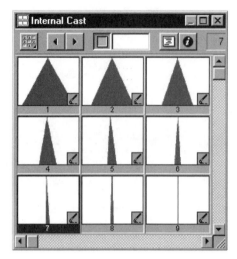

Figure 5–18 Triangular image transforming into a simple straight line over the course of several frames.

Figure 5–19 Turning on the onion skinning feature.

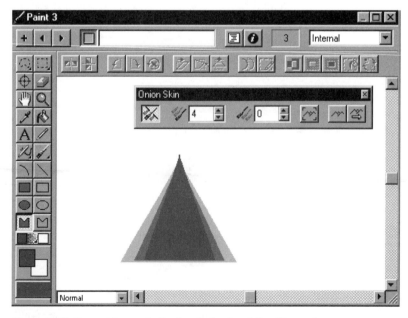

Figure 5–20 Current image is displayed clearly while adjacent images appear ghosted when using the onion skinning feature.

10. Use cast to animate the series of frames:

   A. Click on the first triangle cast member.

   B. Hold the Shift key and select the last straight line cast member. All of the cast members between these should become highlighted.

   C. Hold down the Alt key (Windows) or Option key (Macintosh) and drag the series of cast members onto the stage. This will create one sprite in your score containing all of the various cast members.

11. Rewind and play back your movie. Depending on how many individual frames you drew, your triangle should animate smoothly across the screen, changing into a thin line.

OPTIMIZE YOUR DESIGN TECHNIQUES

You have seen many different types of design techniques implemented to create some interesting effects in Director. There are additional steps that you can take to minimize the work Director has to do to play back your animations. The animated movie in Figure 5–21 utilizes the old style of cartoon animation—designing cels for only the portion of the screen that changes. This technique is especially useful in Director to help reduce both the file size of a project and the amount of memory required to play back the animations. It takes more memory to move a large object across the screen than it does a smaller object.

Figure out which parts of your image are going to be animated before you create the final image. This will save valuable time when you create the animation in Director. Create the animating images on a separate layer from the background.

1. Import all of the images you created for your project into Director (Figure 5–22).

2. Place the background on Channel 1.

3. Add the different elements to be animated on higher channels.

4. Select all of the sprites in the score.

5. Choose Edit Sprite Frames from the Edit menu.

6. Highlight the portion of the lips sprites where you want to begin having the mouth move.

7. Click on the cast member (open mouth) that you want in place of the closed lips.

8. Click on the Exchange Cast Member button in the toolbar at the top of your screen or press Control-E (Windows) or Command-E (Macintosh) on the keyboard.

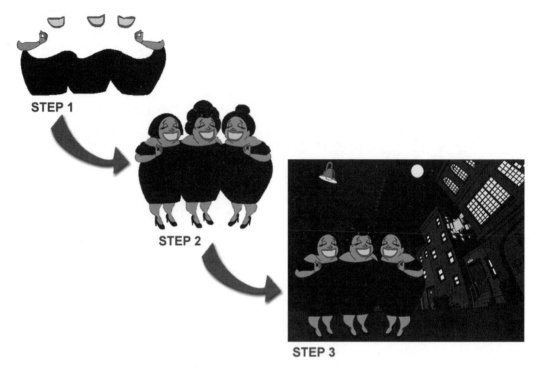

STEP 1

STEP 2

STEP 3

Figure 5–21 Old-school animation technique of layered cels—designing only the aspects that will be changing frame by frame compared to the static background images.

9. Repeat Steps 6 through 8 for all the areas that you want to animate.
10. Rewind and play back your movie.

 Add a music track and try to time the animated sprites to match the beats of the music.

JPEG COMPRESSION

New in Director 8 is the ability to really control the file size of your images (greatly affecting the overall file size and quality of your movie). This is important to be aware of when setting up your images. You can use JPEG compression on bitmap cast members only in a .DCR file (Shockwave movie). You can either apply compression to individual bitmaps or all bitmaps contained in your movie. This is a great feature, especially for those of you who distribute your movies over the Internet. Compression allows you to optimize your bitmapped images to maintain as much of the quality as

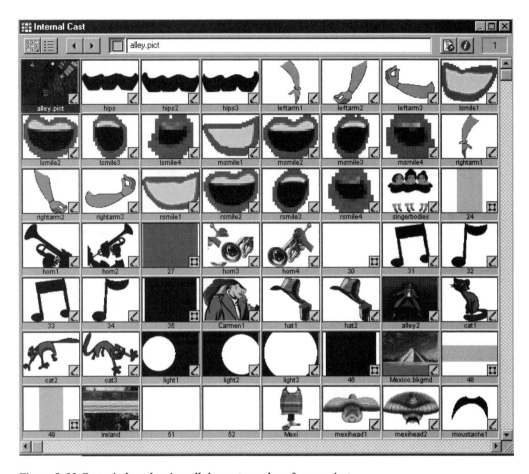

Figure 5–22 Cast window showing all the cast members for a project.

possible while dramatically reducing the size of the file. This, in turn, provides shorter download times for your movies.

Applying bitmap compression at the individual cast member level will take precedence over compression applied at the movie level.

I highly recommend compressing individual cast members even if you are not publishing your movie for the Web. Any application that you develop will always run smoother when trying to open and play smaller file sizes. Be careful not to over-compress your images. You don't want to jeopardize image quality (Figure 5–23, also found in the color section). See Chapter 1 for more information on how to apply JPEG compression to your movie or images individually.

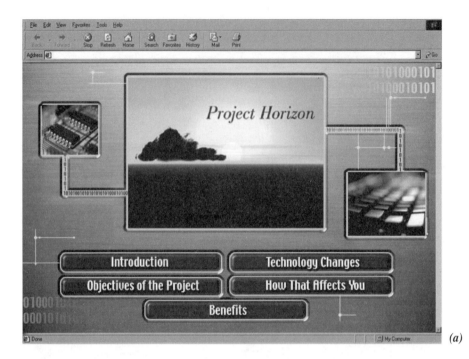

(a)

(b)

Figure 5–23 a & b Comparison of image quality with different levels of compression applied to the image.

SET THE SPEED OF YOUR MOVIE

Now that you are going to begin animating your images inside Director, it is important to understand how to control the playback speed of your movie. In general, the speed at which your movie plays is controlled by the Tempo channel. The tempo sets the speed at which the playback head will play through the score. The tempo is rated at frames per second. Therefore, you can custom-set the speed. If you want the playback head to move very quickly through your score, set a high frame per second rate. If you want to reduce the speed at which it plays, enter a lower frame rate.

You can set one single frame rate for your entire movie or keep altering the frame rate throughout the course of your movie. This allows you to truly customize the playback capabilities of your movie. To set the tempo:

1. Make sure you are viewing the Effect channels in the score. The Tempo channel is the top-most channel, indicated by the Stopwatch icon.

2. Double-click in the Tempo channel on the frame where you want to set the tempo for the following frames (or until the playback head comes across another tempo setting). The Frame Properties: Tempo window appears (Figure 5–24).

   OR

   Select Frame from the Modify menu, then select Tempo from the popup menu.

3. Use the slider to adjust the frame rate between 1 and 999 frames per second.

4. Click OK.

5. Repeat Steps 2 and 3 for each frame where you want to change or alter the existing frame rate.

 The average Director movies that I have seen range between 10 and 30 frames per second.

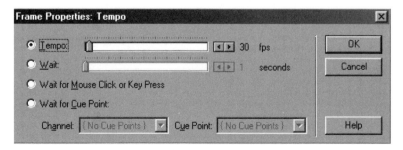

Figure 5–24 Use the Frame Properties: Tempo window to customize the frame rate or speed at which your movie will play back.

FRAME-BY-FRAME ANIMATION

As long and tedious as this process sounds, sometimes it is the only way to get the exact look of an effect you need for your project. Use the following steps to create an effect using the frame-by-frame technique:

1. Model an object using any 3D modeling and animation software (e.g., Infini-D, Extreme 3D, or 3D Studio Max).
2. Animate the object.
3. Export the animations as a series of individual frames from the program showing the progress of movement over the course of time.
4. Import each of these frames into Director.
5. Place them in the score, each for the duration of one frame (Figure 5–25).
6. Rewind and play back the animation. As the playback head travels progressively through each frame of the score, the object created appears to move around the screen into its final position.

ANIMATE MULTIPLE CAST MEMBERS IN A SINGLE SPRITE

Another technique for animating images in your movies is to combine multiple cast members into a single sprite in your score. There are numerous advantages to this technique, but keep in mind that they may not always be the best solution to meet the specific requirements of your movie. One very common reason for applying the multiple-cast-member/single-sprite technique is the ability to stretch or change the span of this single sprite.

 Making changes to frame-by-frame animations can be quite messy if you don't know what you are doing. It can also take far too much time.

Figure 5–25 Frame-by-frame animation represented in score by individual sprites, one frame each.

To create this type of animation takes a few minutes to set up, but again, it offers you the flexibility of working with an animated sequence as a single sprite.

1. Place the first cast member in the score where you want your animation to start.

2. Adjust the span of the sprite to cover the duration that you want the animation to play.

3. Change the Sprite Labels to Changes Only to make changing cast members easier to see (View>Sprite Labels>Changes Only).

4. Choose Edit Sprite Frames under the Edit menu. This makes the score look more like working in Version 5, but it makes it easier to select individual frames within the sprite for swapping cast members (Figure 5–26).

5. Select the frames where you want to play different cast members. To select a continuous span of frames in the score, click on the first frame and then, while holding the Shift key, click on the last frame. All of the inclusive frames should become highlighted (Figure 5–27).

6. Click on the cast member you wish to put in the place of the highlighted area of the score.

7. Click on the Exchange Cast Member button in the top toolbar. Notice how the new cast member fills in the selected area of the sprite.

8. Repeat Steps 5 through 7 to add the rest of the necessary cast members to complete the animation within the single sprite.

9. Once you have added all the necessary cast members, select Edit Entire Sprite from the Edit menu.

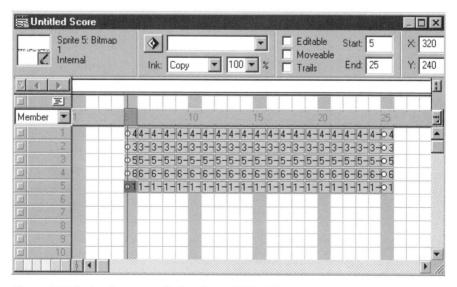

Figure 5–26 Sprites in a score displayed as individual frames.

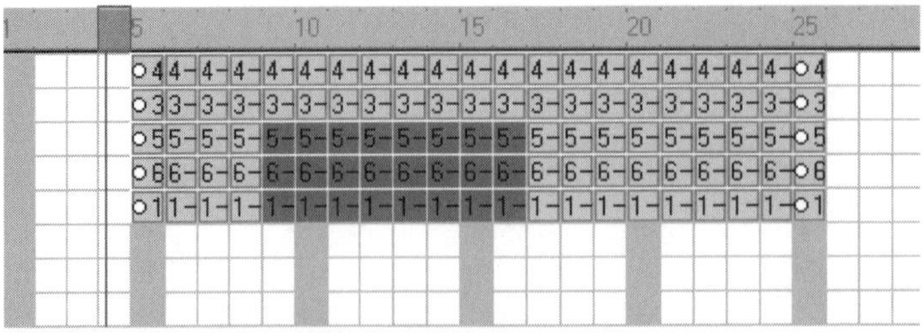

Figure 5–27 Highlighting Portions Of A Single Sprite To Be Replaced With Another Sprite.

Now you can manipulate the sprite (animating cast members) because it functions just like a single sprite made of a single cast member. You can animate it by adding key frames and stretching the span of the sprite in your score.

CAST TO TIME

The best way to animate and get a series of individual cast members to play back in your score is by using a technique called "cast to time." The difference between frame-by-frame animation and cast to time is that cast to time is much faster to implement and provides you with a single sprite in the score instead of many individual frames. To create an animation using cast to time:

1. Import a series of images you would like to animate (Figure 5–28, also found in the color section).
2. Rearrange the images in the order in which you want them to appear. Start with the first image in the first available cast member position, followed by the next successive image in the cast immediately following the previous one.
3. Click on the first cast member of the group.
4. Shift-click on the last cast member of the group.
5. Holding down the Alt key (Windows) or Option key (Macintosh), drag the series of frames onto the stage. A single sprite should appear in the score.
6. Rewind and play back the animation.

Change the length of a sprite to alter the speed of the animation. If you stretch it too far, however, your animation will appear to move with a stuttering motion.

CREATE FILM LOOPS

A film loop is very similar to the end result of cast to time, animating multiple cast members into a single sprite. Film loops are especially effective for animating repetitive motions over time. To create a film loop:

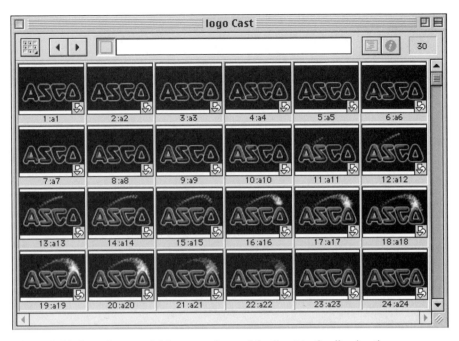

Figure 5–28 Cast of sequential images to be used for "cast-to-time" animation.

1. Select the sprites you want to create into a film loop. One advantage with creating a film loop is that you can select multiple channels, including sound channels, to create one cast member.
2. Choose Film Loop from the Insert menu.
3. Name the film loop. Notice in your Cast window that Director has added a new cast member with the Film Loop icon in it (Figure 5–29).

Another way to create a film loop is to highlight the frames and channels you would like to turn into a film loop. Drag them into an open cast member. Director automatically makes them into a film loop.

Figure 5–29 Film Loop icon.

You can now add any film loop to your movie as a single sprite and manipulate it like you would any sprite. There are a few exceptions:

◆   Film loops do not display the animation while stepping through the sprite , also found in the color sectionframe-by-frame.

◆   The animation will only occur during playback of your movie.

There is a significant difference between lengthening or shortening a film loop sprite and adjusting to a regular sprite. Altering the span of a film loop does not affect the speed at which it plays back, but instead affects the number of times the film loop cycles. If the span of the film loop is shorter than the initial duration of the sprites creating the loop, the film loop will only play the same amount of frames that were in the original sprite sequence covering that same number of frames. For instance, if an initial sprite sequence contained four images each covering 10 frames and a film loop was created, the film loop would have to cover a total of 40 frames to play back the entire sequence. If you then shortened the film loop sprite in the score to only 20 frames, only the first two images would be displayed during playback. The opposite would occur if you doubled the length of the film loop sprite, resulting in the sequence playing twice.

TWEENING

Director's animation capabilities allow you to animate sprites across the stage with very little effort. Tweening (or in-betweening) basically means that the computer will figure out, calculate, and automatically draw in the frames of your animation that fall in between the start and end points that you have set. In its most primitive form, this will produce a linear animation, moving on a straight path between these two points (Figure 5–30). To achieve any type of animation, whether linear or complex, you begin by separating the position of these points by adding keyframes to the sprite in your score.

To establish any type of animation, your sprite must span more than one frame.

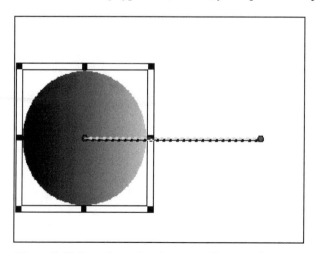

Figure 5–30 Tweening animation over a linear path.

KEYFRAMES

Keyframes can be defined as a set of instructions containing a sprite's characteristics and position information at a specific time (frame number) in a score. That means every time the playback head reaches a particular keyframe, the sprite will be in exactly the same position you set it in whenever your Director movie is playing. In the score, the first frame of your sprite contains a small circle indicating that it is a keyframe, always monitoring the precise location of that image (Figure 5–31).

To add keyframes:

1. Click on the frame of the sprite you are trying to alter.
2. Select Keyframe from the Insert menu. A new circle will appear on the sprite you selected in the frame on which you were parked.

To delete a keyframe:

1. Click on the keyframe.
2. Press the Delete key.

TWEEN ANIMATIONS

Tweening has become one of the most powerful features in animation programs. Through the use of programs like Director, the computer is capable of creating all of the necessary frames to complete the movements between two keyframes. To use tweening:

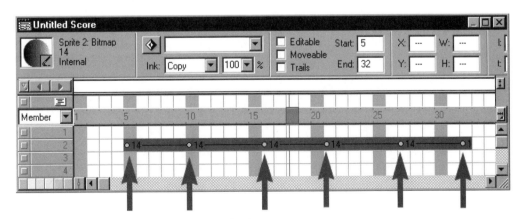

Figure 5–31 Keyframes displayed on sprites in the score.

1. Design any single image.
2. Import it into the cast.
3. Drag it onto the stage and set the sprite's starting position.
4. In the score, add a keyframe on the last frame (Modify>Add Keyframe).
5. Reposition the sprite to its ending position.
6. Rewind and play back the animation.

With the use of Director's tweening capabilities, all you have to do is create a single frame image and set the keyframes for the first and last frames of the sprite. Director will animate your image across the screen by filling in the additional frames needed between the two keyframes.

Setting Tweening Properties

To adjust the way Director animates your sprites, you can select which properties you want to control for the animation (Figure 5–32).

1. Select Sprite from the Modify menu.
2. Select Tweening. The Sprite Tweening Properties dialog box appears. This is where you can set which parameters you want Director to control when it processes each frame of the animation all within one sprite.

Turn off the tween Size control and then change the size of the image on the first keyframe (Figure 5–33). When Director goes to play back the animation, the first frame will appear with the larger size image and the rest will play back with the normal size

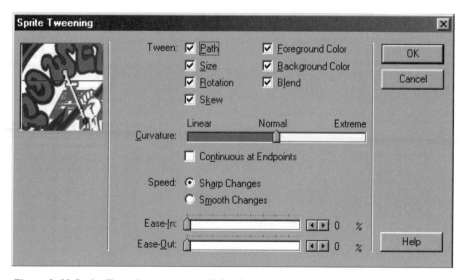

Figure 5–32 Sprite Tweening properties dialog box.

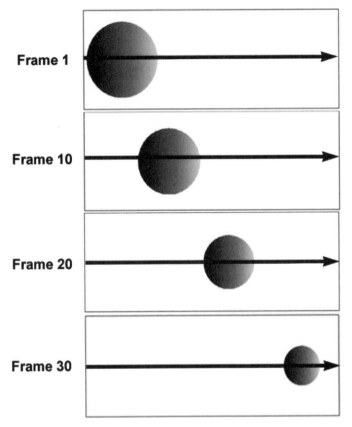

Figure 5–33 Demonstration of how the size of a sprite is displayed during tweening animations.

image. If you loop it, this flash frame will definitely catch your eye, indicating that something is wrong with the animation.

ROTATE YOUR SPRITES

One of the tweening features added in Director 7 was the ability to manipulate your sprites with more control and flexibility. With the addition of the rotation feature, all you have to do is import a single graphic and animate a rotation by setting its variables.

Prior to Director 7, you had to create a new graphic for each frame of a rotation. To rotate sprites:

1. Select the sprite you want to animate.

2. Insert a keyframe (Ctrl-Alt-k for Windows; Alt-Command-k for Macintosh) on the last frame of the sprite (the first frame of every sprite is automatically created as a keyframe).

3. In the Sprite toolbar at the top of the score, enter a variable in the Flip Horizontal—Rotation field for the number of degrees you want to rotate the sprite. For this example, try to make your sprite complete one full revolution.

OR

4. Click the right mouse button (Control-click for Macintosh) to access the Settings popup menu.

5. Select Transform.

6. In the submenu, select Rotate Left or Rotate Right. This will rotate your sprite in 90-degree increments.

Because only the last keyframe had a rotation value entered for it, Director will tween the playback of the sprite between its initial starting point and the final ending point.

When entering a variable to rotate an object that will loop, do not enter a full value of 360 degrees. Notice the image in the first frame (0 degrees) is at the 12 o'clock position and the image in the last frame (360 degrees) is also at the 12 o'clock position (Figure 5–34). When you animate this for a complete revolution and loop it, the animation will actually be playing those two frames consecutively in that same position. This will appear as a slight pause or hesitation in your animation. It will not revolve smoothly. To avoid this problem, enter a degree value less than 360 for the last frame. Depending upon the tempo of your movie (number of frames needed to complete a rotation), an end frame value of

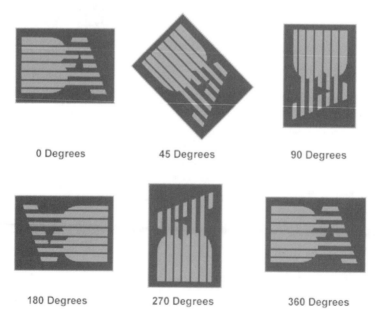

0 Degrees   45 Degrees   90 Degrees

180 Degrees   270 Degrees   360 Degrees

Figure 5–34 Logo rotating 360 degrees (frames 0 degrees and 360 degrees are identical). See also Color Figure 18.

350 degrees seems to allow for a smooth and continuous rotation loop. This may be calculated out if the animation is 20 frames long; rotate each frame by 1/21st of 360 degrees. This will allow the animation to start and complete the looping rotation.

TUMBLE SPRITES IN AND OUT

Those of you who have been developing content on Director for years will probably appreciate the different rotation variables at some point. I have found that rotating the first keyframe slightly and scaling down the size of an image gives the illusion of rotating into position from infinity. The combination of changing the size and transparency level of the image gives it the illusion of flying in from a distant point. If you reverse the keyframes, you can basically move your sprite off-screen, flying it away into the distance. To create the zoom out effect:

1. Select the sprite you want to animate.
2. Insert a keyframe on the last frame of the sprite.
3. On the last keyframe, enter a variable in the Flip Horizontal—Rotation field in the Sprite toolbar for the number of degrees you want to rotate the sprite (Figure 5–35).
4. Set the opacity level to 0%.
5. Rewind and play back your animation.

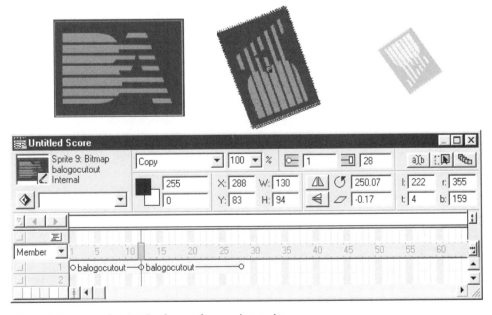

Figure 5–35 Score showing keyframes for rotating sprite.

GO TOO FAR

It is very easy to start playing around with effects, warping and spinning sprites into oblivion. Sometimes experimenting like that is the best way to come up with new effects worth using in your next project. If you do not like the results, simply use the undo feature (Control-Z in Windows; Command-Z on Macintosh). The undo feature can only undo the last step that you have performed. In your quest to see how many ways you can distort your image from its original form, you can choose to reset different variables:

1. Select the deformed sprite.
2. Click the right mouse button (Control-click for Macintosh users) to bring up a Settings popup menu.
3. Click Transform.
4. In the submenu, choose which variables you want to reset (i.e., width, height, or skew). Depending on which variables you changed, reset or revert all of the variables to return to the initial cast member settings.

Duplicating a cast member before making alterations is recommended if you want to experiment with the attributes of that cast member. Some settings, such as converting bit depth, cannot return back to the original state once you proceed with the operation. By duplicating the cast member, you always have a safety copy to use if you are not satisfied with the changes you have made.

ADVANCED TWEENING: USE MULTIPLE KEYFRAMES

With Director, you can use a combination of keyframes and tempo controls to create some intricate non-linear animations. You can make images curve, speed up, or slow down. You can make images change size, change direction, and change transparency levels. Figure 5–36 uses a combination of keyframes and other properties to create more useful animations.

1. Insert keyframes on Frames 10, 20, 30, and 40.
2. Click on the first keyframe.
3. Reposition the sprite on the stage.
4. Repeat Steps 2 and 3 for the other keyframes.
5. Under the Modify menu, select Sprite.
6. Select Tweening from the submenu.
7. Use the various properties in the Sprite Tweening window to adjust the sprite's curvature and speed.

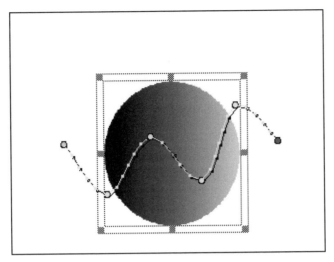

Figure 5–36 Multiple keyframes used for creating non-linear motion paths.

Director only animates on a 2D plane. You need to use combinations of different characteristics for your keyframes to give them the illusion of traveling in the third dimension.

CREATE BETTER TRANSITIONS

Director provides you with a set of standard single-frame transitions to be applied in the Transition channel of the score. Normally, you place a transition in the end frame of the outgoing scene to transition into the next scene. The standard effects are rather blocky and generic. The dissolve transition is probably the most common transition used in any project, yet is quite possibly the most pixilated effect within Director (Figure 5–37, also found in the color section). Instead, work with other tools inside Director to create better looking transitional effects without actually applying a transition. Use the following procedure to create a smooth, non-pixilated, one-second cross-fade transition (for this example, the movie frame rate is 30 frames per second):

1. Click on the sprite you want to animate using the tweening technique.
2. Select Sprite from the Modify menu.
3. Select Tweening from the Sprite submenu.
4. Make sure the Blending option in the Sprite Tweening window is selected and close the window.
5. Place the outgoing sprite in Channel 1.

 *(a)*

 *(b)*

 *(c)*

Figure 5–37 a, b, & c Steps showing Director's standard pixilated dissolve.

6. Extend the sprite for 40 frames.

7. Place the incoming sprite in Channel 2.

8. Extend this sprite for 40 frames.

9. Position the sprite on Channel 2 to start 10 frames later than the sprite in Channel 1 (Figure 5–38).

10. On both channels, insert keyframes at Frames 10 and 40.

11. At Frame 10, change the opacity value on Channel 2 to 0% (invisible).

12. At Frame 40, change the opacity value on Channel 1 to 0% (invisible).

13. Rewind and play back your movie. You should notice a smooth gradual cross-fade from one image into the other as opposed to the pixilated effect produced using the dissolve effect transition (Figure 5–39).

SPRITE TRANSITIONS

The need for ever-increasing functionality, flexibility, and creativity has gone the way of new transitions. I'm not just talking about the standard transitions that you add to the Transition channel of the score. I'm talking about some new transitions that get added directly to sprites. To access these transitions:

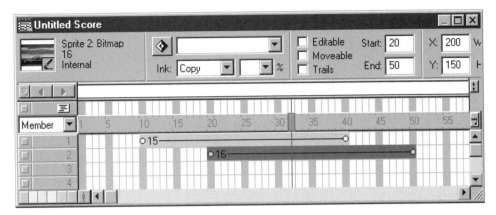

Figure 5–38 Sprites with offset starting positions.

Figure 5–39 A smooth transition showing an even blend (not pixilated).

1. Select Library Palette from the Window menu. The Library Palette will appear.

2. Select Animation from the Library List.

3. Select Sprite Transitions from the popup menu (Figure 5–40).

4. Drag one of the Sprite Transition behaviors directly onto the sprite to which you want to apply the transition. The "Parameters for…" window appears (Figure 5–41).

5. Set the appropriate variables.

6. Click OK.

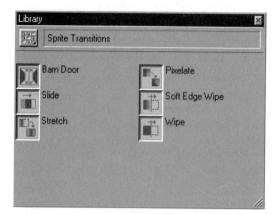

Figure 5–40 The Sprite Transitions behaviors in the Library Palette.

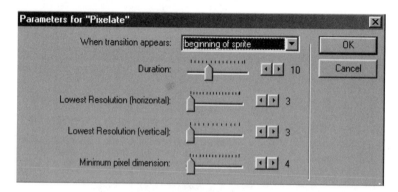

Figure 5–41 Use the "Parameters for..." window to customize the new sprite transitions for whichever Sprite Transition behavior you applied.

SUMMARY

Imagery really is important to Director. Don't worry if you're not very talented. You can create some incredible-looking graphics with the help of some of Director's tools. You can also see how much work goes into creating a simple animated scene for a Director movie. Do not be overwhelmed. Think creatively and break down your ideas into smaller elements. It is amazing what you can build by analyzing the designs and effects of your favorite multimedia pieces and by trying to emulate similar effects in your productions.

chapter 6

CREATING KILLER

VISUAL EFFECTS

We live in a culture of Hollywood-style productions and million-dollar effects. Every movie, TV show, and commercial tries to outdo the previous one by adding higher budgets and more realistic visual effects. It has gotten to the point where most of us are not impressed unless the image pops off the screen and grabs us. It is our duty as developers to keep up with the changes in technology and learn how to integrate Director to design effects that would make George Lucas, James Cameron, and the entire Disney animation team jealous.

This chapter will cover a number of different design element styles and how to effectively implement them. There are three main points that every developer should focus on when creating a new project:

1. Quality.
2. Functionality.
3. Timeliness.

Always remember there are many variables when working with multimedia applications that can affect the outcome of your projects in the way they look and perform. Throughout this book, we cover many of the key requirements that will ultimately determine what type of design elements you will be able to utilize or whether your Director movie will even play.

LAUNCH AND EDIT

Creating multimedia programs is never easy and changes are bound to occur. Director makes these changes simple through a feature called Launch and Edit, which allows you to quickly edit your changes using the design program you prefer.

Use Launch and Edit to automatically open up your favorite bitmap image or sound editor programs directly from Director. The editor program will open with the file you selected. When you are finished making the necessary changes, Director will automatically update that file in the cast and the score, eliminating the old process of re-importing new files, finding and replacing them in the score, and deleting old cast members.

To set up Director's list of editors:

1. Choose Preferences from the File menu.
2. Select Editors from the submenu. The Editors Preferences window appears displaying a list of file types Director uses (Figure 6–1).
3. Select one of the bitmap or sound file formats and click the Edit button.
4. Click the Scan button to display a list of applications available to edit this file on your computer.

    OR

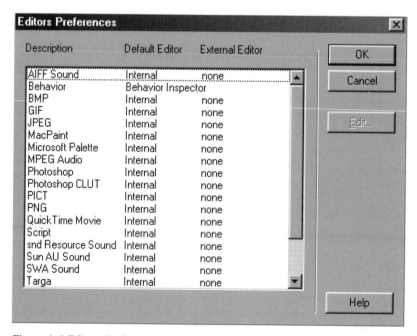

Figure 6–1 Editors Preferences window.

Click the Browse button to manually search through all of your computer's files.

5. Choose an application and click OK.

To launch a pre-selected editor:

1. Import files that you would prefer to change using an external editor.
2. Double-click on a bitmap or sound file cast member. The editing application should open with the file ready to be edited.
3. Make the necessary changes.
4. Save the file and close the editing application.
5. Return to Director.
6. Click the Done button to automatically update your changes in the cast, stage, and score.

If you plan to use external editors to change your files, you must first select Include Original Data for Editing from the Media pull-down menu at the bottom of the Import window (Figure 6–2). With this option selected, Director records a copy of the original data of a file. Then, when you choose a cast member that has an external editor selected for that file format, all of the stored information is sent to the external editor. This ensures the most accurate data transfer between the programs to preserve the quality of your images. This additional information is not translated over into your projector or Shockwave files to eliminate any unnecessary file space.

For a quick design fix, even with external editors selected as the preferred application, you can choose to edit your image in the Paint window. To choose Director's internal Paint window:

1. Single-click on the cast member you wish to alter.
2. Choose Edit Cast Member from the Edit menu. Director places that cast member into the Paint window.

ADD JUST THE RIGHT COLOR

When working with any type of image in Director, setting the right color palettes is critical. What actually determines the way an image is displayed is the types of colors available in its associated color palette. This is especially true when working with images created as 8-bit color depth or less. Working in Director involves two types of color depth settings:

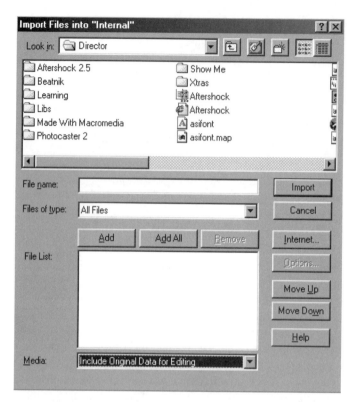

Figure 6–2 Make sure to select Include Original Data for Editing when using external editors.

◆   Setting a general palette for the entire movie.

◆   Setting color palettes for individual sprites or cast members.

Director offers the unique ability to change color palettes along the way (via the Color Palette channel) or to import custom palettes associated with individual graphics (Figure 6–3). Director has the ability to create customized palettes by selecting the most commonly used colors and then saving them for the most optimal playback display of all your images. (Check out the color section in this book to see some examples of how custom color palettes can work for you.)

OPTIMIZE YOUR GRAPHICS

Every bitmapped image imported into Director has its own color depth setting. When you import a graphic into Director, if the color depth is not the same as the color depth set for your Director movie, an Image Options window appears, prompting you to

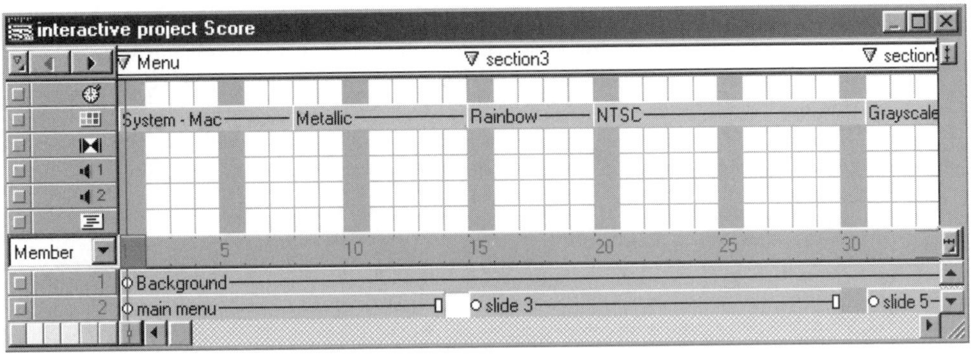

Figure 6–3 Various color palettes can be applied directly in the score.

choose which Color Depth setting you want to apply to the graphic being imported (Figure 6–4). If the image has a higher color depth than that set for your movie, Director will automatically strip out the extra colors not found in the movie's color palette. The downside is that the graphic will still sustain the same characteristics of the larger file, meaning that the image will use up more RAM as if it still contained all the discarded colors, causing it to animate more slowly across the screen. If you want to display an image at its natural color depth, you must change the color depth setting of the movie.

◆ 1-bit = 2 colors (black and white only).

◆ 2-bit = 4 colors.

◆ 4-bit = 16 colors.

◆ 8-bit = 256 colors.

◆ 16-bit = thousands of colors (32,768).

◆ 24-bit = millions of colors (16.7 million).

The color depth of your movie is set outside Director. How you set the color depth for your monitor determines the color depth available for your movies. Therefore, if

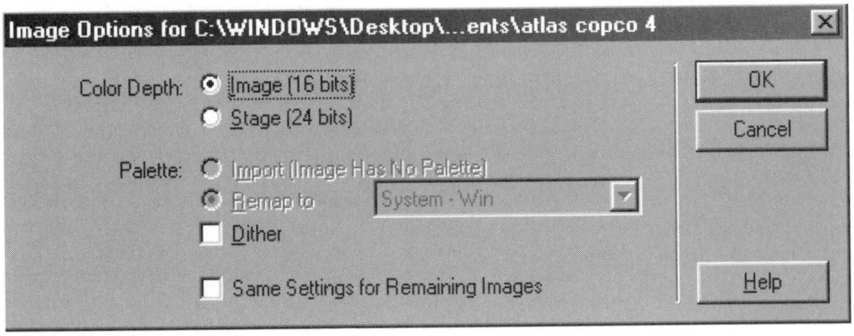

Figure 6–4 Image Options (Color Depth settings) during import.

you only set it for 256 colors, you will only be able to display 8-bit images. For Windows systems, use the Display Properties Settings in the Control Panel to set the color depth of your monitor. For Macintosh systems, use the Monitor and Sound Settings found in the Control Panels folder.

Inside Director, graphics with a 2-, 4-, or 8-bit color depth identify with colors set to a particular position of a color palette, referred to as index colors. Higher bit depths do not rely on color palettes to display accurate colors and use the adjustable Luminance, Hue, and Saturation levels of the color wheel (Figure 6–5).

Map your images to as few color palettes as possible. This will increase the quality and performance of how Director displays your images.

CHANGE IMAGE COLOR DEPTH

To get your images to look their best, create a custom palette optimal for most of the graphics you have imported as cast members. This may be the best solution for working at lower bit depths with reduced file size, and still having images look as close to normal as possible. This new optimized palette will allow you to remap all of your cast members and have them utilize one color palette instead of trying to load a new one for each individual cast member displayed. To set up an optimized custom palette (your stage must be set for 8-bit (Windows and Macintosh) or 4-bit (Macintosh only) color depth to create a custom palette in Director):

1. Select a cast member to utilize its color palette as the basis for the optimized palette.

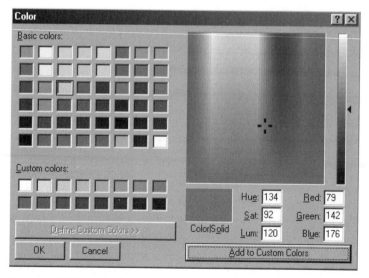

Figure 6–5 Color wheel with adjustable Luminance, Hue, and Saturation controls.

2. Choose Color Palettes from the Window menu. The image's color palette appears.

3. Choose Duplicate from the Edit menu. This way, you will not destroy the original color palette of the selected cast member.

4. Enter a name for the new palette in the Create Palette window that appears.

   In Director or any other program, get into the habit of naming files in a manner that makes them easily recognizable. Name the new palette you created in Step 3 something descriptive and easily identifiable, such as "custom palette" or "optimal palette."

5. Click the Select Used Colors button at the top of the Color Palette window (Figure 6–6).

6. Click the Select button in the Select Colors Used In Bitmap window. Director will put a black outline around the colors of the palette present in the cast member.

7. Use the Hand tool and drag one of the selected colors to the second color panel in the top row (next to the white color chip). Director automatically rearranges the selected colors in a continuous row next to the one you just repositioned (Figure 6–7).

8. Click the Invert Selection button to highlight the unused colors of the palette.

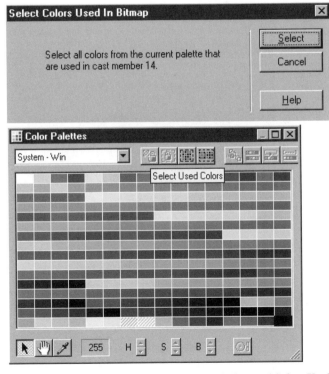

Figure 6–6 Select Colors Used In Bitmap window and Select Used Colors button.

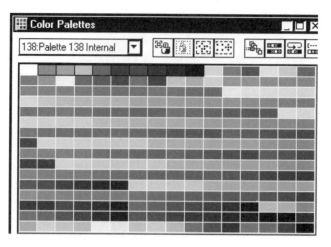

Figure 6–7 Rearrange used colors in the color palette.

9. Click the In-Betweening button to convert the unused colors into an even-toned color blend to make it easier to identify and separate the actual colors used in the original cast member (Figure 6–8).

10. Click the Palette popup menu in the Color Palettes window. Choose a color palette used by other cast members.

11. Select another cast member and click the Select Used Colors button again.

12. With the new selection highlighted, choose Copy Colors from the Edit menu.

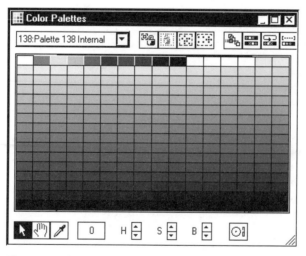

Figure 6–8 The In-Betweening button separates unused colors into an even color blend.

13. Select Optimized Palette from the Palette popup menu.

14. Select the first chip after the colors used in the original cast member.

15. Choose Paste Into Palette from the Edit menu to add these newly selected colors from the second chosen cast member to your optimal palette.

16. Repeat Steps 10 through 15 for each cast member or until the optimized color palette is full.

Now, you must remap all of your images (graphical cast members) to this new optimized color palette you just created:

1. Select the cast member you want to remap.

2. Select Transform Bitmap from the Modify menu. The Transform Bitmap window appears.

3. Select the Remap Colors radio button.

4. Select the optimized palette you created from the Color Palettes popup menu (Figure 6–9).

5. Click Transform to apply the new color palette.

It is important to plan this procedure from the beginning of your project to get the best quality images while creating the most optimal Director movie.

There are only two color depths that have customizable palettes. Both Window and Macintosh systems allow you to modify an 8-bit color palette. Only Macintosh systems allow you to modify a 4-bit color palette.

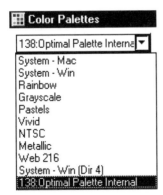

Figure 6–9 Color Palettes popup menu containing new custom-made optimized palette.

DESIGN EFFECTIVE NAVIGATIONAL ELEMENTS

As a developer, the navigational system is probably one of the first features you look at when examining any multimedia package. Is it effective? Does it impress you? Can you maneuver around the program easily and accurately? Director allows you to design your interactive links almost any way you can imagine. The creativity is up to you. Before you begin programming your Director movie, you must first design the elements that are going to be used in your application.

It is a good idea to sketch out on paper how and where you would like your navigational elements to be placed on the screen.

CREATE FLASHY BUTTON DESIGNS

My personal preference (depending on the purpose of the project) is to give the navigational elements as much life as possible. These "buttons" are what the end-user will ultimately be interacting with. Make them easy to use, but don't forget that they can also be exciting. How impressed would you be if you saw a program that contained only generic gray buttons with Arial 10-point font text in them (Figure 6–10)? Or would the interfaces in Figure 6–11 catch your attention? Even if you do not have access to any third-party design programs, you can still create some exciting buttons using Director's Paint window.

Because Director Paint does not have the same type of layering capabilities as Photoshop, it is easier to work with the outline portion of an object first and then fill in the space, as opposed to trying to put a border around a solid object.

1. Open the Paint window.
2. Select a color to use as your border color in the foreground color chip. (If you are placing this object over a dark background, use a light color. If you are placing it over a light color background, use a dark color to give your object some separation.)
3. Using the Hollow Oval tool, drag the shape of your button.
4. Pick a color to make the background portion of the button.
5. Use the Paint Can tool to fill in the oval.
6. Select the border color again and draw a smaller oval inside the original.
7. Using the Gradient tool, select two different shades of the same color and fill the inner oval.
8. Select black as the foreground color and use the Text tool to type in the name of the button.

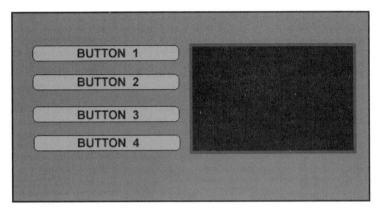

Figure 6–10 Generic interface with default gray buttons.

9. Select white as the foreground color and type out the same word with the same attributes.

10. Place it slightly offset from the black text to give it a drop shadow effect. This will be used as our "Up" button.

11. Copy and paste the button into a new cast member.

12. Repeat Steps 6 and 7 over the new cast member. This time, reverse the direction of the gradient colors.

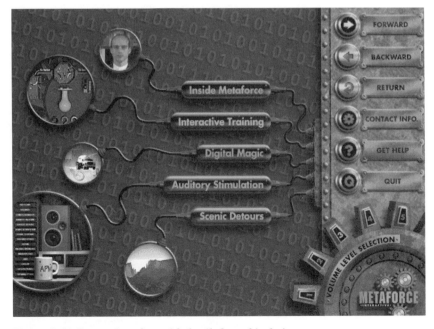

Figure 6–11 Custom interface with detailed graphic design.

13. Type the same word using only the white color. This will be used as our "Down" or "Clicked" button.

14. Copy and paste the original image one more time into a new cast member.

15. Change the hue and use this button for the "rollover" state (Figure 6–12).

Use the first cast member as your stationary button. Using behaviors, add the inter-activity to change cast members on a `mouseDown` command to the second button you created. This procedure will give the illusion that the button is being clicked.

To assist in building objects in the Paint window without layers, create each element in the outside white area around the main object. Use the Marquee tool set to Lasso and grab your image and place it exactly where you would like. If you put it in the wrong area, select Undo from the Edit menu before performing any other steps.

There are no rules for creating buttons. Creating a button can be as easy as creating geometric shapes in any paint program or as complex as rendering a custom-modeled 3D object. Be creative, but always keep in mind the intended audience and the scope of the project.

TRIM DOWN NAVIGATIONAL ELEMENTS

Director looks at the entire bounding box area of a cast member, including its background, even after you apply ink effects. If you have been experiencing strange behavior patterns with rollovers or buttons, it could be more of a graphic design issue than a

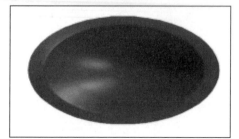

Figure 6–12 The three states of a button—normal (A), rollover (B), and down (C).

navigational script problem. Notice the large white bounding area around the actual object. If you apply a rollover behavior or navigational command to this object, you will experience these interactions even within the bounding box areas of this object. If you have several navigational elements close together, the overlapping background areas may cause a different interaction than you intended. The best solution is to clean up your images.

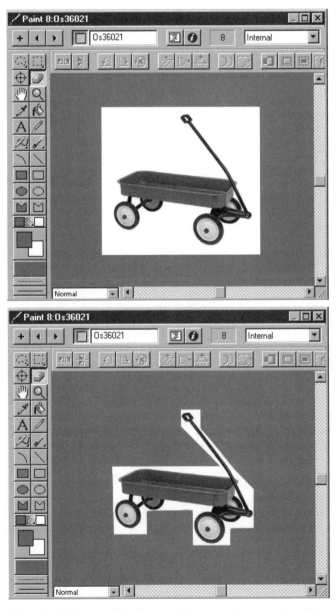

Figure 6–13 Unwanted background image and how to reduce it.

1. Open a bitmap cast member in the Paint window.

2. Use the Erase tool to eliminate any unwanted background area (Figure 6–13).

Hold the Shift key down to constrain the cursor to a horizontal motion to work with straight edges.

DESIGN BUTTONS WITH THIRD-PARTY HELP

You do not have to be an artist to design any type of interactive controller. A simple square created in Director's Paint window is all it takes to create a button. If designing your own buttons is just not working and you cannot afford to pay a designer an hourly rate to create these elements for you, you might want to consider purchasing some third-party Xtras that have buttons already created. Some of these Xtras contain 2D and 3D animated buttons complete with sound effects and Lingo scripts. My favorite program, Instant Buttons and Controls (IB&C) by Statmedia, contains over 4,000 images and objects that you can use in your Director movie. They range from simple, generic buttons to the wildest animated 3D buttons you have ever seen. Visit Statmedia on the Web at www.statmedia.com (Figure 6–14). The majority of third-party Xtras are easy to use and save you hours of designing and coding.

1. Once installed, select IB&C from the Xtras menu.

2. Cycle through the display of images.

3. Drag the selected button to the stage. Notice the cast is automatically filled with each individual cast member and scripts.

4. Open the Script window (Lingo scripts already written by IB&C). You only need to enter the specific variables that will complete the Lingo commands (i.e., how and where you want these links to interact). Examples of scripts you will need to fill in may include frame number or marker name (where to link to when clicked or rolled over; see Figure 6–15).

QUICK SHORTCUT TO HIGHLIGHT BUTTONS

If you did not make an alternate version of your button or navigational object when designing your images, Director has a shortcut method to give your buttons the look of actually being clicked on by highlighting (inverting their color) when the mouse button is pressed. To set up this feature:

1. Select the sprite or cast member that you want to highlight.

2. Open the Property Inspector.

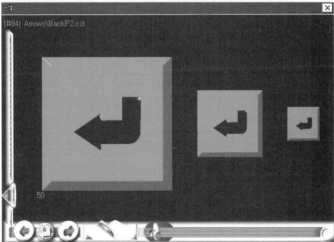

Figure 6–14 IB&C interface screens.

3. Select the Bitmap tab.
4. Select the Highlight When Clicked checkbox.

If you select this option but have not programmed any type of navigation, the object will not be highlighted when it is clicked.

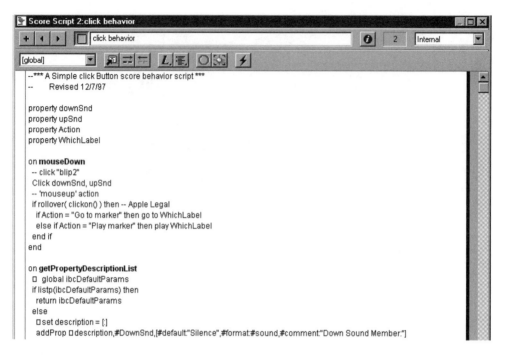

Figure 6–15 Sample script prewritten by IB&C.

COOL EXAMPLE USING ROLLOVERS

The best way to learn how to create new and exciting rollover effects is to look at other peoples' projects and try to emulate and vary their effects. One effect that I use involves a series of words running down the side of a screen that functions as the navigational controls for the program. What is intriguing about this is that all of the text is out of focus. As you roll your mouse over each of these areas, the blurry text changes into clear words (Figure 6–16). For my company's demo CD-ROM, we incorporated the changing of blurry text with an added feature that offers the user more interactivity. We implemented a "decoder window" that as you drag it over an out-of-focus image, the clear text appears in the window. Here is how to implement this effect:

1. In the graphics program of your choice (we used Photoshop), create all of the text you need in focus.
2. Create the "decoder window" graphic with a completely white center.
3. Save each element individually or use PhotoCaster and skip to Step 9.

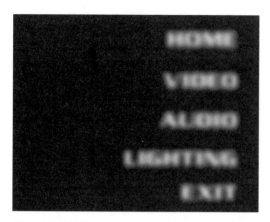

Figure 6–16 Blurry text displayed as normal, and clear text displayed when cursor rolls over image.

4. Apply a Gaussian Blur (or any blur filter) of about 30% to each text image.

5. Use the `Save As` command to save each image as a different name from the original file.

6. Launch Director and import all of these images into the cast.

7. Drag the out-of-focus cast members onto the stage.

8. Position the out-of-focus sprites into their desired locations.

9. Assign a new behavior to each sprite, choosing the in-focus sprite under the Change Cast Member action for the `mouseEnter` command.

10. Add to the behavior of each sprite and choose the out-of-focus sprite under the Change Cast Member for the `mouseLeave` command in the Behavior Inspector window.

11. Select the "decoder window" cast member and drag it to the score.

12. Place the "decoder window" in the highest channel to be displayed over all of the out-of-focus sprites.

13. Apply a Background Transparent ink effect to the "decoder window" sprite (Figure 6–17).

14. With the sprite still selected, select Moveable in the Property Inspector located in the Sprite tab (Figure 6–18).

15. Rewind and play your movie.

As you play your movie, drag the decoder window around on the screen. The Moveable command allows you to click on and drag the sprite while your movie is in play mode. The Background Transparent ink effect makes the center, white portion of the decoder window transparent, displaying the images beneath it. The secret to this effect is that your rollover commands are activated when the mouse comes in contact

Figure 6–17 Decoder window used to roll over blurry sprites. Clear text appears in window.

with the out-of-focus sprites. To drag the decoder window into position to "decode the hidden message," the mouse is positioned over the sprite, changing the cast member to display the in-focus sprites through the window.

When creating altered versions of the same image as in the case of rollovers and click-down buttons, come up with a file naming system that will help you recognize which file you are working with by the code you use. Keep it consistent for every project you develop to decrease wasted time opening the wrong files while searching for the correct version. For buttons and other linkable objects, we use a number 1 at the end of the filename to indicate the "normal" version, a number 2 for the "down" version, and a number 3 for the "rollover" version. It's simple, easy to remember, and saves us time searching through a mess of files. In addition, by using the same filename followed by a numbering system, the computer's internal filing system groups the like images together as follows.

Help 1

Help 2

Help 3

Exit 1

Exit 2

Exit 3

SUPPORT FILES WITH THIRD-PARTY APPLICATIONS AND XTRAS

As with many applications you create, you will need to add different types of file formats that require additional programs to run or view the given files. Director has the ability to automatically launch the required applications through Lingo scripts and Xtras, as long as the required applications are installed on your hard drive. There are many different types of small applications and Xtras that can be used to open, view, or work with a wide variety of files and documents. Some applications can be distributed along with your movie; others are downloadable from the Web.

> **Before including or distributing any Xtras or other programs, check with the developers of those applications for any licensing or copyright issues.**

A common request is to include .PDF files in the electronic programs you create. .PDF files require Adobe Acrobat Reader or Viewer to open and view these compressed documents (Figure 6–19). Director now has the ability to work with .PDF files packaged

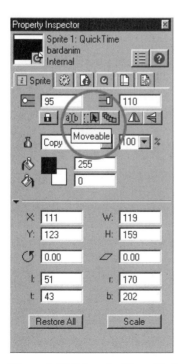

Figure 6–18 Select the Moveable button in the Property Inspector.

within your movie by using such Xtras as the AcroViewer Xtra by XtraMedia. The advantage is that you can now have cross-platform electronic files, catalogs, presentations, and tutorials all controlled from your Director movie. Check out AcroViewer on the Web at www.xtramedia.com/AcroViewer.html.

Another type of application used to support integrated multimedia files is a small executable application known as a Whip reader. To view CAD drawings in your Director or Shockwave movies through a Web browser, install this application onto your system. This reader gives your viewers full access to CAD drawings, including the ability to zoom in and out and pan left and right without losing any quality in the image (Figure 6–20). You can download this application from the Autodesk Web site at www.autodesk.com/products/whip/index.htm.

Using custom Xtras with your Director movie instead of just relying on the application itself can help minimize potential conflicts trying to launch and execute these other programs.

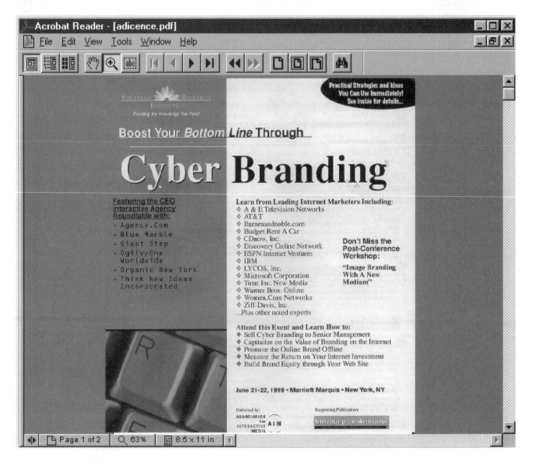

Figure 6–19 .PDF files can be read with Adobe Acrobat Reader inside Director.

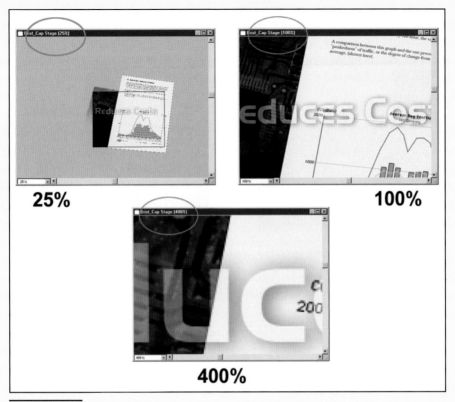

FIGURE 1–3

Director now allows you to increase or decrease your view of the stage.

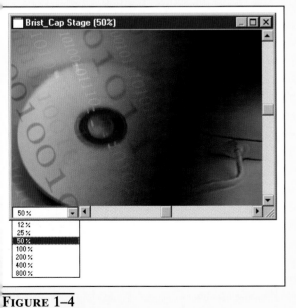

FIGURE 1–4

Use the Zoom Menu pulldown box to select one of the present viewable stage areas.

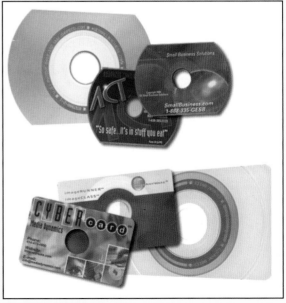

FIGURE 1–10

Business card-shaped CD-ROM that contains up to 40 MB per disc.

 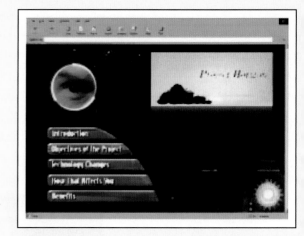

(a)

(b)

FIGURE 1–11 a & b

Notice the difference between quality settings. Images quickly degrade with the more compression you apply.

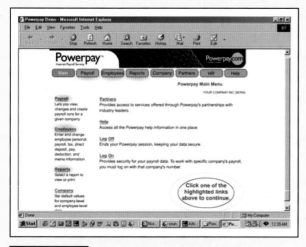

FIGURE 1–15

Publishing your movie defaults to opening in a browser to display your new Shockwave movie.

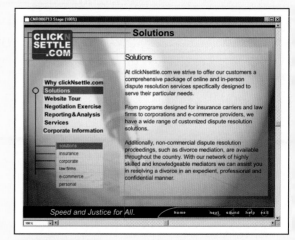

FIGURE 1–20

A comparison between working with Guides vs. the Grid. Notice the clean and accurate results with Guides.

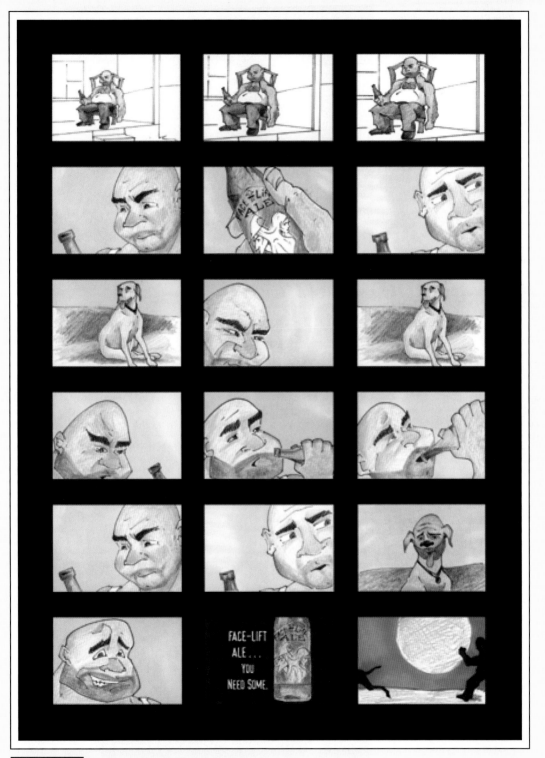

FIGURE 2–6

Sample storyboard layouts.

FIGURE 2–10 a, b, & c
Clients generally like to see alternate versions of the same basic thematic design before selecting the final layout.

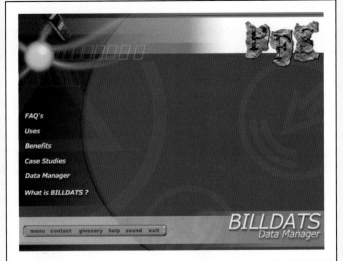

(a)

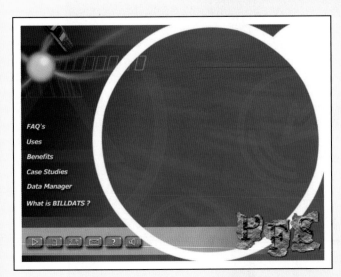

(b)

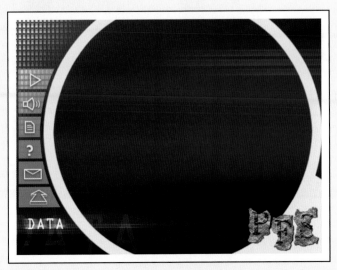

(c)

FIGURE 2–12
Single frame from a vector-based image created in Flash.

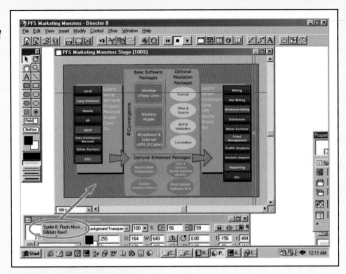

FIGURE 3–8
Previous, repeat, and next buttons for navigation.

FIGURE 3–20
Various types of interactive multimedia interfaces

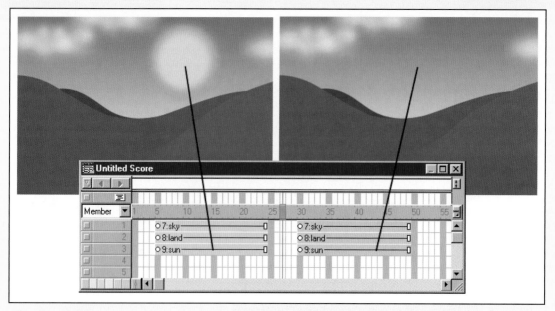

FIGURE 4–13

Sprite "sun" visibility set to true on left image, and false on right image.

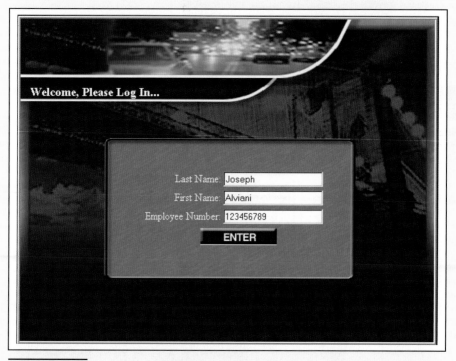

FIGURE 4–18

Area for user to enter his name, which will be displayed in other areas of the program.

(b)

FIGURE 5–1 a, b, c, & d
Effects of different inks applied to the same images.
(Shown: (a) lightest, (b) not copy, (c) not transparent,
and (d) subtract.)

(d)

FIGURE 5–7b
Background transparent ink does not always work if the image contains the same color that you want to remove from the background

(a)

(b)

FIGURE 5–23 a & b
Comparison of image quality with different levels of compression applied to the image.

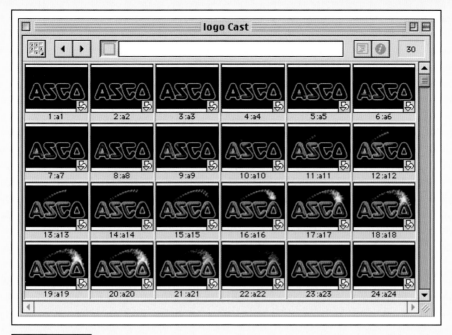

FIGURE 5–28

Cast of sequential images to be used for "cast-to-time" animation.

(a)

(b)

FIGURE 5–37 a, b, & c

Steps showing Director's standard pixilated dissolve.

(c)

FIGURE 6–24

Create an orange-red image in Photoshop to be used for a fire effect in Director.

FIGURE 6–25

The Effector Set II Behavior Cast Window.

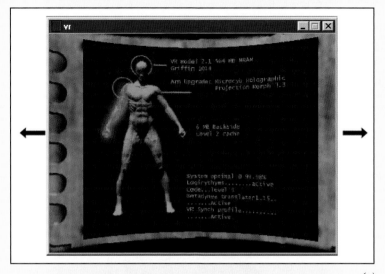

(a)

(b)

(c)

FIGURE 6–28 a, b, & c
Sample QTVR files.

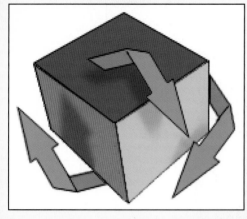

(a)

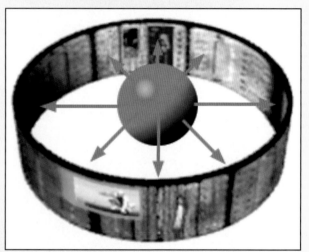

(b)

FIGURE 6–29 a & b
*Panoramic vs. objects virtual reality is determined
by the viewer's position relative to the image.*

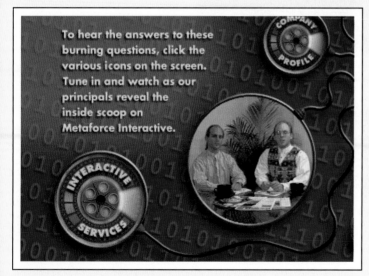

FIGURE 7–30
*No more rectangular video displays.
Video clips can be displayed in just
about any shape.*

(a)

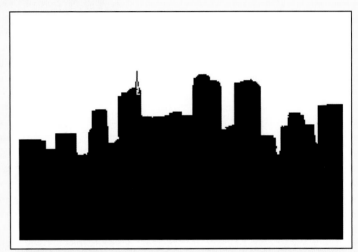

(b)

FIGURE 7–32 a, b, & c
Mask cast member placed directly after original cast member.

(c)

FIGURE 9–20

Joe G's Famous Frog Bog Game, developed for OnlineBoardwalk.com.

FIGURE 10–11
Full-screen display projectors cover the entire screen, regardless of resolution.

FIGURE 10–30
Add a Quit button to any screen saver that allows user interactivity.

FIGURE 11–1
Shockwave movie running inside a web browser.

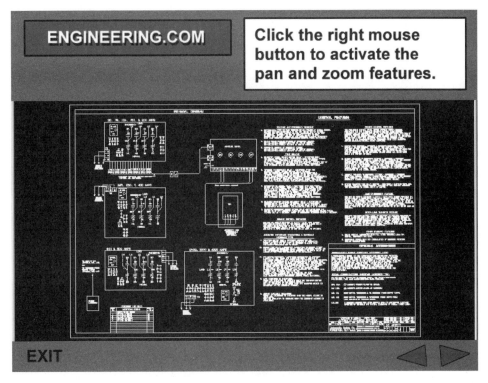

Figure 6–20 AutoCAD drawings can be accessed through a Director movie and the Web.

As technology grows, clients are demanding that more complex functions be added into the software you design for them. Look around to find out which Xtras developers have used or created to allow for these complex features to be easily added into your Director applications. You can find a list of custom third-party Xtras, a description of their functions, and a link to the companies that created them at the Macromedia Web site at www.macromedia.com/software/xtras/director.

A CLOSE-UP LOOK AT AN IMAGE

I was working on a project that required a feature I had always done the hard way. And of course, the hard way never quite works just the way you want it to. The program needed the user to have the ability to enlarge various portions of the image on-screen, as if looking through a magnifying glass. What we simulated was giving the user the ability to move the magnifying eyepiece around on the screen to uncover a larger, clearer portion of the image that the user wished to see (Figure 6–21).

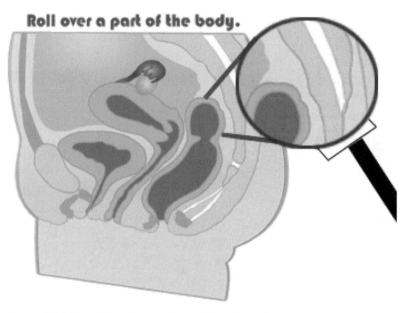

Figure 6–21 Magnifying images from a Director movie.

I was recently introduced by one of my co-workers to a method that would take our same concept and make it happen exactly as we needed it for that particular project … faster, easier, and better-looking. I have to give the credit to Gary Rosenzweig, a true Director guru. He posted a method on www.director-online.com how to use Director 8's Imaging Lingo to simulate magnifying images with only a few lines of code. The basic concept here is to import an image at a larger resolution (image size) than you want to show when displaying the smaller, less detailed version of the image. I recommend three to four times the size. This is necessary because Director cannot actually enlarge portions of a smaller image. They would only pixilate, showing you less detail rather than more. As you move the magnifying eyepiece over the image, Director calls out to the original size of the file, displaying the "magnified" viewing area at the resolution you initially imported the image into Director.

The key to this illusion is to use the `mapStageToMember ( )` command. This determines where the user's cursor is positioned over the smaller image to determine what portion of the larger image to display.

Here is what you will have to do to implement this feature:

1. Create an object to be used as the magnifying eyepiece.
2. Duplicate the image to create a mask from a smaller area of the object you just created. Always place masks in the next cast member slot at 1 bit. (Check out Chapter 5 for more information on creating masks.)

3. Import the large image and place it into your score.

4. Scale it down at least 50% for this effect to work properly. Depending on the original image size, scaling it down to 25% to 35% works very well.

5. Type in the following code (remember to put in the proper names of your cast members):

```
property pEyepieceImage, pEyepieceMask, pEyepieceRect, pRegPoint, pLastLoc, pOrigImage

on beginSprite me
  — get the image to use as the magnifying image (next sprite)
  pEyepieceImage = sprite(me.spriteNum+1).member.image

  — get the original image
  pOrigImage = duplicate(pEyepieceImage)

  — take the matte image from another member
  pEyepieceMask = member("Eyepiece mask").image.createMask()

  — determine the rect of the Eyepiece mask, with the center at 0,0
  pEyepieceRect = rect(-member("Eyepiece mask").width/2,-member("Eyepiece
mask").height/2,member("Eyepiece mask").width/2,member("Eyepiece mask").height/2)

  — get the registration point of the Eyepiece
  pRegPoint = sprite(me.spriteNum+1).member.regPoint
end

on exitFrame me
  — get new mouse location
  ml = the mouseLoc

  — only update image if the location has changed
  if ml <> pLastLoc then

    — get the relative location inside the image
    loc = mapStageToMember(sprite me.spriteNum, ml)

    — if outside the image, hide Eyepiece
    — otherwise, show Eyepiece with new image imprint
    if voidP(loc) then
      sprite(me.spriteNum+1).loc = point(-1000,-1000)

    else
      — get the area inside the image
      sourceRect = rect(loc,loc) + pEyepieceRect
```

```
    — determine the area of the Eyepiece to use
    destRect = rect(pRegPoint,pRegPoint) + pEyepieceRect

    — figure out the mask offset so things line up correctly
    maskOffset =  loc - point(pEyepieceRect.width/2,pEyepieceRect.height/2)

    — copy pixels from image into Eyepiece using the mask
    pEyepieceImage.copyPixels(pOrigImage, pEyepieceImage.rect,pOrigImage.rect)
    pEyepieceImage.copyPixels(sprite(me.spriteNum).member.image,
destRect,sourceRect,[#maskImage: pEyepieceMask, #maskOffset: maskOffset])

    — position the sprite under the cursor
    sprite(me.spriteNum+1).loc = the mouseLoc

    — remember the current location
    pLastLoc = ml
  end if
 end if
end

on endSprite me
  — restore original image
  pEyepieceImage.copyPixels(pOrigImage, pEyepieceImage.rect,pOrigImage.rect)
end
```

6. Apply this script to the Eyepiece sprite.

7. Add all of your cast members to your score.

Play your movie. As you drag the eyepiece around the screen, you should see an enlarged version of your original image appear. I must say Gary made this trick work very well and it looks great. If you want to see more of Gary's tips, check out www.director-online.com.

MY FAVORITE XTRAS

If there is one set of Xtras that you need to have in your "Director toolbox," it would have to be Media Labs' PhotoCaster, AlphaMania, and Effector Sets I and II. Check out Chapter 5 for more information on PhotoCaster. In this section, I want to focus on AlphaMania and some of the funky effects that you can get with the Effector Set behaviors (See "Smoke, Fire, and a Bit of Rain" below). AlphaMania allows you to import Photoshop files (or other graphic files) that contain alpha channels. AlphaMania allows you to select which layers you want to import into your Director movie, preserving 100% of the image's transparency and alpha channel properties (Figure 6–22).

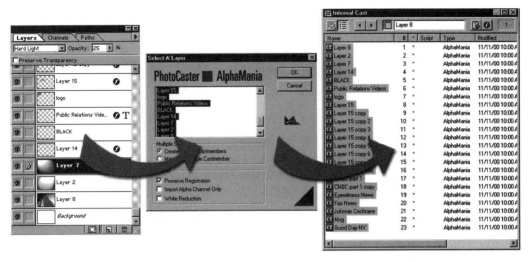

Figure 6–22 Photoshop layers are transferred over to Director seamlessly via AlphaMania, preserving all transparency layers.

To use AlphaMania (once you have registered your copy):

1. Create an image in Photoshop that has an alpha channel and save it.
2. In Director, select Media Lab Media from the Insert menu.
3. Select AlphaMania from the popup menu. The AlphaMania window should appear (Figure 6–23).

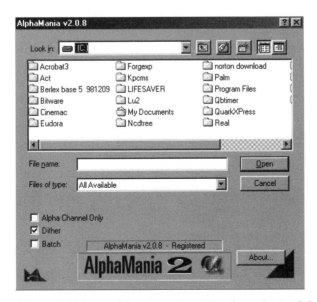

Figure 6–23 Import files supporting alpha channels via AlphaMania.

4. Browse to find the image containing the alpha channel you just created and click Open. The Select A Layer window should appear.

5. Select which layer(s) you want to bring into Director. You can choose to create each layer as a separate cast member or merge the layers into one cast member (still maintaining the alpha channel).

Your image should appear in Director maintaining the same alpha channel you saved back in Photoshop (or another application). This is the only way to get images with true, clean alpha channels into Director. This method will give you the cleanest edges, especially with cut-out sections or when feathered.

An alert window will warn you if you have selected part of an image that is not layered or contains an image mask.

SMOKE, FIRE, AND A BIT OF RAIN

There are so many cool things that you can do inside Director. There are even more neat things to do when you use some outside help from the Effector Sets of Media Lab. The Effector Sets are a series of Xtras or behaviors that you can apply to images to create unbelievable effects. My two personal favorites are the ability to create fire (or smoke, depending on the colors of the image) or have it rain on your stage. These effects are so easy to create. First the fire:

1. Create an odd-shaped image with a red and orange gradient in Photoshop (Figure 6–24, also found in the color section). Make sure to save it with an alpha channel.

2. Bring it into Director through AlphaMania (see "My Favorite Xtras" above for more information on using AlphaMania).

3. Place the image on your stage.

4. Select Media Lab Xtras from the Xtras menu.

5. Select Effector Set II Behavior Cast from the popup menu. A new Cast window appears, containing all of the Effector Set II behaviors (Figure 6–25, also found in the color section).

6. Find the behavior named "Roil" (default cast member #31).

7. Apply it to the image containing the alpha channel. The Parameters for "Roil" window appears.

8. Adjust the Speed and Stretch sliders as desired.

When you play your movie, the image effect should appear to be a series of random waves moving across your image, creating the illusion of flames. If you create your image with various grayscale shades, the image effect will appear more like smoke. You can even apply a bit of a blur effect to really enhance the look.

Figure 6–24 Create an orange-red image in Photoshop to be used for a fire effect in Director.

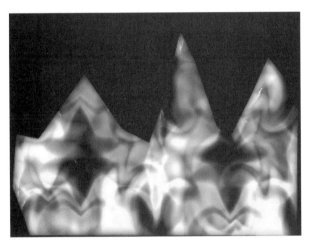

Figure 6–25 The Effector Set II Behavior Cast Window.

To add raindrops (a simple spring shower) to your movie:

1. Create an image in Photoshop. Make sure to save it with an alpha channel.
2. Bring it into Director through AlphaMania (see "My Favorite Xtras" above for more information on using AlphaMania).
3. Place the image on your stage.
4. Select Media Lab Xtras from the Xtras menu.
5. Select Effector Set II Behavior Cast from the popup menu. A new Cast window appears, containing all of the Effector Set II behaviors.

6. Find the behavior named "Ripple-Rain" (default cast member #42).

7. Apply the behavior to the image containing the alpha channel. The Parameters for "Ripple-Rain" window appears.

8. Adjust the sliders as desired.

When you play your movie, the image effect should appear to be a series of random raindrops hitting your scene (Figure 6–26).

AUTOMATIC ANIMATING BEHAVIORS

In the last few sections, I covered some great effects you can create outside Director. That's not to say that there aren't some neat behaviors that come bundled inside Director. This is one of those areas where I can only recommend to play around and try some of the various combinations. You'll be surprised at the results. If your experiments don't give you some creative ideas that you can apply to future projects … well, let's hope they will.

To try some simple, neat effects with behaviors within Director:

1. Drag any image onto your stage (either a bitmap image imported in or a vector image created in Director Paint).

2. Select the Library Palette from the Window menu.

3. Select Animation from the Library List.

4. Select Automatic from the popup menu.

5. Drag a behavior (such as "Random Movement and Rotation") onto the sprite (Figure 6–27).

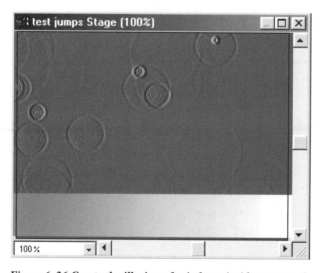

Figure 6–26 Create the illusion of raindrops inside your movie.

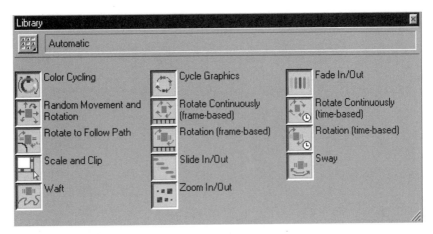

Figure 6–27 You can create some interesting effects from color cycling to random sprite rotations without any programming knowledge.

Play your movie and notice the interesting effects that you get ... all without any programming. I've found these effects work great when applied to background images, to add some life to a static interface. Use them, but don't go crazy. Too many effects can ruin a project.

INTEGRATE QUICKTIME VR

The days of merely adding still graphics to a presentation are quickly fading. Users today want more; they want the ability to interact with their movie and choose for themselves what they are looking at on the screen. The answer to this desire is the use of QuickTime VR (QTVR; Figure 6–28, also found in the color section). QTVR is a unique type of digital video file that allows the user to pan and zoom within a file to view different aspects of the movie. This feature gives the user full control of what is being displayed while providing the illusion of viewing a 3D world. There are basically two types of QTVR movies (Figure 6–29, also found in the color section):

1. Panoramic scenes—Where you view an image wrapped around you in a full 360-degree display.

2. Objects—Where you can view all possible angles of an object by rotating it in front of you.

QTVR files work on both Macintosh and Windows platforms and can easily be imported into your Director movies. These files work like most other digital video files. They are imported into Director as linked cast members and can be integrated as part of your movie as a regular sprite. You must have the proper Xtras (such as the QTVR Xtra) installed on your system to view these files in your Director movie.

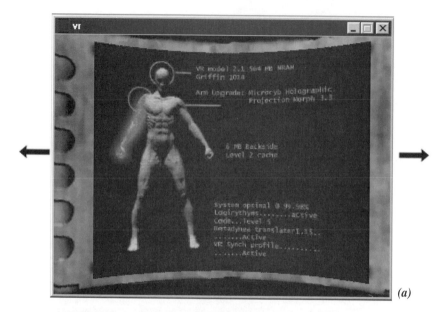

(a)

(b)

(c)

Figure 6–28 a, b, & c Sample QTVR files.

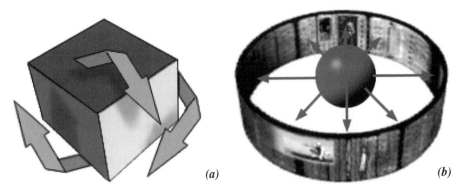

(a)

(b)

Figure 6–29 a & b Panoramic vs. objects virtual reality is determined by the viewer's position relative to the image.

It is a good idea to include the required Xtras when distributing your movie or provide instructions on how the user can obtain these applications from the Web to properly view your movie. Check with the makers of any Xtras you plan to distribute to see if there are any licensing agreements that you need to secure before passing out the required Xtras.

There are three basic steps required to use QTVR files in your Director movie:

◆ Setup—Registers the QuickTime VR components that will recognize the QTVR Xtra.

◆ Open—Opens the movie.

◆ Display—Shows the movie on-screen, constantly updating the screen based on the user's interactions.

It is important to understand that opening a QTVR movie does not display the movie. These are two distinct commands that must be included.

Following are some of the basic scripts you need to implement to run a QTVR file in your Director movie:

```
on startMovie
    global gQTVRObj

    QTVREnter(xtra "QTVRXtra")

    set gQTVRObj = new(xtra "QTVRXtra")
    —creates a new instance of the xtra
end
```

```
on stopMovie
   global gQTVRObj

   QTVRClose(gQTVRObj)
   —closes any open QTVR movies

   QTVRExit(xtra "QTVRXtra"
end
```

To open and display a QTVR file and convert Lingo variables to strings for use by the Xtras; for example, QTVROpen(gQTVRObj, "Hard Disk:folder:Pano.mov", "0,0,300,150", "visible":

```
on openQTVRMovie, pMovieName, pSprite
      —where pMovieName = full system pathname
      —pSprite = sprite placeholder with size and location
   global gQTVRObj

   set tRect = rectToStr(the rect of sprite pSprite)
   put QTVROpen(gQTVRObj, pMovieName, tRect, "visible")
end

on rectToStr myRect
   set myString = string(myPoint)
   delete char 1 to 5 of myString
   delete char (the length of myString) of myString
   return myString
end

on pointToStr myPoint
   set myString = strig(myPoint)
   delete char 1 to 6 of myString
   delete char (the length of myString) of myString
   return myString
end

on exitFrame
   —Display the movie
   global gQTVRObj

   if isQTVRMovie(gQTVRObj) then
      if rollover(10) then --the QTVR movie
         QTVRMouseOver(gQTVRObj)
   —have QTVR controls take over
   —allows the user to interact via mouse
   else
         QTVRIdle(gQTVRObj)
         cursor 200
         cursor -1
      end if
end
```

Keep in mind that QTVR files are brought up as "direct-to-stage" movies. They are displayed as the highest in priority on your screen; often, Director cannot even recognize these files on its own. You must tell the Xtra when to recognize and respond to the user's interaction with the QTVR movie.

There are many other Lingo codes that may be required, depending on the exact application for which you plan to use your QTVR file. To find out more about using QTVR, check out the QuickTime VR Web site at www.apple.com/quicktime.

SUMMARY

With a little creativity, you can make design work fast and easy when you know the techniques described in this chapter. As you know, the less time you waste doing cumbersome tasks, the more time you have to be creative. The topics and suggestions covered in this chapter are by no means the only effects you can create. There are virtually thousands of other ideas you can implement. I just wanted to wet your palate, get the ideas flowing, and lead you in the right direction. Let your creativity take you where it wants to go. In other words, have fun with it.

AVOIDING AUDIO AND VIDEO NIGHTMARES

The first video-on-computer piece that I ever saw (over a decade ago) was a 10-second clip that was not much larger than a postage stamp with a frame rate (if you want to call it that) barely fast enough to be considered a video file and not a slide show.

Fortunately, things have come a long way since then. Today's technologies allow for full-screen, full-motion video and CD-quality audio to be played on your computer. As much as you would like to have these features in every multimedia project you create, it is not always feasible. The real challenge with developing for multimedia is presenting the best quality product within the limitations set by the guidelines of the project, especially within the client's system requirements. The challenge lies in knowing what guidelines you have to follow and how to then provide the best types of files for the project.

OPTIMIZE DIGITAL MEDIA FILES

When you are working with digital video and audio files, it takes time to set up the different attributes and compare the results. You will quickly learn the best settings for certain aspects and how to make your adjustments accordingly. Unless your clients tell you specifically how they want their audio and video files, you need to be the expert on knowing what will work best for their particular situations. Clients rarely understand that there *are* limitations when it comes to putting video and audio in their projects.

Rule #1—Always start with the best quality source material. (The better the starting quality, the cleaner the end result.)

Rule #2—Always start with the best quality source material. (I wonder where you heard this rule before? Obviously, ideal situations don't always exist. But now that we are going to be compressing files, we need to understand that putting garbage in only gets you garbage out.)

TEMPO CONTROLS

Initially, you might think the logical place to adjust the playback of sound and video files is by using the Tempo slider found in the Tempo channel of the score. Actually, digital audio and video files are brought into Director with the duration already set from when you compressed the clips. Director does not have the ability to customize the playback of your files faster or slower than the overall duration at which you created them prior to import. Director looks at these files, calculates the total duration time, and plays back each file as best it can, to finish within a given duration. Director will not slow down the speed of any digital audio or video file to make sure it plays every single frame of a file. Instead, Director is more concerned with the total duration time of a clip and achieving that time on playback. If a system cannot handle the frame rate that has been set for a file, Director will begin to randomly drop frames when it cannot keep pace with the set frame rate.

If your audio or video files are getting cut off:

◆ Stretch the sprites far enough to span the necessary frames in the score.

◆ Implement a Wait command using the properties in the Tempo channel (Figure 7–1).

◆ Use the Wait for Cue Point setting.

WAIT FOR CUE POINT

The Wait for Cue Point setting is designed to synchronize digital media files (for timing) and deal with the aggravation of digital audio and video files being chopped off or cut short. Using this feature instructs Director's playback head to wait at the frame where you have placed this command in the Tempo channel for the media file you have selected to catch up to that specified point.

 You'll need to use a third-party program such as Sound Forge 4.0 (Windows) or Sound Edit 16 (Macintosh) to add cue points to your digital media file.

Figure 7–1 Frame Properties: Tempo window.

I set a cue point at the end of every video clip to make sure that it plays through to the end before the playback head moves on to the next frame. This works regardless of how long or short you set the span of the sprite. Generally, the best place to set this command is on the last frame of the sprite. Otherwise, there will still be portions of the sprite that the playback head will read after the audio or video file has completely played. Putting a Wait for Cue Point command in an early part of a sprite can have some unpredictable behaviors. To add a Wait for Cue Point command:

1. Place your media clip in the score.
2. Double-click on the Tempo channel in the same frame where your sprite ends.
3. In the Frame Properties: Tempo window, click the Wait for Cue Point button.
4. In the Channel pull-down menu, select the channel and sprite that are utilizing this command.
5. In the Cue Point pull-down menu, select End (this will command Director to wait until the end of the media file before continuing on).

Synchronizing digital media files using cue points can be great when timing out text to go along with an audio track. The cue point settings will trigger the text to appear in time with the narration.

 AVI digital video clips do not work with cue points.

WORK WITH DIGITAL MEDIA FILES

Before you consider using digital video or audio files in your next project, you should first understand some basics about where to get these files and how to work with them. You may experience situations where, due to one factor or another, you need to sacrifice one facet of the file to meet the requirements of another technical specification. These types of trade-offs are frequent when you are developing for systems without the ideal performance levels. The more you begin to work with digital media files, the more you will be able to know which factors will be acceptable to reduce to execute the project successfully.

AUDIO

Source Material and Digitized Sound

With most of the projects you work on, your audio elements will not be ready for use in Director. It is very likely that you will be provided with the original raw elements that were used to record the sound initially. You will usually be working with some sort of audio media such as:

* Audio cassette.
* DAT.
* Compact disc.
* MiniDisc.

If this is the case, you will need to get access to some additional hardware and software for capturing the sound elements and converting them into digital media files on your computer system. You may also want to look into some type of audio editing program. I suggest adding a standard sound card (SoundBlaster or equivalent) that has audio capturing capabilities. Most consumer sound cards come with a stereo mini-connection input jack, output jack, and ports for your audio speakers. You can then use a basic audio editing program to record and manipulate your sound files, like Macromedia's Sound Edit 16 (Mac) or Sonic Foundry's Sound Forge XP, which both come bundled with the Director Multimedia Studio package.

There are many books on the market that describe the best procedures for capturing and editing these sounds that go beyond the scope of this book.

Even if you are not the person responsible for capturing and editing the sound files, you will need to have an audio card installed in your system and a set of multimedia speakers (any brand is usually adequate) to play back the files.

File Types

Once you have a digital sound file in your system, you must make sure it is in the proper format for Director. Just as there are many different types of file formats for graphics and each has its own unique qualities, the same holds true for audio files. Depending on the criteria of your projects (this goes back to the pre-planning stages discussed in Chapter 2), you must be aware of the different characteristics and applications that each type of file holds unique to itself. Issues such as file types and cross-platform compatibility seem to pop up with projects that use multiple operating systems. The good news is that Director supports most of the basic sound files for both the Macintosh and PC environments.

Director supports the following digital sound files:

◆ AIFF (for cross-platform use).

◆ WAV (Windows).

◆ MP3.

◆ System 7 Sound (Macintosh).

◆ QuickTime (sound-only movies).

◆ Video for Windows (sound-only movies).

◆ MIDI.

◆ SWA (ShockWave Audio).

If you are not sure what platforms you are going to be developing for, then go with a file format that can be used on more than one operating system or is supported by the computers that will be playing your movies, such as AIFF.

The decision for which file type to use depends on:

◆ Cross-platform compatibility.

◆ Xtras or plug-ins required.

◆ Type of capture card.

◆ Type of editing software.

◆ File conversion capability.

 Remember to flatten your QuickTime movies. This is what makes them applicable for cross-platform use.

Convert Files

As a multimedia developer, you should have several different programs available for converting files, audio, and video. If you do not, I strongly recommend getting them. Many of these types of programs are not very expensive. There are some you can download from the Internet. Some of them are even free. The greatest program worth purchasing is called Media Cleaner Pro from Terran Interactive. This program is designed for converting and compressing just about every digital media file known (Figure 7–2). Check out their Web site at www.terran.com.

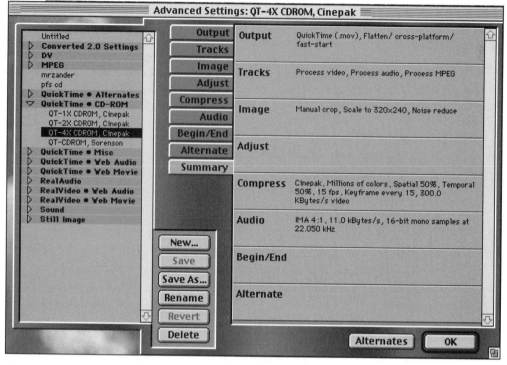

Figure 7–2 Media Cleaner Pro Advanced Settings interface.

Because video clips usually have audio with them, don't overlook your video editing programs (Avid and Premiere) as a means for editing, compressing, and converting your audio files. Some video editing packages come with outstanding audio formatting capabilities. Check out *Premiere To Go* for tips on audio editing, written by yours truly.

Downsample your Audio Files

The problem with audio when developing for multimedia is that it is not always necessary to have the highest quality audio. Limitations abound when working in the multimedia world, including:

◆ Limited storage space.

◆ Delivery platforms.

◆ Client's computer system.

Because there are still many limitations in technology when developing multimedia with Director, compress your files into the smallest possible size without reducing the quality beyond the acceptability level. Fortunately, compression for sound and down-sampling rates hold up the quality of the original files remarkably well.

So What Is a Sample Rate?

The quality, or clarity, of an audio file is a result of the sampling rate and bit depth. The higher the sample rate, the better the sound quality of the file. A better quality sound file is generated with higher sampling rates because the sampling rate determines the highest frequencies that can be reproduced. Therefore, the lower you go with the sampling rate, the more high-end frequencies you will lose. That is why you can sample good quality voices at a lower sample rate than the New York Philharmonic. A more detailed explanation of sample rates and bit depth qualities goes beyond the scope of this book.

   CD-quality audio takes 44,100 samples, or "snapshots," of the sound file for each and every second the sound is being captured. You will generally see this represented as 44.1kHz. Rarely will you use audio files of this quality. In most cases, you will want to sample down your file to 22.05kHz, or even 11.025kHz. I generally try to use 22.05kHz whenever possible. It is about half the size of the original file, yet retains enough of the quality to be acceptable for multimedia productions. A huge drop in quality occurs if you sample music at 11.025kHz. It sounds like you are listening to an AM radio station over a telephone. However, due to the more consistent dynamic range and minimal variation in tonal range, sampling voiceover narrations at this rate, especially female voices, seems to be acceptable for many applications. You can usually set the sample rate for your audio files when actually digitizing and creating them. Otherwise, there are a number of third-party applications, including Media Cleaner Pro, that can downsample your files for you. Another variable that affects the clarity of your audio file is the bit depth. The best way to understand the difference is to take several different files, make two copies of each, convert one to 16-bit and the other to 8-bit, and then play and compare the same exact file at the different bit rates to hear the difference.

 16-bit files are of much higher quality than 8-bit sound files.

Mono or Stereo?

Another factor that will determine the size of a file more than the quality of a file is whether it is saved as a mono or stereo file. The difference lies in the number of audio tracks and the placement (panning) of the sounds on those tracks. Keep in mind the application that you are creating this Director piece for. Most of the time, you will opt for using a single-track mono sound file. This does not mean that your sound will only be played out of one speaker. It means that all of the sounds in your audio source will be played back out of both your left and right speakers equally. The advantage is that when storage space and delivery platforms are issues, reducing the file size to a mono signal can help your Director movie play back with more efficiency.

Import Files

There are basically two ways Director approaches the importing of audio files:

1. Import the sound file into the Director movie internally. Importing sound files internally stores all of the sound information inside the Director movie, within the Cast file.

2. Link a cast member to a file that remains external from the Director movie. With this method, Director does not store any of the actual sound information inside the movie, only the link to the external file.

When you go to import a sound file into Director, you need to choose whether you prefer to have this sound file as an internal fire or an externally linked cast member. Because internal sound files are stored inside the Director movie, they increase the size of your movie. External files reside outside your movie, having very little effect on the size of the Director movie. External cast members are represented with an added ellipsis icon in the cast (Figure 7–3).

To import a sound file:

1. Use the Standard Import option located at the bottom of the Import Dialog window.

2. Use the Link to External File option when importing external sound files (Figure 7–4).

See Chapter 10 for more information about packaging your Director movie with externally linked files.

Figure 7–3 Comparison of internally and externally linked file cast icons.

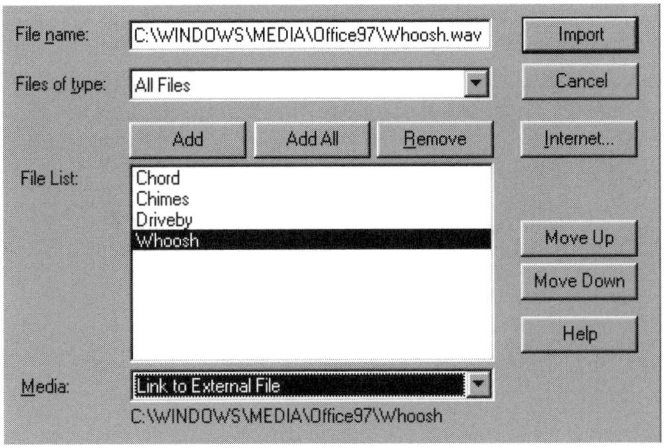

Figure 7–4 Import digital media files using the Link to External File option.

Glitched Sound Files

You may have experienced a project where the sound files did not play back smoothly. This can be due to both the size and type of file you are using. Depending on the hardware configuration of your system and the size of your audio file, you may have some trouble with the sound file playing through completely, without any pauses or hesitations. Internal sound files tend to play back better if they are kept short. Long internal audio files have a hard time playing back smoothly because the entire file is loaded into RAM before it begins to play. Director handles the playback of larger files better externally, but there may be a slight delay with initial playback. Director uses a feature known as file headers, which tells Director how large the external audio file is, to assist with a quicker response for playback.

Quick Response Sounds vs. Long Tracks

As a developer, you will quickly realize when your sound files are responding to their commands and playing properly. If you are uncertain about which way to import your audio files, test them out both ways and see which works better for your application. Experiment with different file sizes (both in quality and duration). Director works with short, quick sound files internally very well. A good example is any type of file that requires precise playback timing. It can load into memory quickly and play the instant you activate the command. Small file sizes, such as sound effects for rollovers and mouse clicks, are the types of files you need to keep internally. If you are planning on looping any audio files, these must be stored as internal cast members. Director cannot loop a file stored externally.

   Longer sound files such as voiceover narrations and full music cuts will be too large to play from RAM smoothly and will have better playback capabilities coming from a hard drive or CD-ROM.

If you need to import long sound files instead of using external links to the files, consider breaking up the files into smaller sections. Find clean break points and edit a long clip into several subclips. This works especially well for voiceovers, by cutting files at the end of a sentence or paragraph. Your system will perform much faster by working with smaller files. Cutting out the pauses in between sentences will help eliminate any noise or hiss that might occur during these silent periods.

Reduce Access Time to Linked Files

One way to decrease file access time is to assign a meaningful and efficient naming structure to your files. Because the computer generally writes files in alphabetical order, naming associated files with a similar beginning structure can help reduce the amount of work and search time that your computer or CD-ROM's playback head needs to take to find the files. To demonstrate:

1. Name your Director movie "Test.dir."
2. Whenever possible, name the audio files externally associated with this movie "Testaud1.aif" and "Testaud2.aif."

These filenames will be copied from a CD-ROM or other media and saved on the hard drive closer together (physically on the disc), helping avoid the drive's playback head from bouncing all over to search for files to play. This may not always be the most convenient or even preferred way of naming files; however, it can be used as a means of troubleshooting if the playback system is getting hung up trying to access files with random filenames. For older systems, it can make enough of a difference on whether or not your movie will be able to play without any glitches.

Contiguous drive space on the end-user's computer may not be available and results may vary, especially if her drive is full or has not been defragged recently.

Loop Audio

The shorter the duration and size of the actual file, whether it is stored internally or externally, the quicker Director will be able to access and play the sound, no matter what type of system you are on. What can you do then if you need a music bed to span the duration of your entire presentation? The best way to handle this type of situation is to incorporate a shorter piece of music that can be smoothly looped without any abrupt connection points. Finding a piece of music that can be looped easily can be difficult.

There are stock music libraries out there that contain short sound bites geared toward being looped in multimedia applications.

Making a music file loop in Director is easy. To make an audio file loop:

1. Select the sound file (cast member or sprite).
2. Click the Sound tab in the Property Inspector.
3. Click the Loop checkbox in the Property Inspector (Figure 7–5).

Volume Controls

The volume of sound files in the score of your Director movie is initially determined by the volume set in the computer sound level control. You can use Lingo controls to readjust the level of your sound files. Why would you use Lingo commands? Lowering the speaker volume will not work if you need to adjust the level for only one of two sound files playing at the same time.

For example, assume you were given two audio tracks to work with, a narration and a music bed. Suppose the music was too loud in comparison to the narrator's voice. The easiest way to fix this in Director is to alter the level of one of the audio channels. To set the volume for a particular channel, use the following Lingo script:

```
set the volume of sound whichChannel
```

You can enter a value for the volume between a 0 (mute) and 255.

For example, to change the volume of the sound in the score on Channel 1 to a medium level, you would use the following command:

```
set the volume of sound 1 to 140.
```

The lower you set the value of the volume of sound, the more likely you will hear noise or the hum of your speakers. Setting a value of the volume of sound too high, especially on a Windows system, may distort the sound.

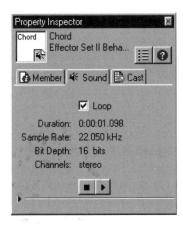

Figure 7–5 Loop checkbox located in the Property Inspector.

Create Adjustable Volume Controls

Every end-user has his own comfort level for sound. Instead of trying to program your movie to please everyone, why not give the user the ability to adjust the volume of the sound tracks? Figure 7–6 shows a screen from my company's demo CD-ROM, including a volume remote control. This interactive feature uses a combination of some creative graphics and technical Lingo to adjust the volume of the movie in small increments.

To design a functional volume control application in your Director movie:

1. In the graphics program of your choice, design at least two buttons (one for raising the volume, the other for lowering it).

2. Import your graphics and position them on the stage.

3. Select the sprite that will raise the volume.

4. Open a sprite script and type the following `if-then` Lingo command:

```
on mouseUp
    if soundLevel = 0 then
    set the soundLevel = 1
else
    if soundLevel = 1 then
    set the soundLevel = 2
else...
```

(and so on for as many increments as you would like to set).

The same script in reverse would then be applied to the down button sprite:

```
on mouseUp
    if soundLevel = 6 then
    set the soundLevel = 5
else
    if soundLevel = 5 then
    set the soundLevel = 4
else...
```

(and so on for as many increments as you set to raise the volume; continue the pattern to return to 0).

Make sure to add the end **command as the last line of your script.**

Figure 7–6 Audio volume control.

In essence, this `if-then` statement tells Director to look at the value set for the volume of the movie. For each click of the mouse, update the variable to the next value. If raising the volume, add to the value to make the volume louder; if lowering the volume, decrease the value to soften the volume. A value of 0 will mute the sound and play nothing but silence.

Wanna Be a DJ Using Volume Sliders?

This new feature in Director 8 wins the award for coolest new feature in a behavior. I can't believe how easy they are making adding neat new features to your movies with almost no programming whatsoever. And the winner is ... the Channel Volume Slider behavior. This behavior allows the user to use any sprite as an audio slider (volume control slider), similar to what a DJ would use when mixing songs. Adding this feature allows the user to control the volume of your movie or individual audio tracks. You can make one sprite control the volume of a sound file in Audio Channel 1 while another controls the levels for Audio Channel 2. This is how easy it is to do:

1. Add any sprite to your stage.
2. Import an audio file into your movie. (It can be linked to external media.)
3. Add the sound cast member to an audio channel in your score.
4. Select Library Palette from the Window menu.
5. Select Media from the Library List menu.
6. Select Sound from the popup menu.
7. Drag the Channel Volume Slider behavior onto the sprite. The Parameters for "Channel Volume Slider" window appears (Figure 7–7).
8. Select the sound channel and initial volume setting.
9. Click OK.
10. Repeat Steps 1 through 9 for each volume slider you want to add.

Now when you play your movie, you can raise and lower the volume of the sound file in the audio channel you assigned to that particular sprite. This is a great way to independently control the volume of each sound file in comparison to any others playing at the same time (Figure 7–8).

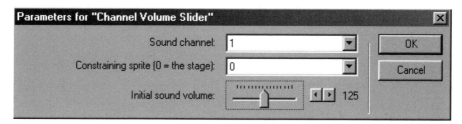

Figure 7–7 The Parameters for "Channel Volume Slider" window.

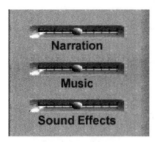

Figure 7–8 Volume control sliders for various audio tracks.

Digital Video Volume Controls

The previous examples affected the volume levels for the audio channels of your movie. What happens when you need to adjust the volume levels for a digital video file in a sprite channel? You can use a Lingo command to adjust the volume of a particular sprite similar to the way you adjusted the volume of the entire audio channel. Use the following command to control the volume of a digital video movie cast member:

```
set the volume of sprite (channel number) to (value)
```

This command tells Director which channel of the score the digital video sprite is in and adjusts the volume accordingly. You can enter values for the volume ranging from 0 to 256. Zero and any value below will mute the sound completely.

For example, to set a different volume for a QuickTime movie in Channel 4, we might use the following script:

```
set the volume of sprite 4 to 200
```

Fade Sounds In and Out

Having a sound file start or end suddenly may seem too abrupt for your viewer. If you know the specific beginning or ending points of your sound file, you might choose to add Fade-In or Fade-Out effects using your audio editing software such as Sound Edit 16 or Sound Forge.

If you create a sound file in an audio editing program and loop it inside Director, it will always play with the Fade-In effect. That is why it is better to create the Fade-In and Fade-Out effects in Director using a simple Lingo command.

Most of the time with an interactive movie, you will not know when you need a sound file to fade out. The timing is determined by the user's interaction with the program. For instance, you want a sound to fade out when the user clicks on a button to jump to another section of the movie. Without a Lingo script to tell the sound file to gradually fade out, the sound file will stop playing abruptly when the playback head jumps into a new section of the score. Therefore, you must add a Lingo script for fading in or fading out sprites in sound channels.

To fade a sound channel in, use the following Lingo command:

```
sound fadeIn which channel
sound fadeIn which channel, ticks
```

Ticks are used as timing elements in Director. Each tick is equivalent to 1/60 of a second. Lingo can accept mathematical functions for certain commands (2*60 tells director to multiply 2 times the 60 tick counts to produce a two-second effect).

For example, to fade in a sound sprite in Channel 1 over the course of three seconds, you must write it in one of two ways:

```
sound fadeIn 1, 180 OR sound fadeIn 1, 3*60
```

Some commands do not always work correctly on the first frame of your score. This is because certain Lingo commands call for an action to take place upon entering the frame. Director may not execute that command due to the fact that it may not be able to read that script ahead of Frame 1 and actually start playing your movie from the perspective of already being in Frame 1.

As a workaround, to fade a sound file in, move everything else over one frame and begin on Frame 2. This way, you can place your `fadeIn` script in Frame 1 (Figure 7–9).

The script command would read:

```
on exit frame
   sound fadeIn 1, 180
end
```

To give the user control of fading sounds in and out, see the section above entitled "Wanna Be a DJ Using Volume Sliders?"

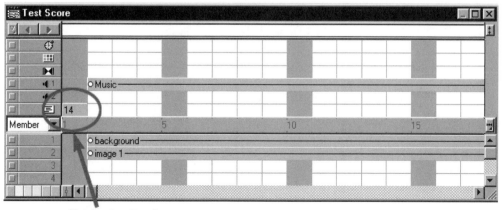

Fade-In Script

Figure 7–9 Placing the `fadeIn` *script before the other sprites allows Director to perform the task correctly.*

Use Lingo to Play External Sounds

Director uses a Lingo command to play external audio files that are not in the cast. The `sound playFile` command tells Director which audio file to play and in which channel. These external sound files must be in either AIFF or WAVE file format. For example, to play a sound file named `jazz.aif` in the `music` folder on the main hard drive on Channel 2, enter the following script:

```
sound playFile 2, "C:\music\jazz.aif"
```

Playing external sound files helps minimize the size of your Director movie. The advantage is that the external sound file minimizes the amount of RAM that is used to play the file, because external sound files do not get completely loaded into RAM. The disadvantage is that the computer can physically only read one file at a time from your disk. Director may experience a delay because it cannot load up or play any other cast members.

Turn Sound On and Off

Some applications require the ability to turn the sound on and off for a specific channel or for the entire movie. Most computer-based training projects that my company develops incorporate at least a button to toggle sound on and off. Consider, for example, a training application that is developed and installed on a large company's intranet site (Figure 7–10).

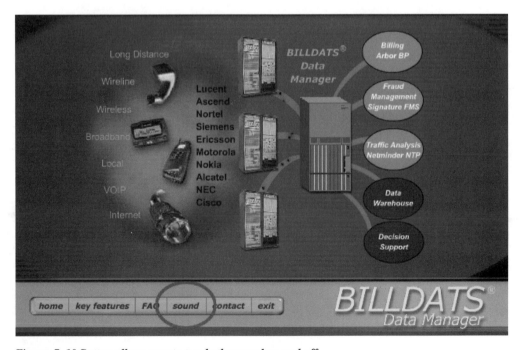

Figure 7–10 Button allows user to toggle the sound on and off.

The application may be used in a classroom-type environment where employees work on exercises at their own pace. Imagine 20 people in a room working on different sections of the program. Any audio playing would be a major distraction to the rest of the group. You will need to include audio capabilities for those employees who choose to work alone at their own workstation. Listening to the narrator's audio while maneuvering through the program would be very beneficial in this type of situation.

To turn off all sound in a movie, use the `soundEnable` command:

```
set the soundEnabled to False
```

Director 8 has added more sound control features into the Library Palette. These new behaviors function with drag-and-drop capabilities (Figure 7–11). Just drop the appropriate behavior on the desired sprite. The Parameters window for that specific behavior will appear (Figure 7–12). Just set the variable according to the function you want the sprite to control. Now you have an easy way to start, stop, and pause sound files like on an audio CD player.

Toggle Channel Sound On and Off

Use the following command to have Director play the opposite of the current setting. So, if the current sound is set to off, this script will turn it on. If the current setting is on, it will turn the sound off.

```
set the soundEnabled to not (the soundEnabled)
```

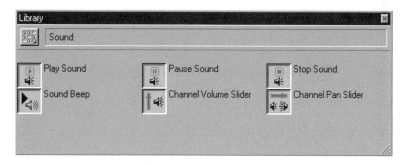

Figure 7–11 Sound behaviors in the Library Palette.

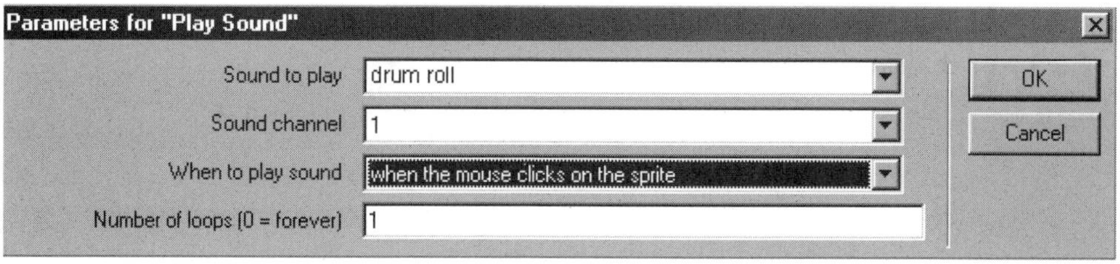

![Parameters for "Play Sound" window]

Figure 7–12 The Parameters for "Play Sound" window.

Sometimes, you will need to shut off sounds in a particular channel as opposed to turning the sound off for an entire movie. For example, you may want to turn off the narration set on Channel 1, but do not want to turn off the sound effects and button clicks on Channel 2. For this type of situation, use the `sound stop` command:

```
on enterFrame
    sound stop 1
end
```

Control Sound Files

Sound Edit and QuickTime files support cue points that are used to track the time and position of a sound file. This means Director can continue to play a file from the point at which it was stopped. If you click Play again, the sound file should continue from where it left off when it was stopped initially. AIFF and WAVE sound files do not support any control of time. If one of these files is stopped before it plays through completely, Director has no way to determine where and when a sound file was stopped, leaving you very little control over the file.

A good workaround for this problem is to associate WAVE and AIFF sound files as if they were audio-only digital video files. You can use Lingo commands to gain better control over these files. Use the `movieTime of sprite` command to track where and when a file stopped playing so it can begin playing the rest of the sound file from that point.

```
set the movieTime of sprite (which sprite).
```

To gain even more control over your sound file by associating it as an audio-only digital movie file, you can control the rate at which the sound plays forward, backward, or just stops. Use the `movieRate` command to determine the playback property of a particular sprite in a designated channel. A value of 1 means the file will play at normal speed forward; a value of –1 means the file will play in reverse; and a value of 0 stops the movie. You can use other variables, such at 0.5 or 2.0, but the results will vary from system to system as to the playback capabilities of your file.

The puppetSound Command

The more advanced your programming becomes, the more you will need to rely on Lingo scripts to execute playing through complex situations successfully. Puppet files are usually referred to as channels under Lingo's control. As with the rest of Director, Lingo continues with the metaphor of the theater. Lingo acts as the puppeteer, controlling the actions of the sprite in a channel.

The `puppetSound` command can be used either to play sounds or turn them off, overriding whatever is set in the sound channels of the score. The correct syntax for setting up a puppet sound is the command `puppetSound`, followed by a channel number, a comma, the name or number of the sound file cast member, and finally the cast with which it is associated if there are multiple casts.

```
puppetSound 2, member "Music" of castLib "Audio Cast"
```

This command is telling Director to play the sound file called Music from the cast called Audio Cast in Channel 2 of the score. Puppet sounds are useful when you need to play a sound while a new movie is loading. This Lingo command enables Director to continue with one sound file while another is being activated. You need to keep these puppet sounds as internal cast members so they can be played directly from the RAM buffer. A typical puppetSound command (Figure 7–13) for having a sound file play while jumping to another section of the score is:

```
On mouseUp
    puppetSound "Sound Effect"
        go to "Scene 3"
end
```

This script tells Director to play a sound file called "Sound Effect" while the playback head jumps to the frame indicated by a marker called "Scene 3" when the user clicks and releases the mouse button. This type of command is very common and allows the movie to play more naturally. Otherwise, the playback of your movie might seem a bit jarring if no sound or visual is playing while Director navigates to the next section.

Once you put a puppetSound command in your script, no sound sprites will play in that sound channel until the puppet sound finishes playing.

Add Sound Effects to Rollovers

You can enhance any interactive movie by adding sound effects in the right places. Warning: Do not go crazy adding them to everything that moves, shakes, or rattles. Too many sound effects can destroy a movie and make it "cheezy." Simple sounds, beeps, and tones are pleasant to hear and do not detract from the content of a movie. Adding sound effects to buttons and other interactive links is very easy with the Play Sound behavior.

For best results, the sound file should be small and it should be imported as an internal cast member.

Figure 7–13 Puppet Sound in Audio Channel 2 allows for sound to continue playing during jumps to other sections of the movie.

For example, to add a sound effect as a rollover feature to the logo sprite shown in Figure 7–14:

1. Import the sound effect file into your internal cast.
2. Open up the Behavior Inspector window for the sprite.
3. Choose New Behavior and name it.
4. In the Events column, select mouseEnter.
5. In the Action column, select Sound.
6. Choose Play Cast Member from the popup menu (Figure 7–15).
7. In the dialog window, select the sound cast member you want to activate when the mouse enters the area of the selected sprite.

   OR

Use the Library Palette:

1. Select Library Palette from the Window menu.
2. Select Media from the Library List menu.
3. Select Sound from the popup menu.

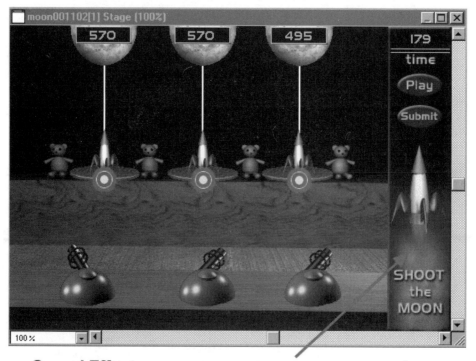

Sound Effects occur as you move cursor over logo.

Figure 7–14 Adding sound effects to rollovers.

4. Drag the Play Sound behavior onto the desired sprite.

5. Set the sound file and when to play it in the Parameters for "Play Sound" window.

   OR

   Use actual Lingo scripts instead of behaviors.

6. Enter the cast member script or sprite script for the small square image:

```
on mouseEnter
    puppetSound (name of cast member)
end
on mouseLeave
    puppetSound 0
end
```

Whatever way you choose to set up your commands, Director will play back the sound cast member (Thunder sound effect) when the mouse rolls over the area of the logo. Adding sound effects to mouse clicks and other interactions works the same way as these behaviors and Lingo commands work for rollovers. Simply substitute the `mouseEnter` commands with `mouseUp` commands. This way, when you click the left mouse button and release it, the selected sound effect will play.

Due to the internal architecture of the machines, Macintosh systems handle the playback of multiple audio files better than Windows systems. To play back more than one sound file in a Windows system, you must have the Macromix.dll (Xtra) file installed on your system (Figure 7–16). This file mixes multiple audio files and plays them back as one file.

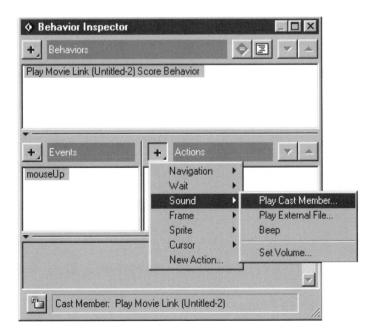

Figure 7–15 Applying the Sound: Play Cast Member command using the Behavior Inspector.

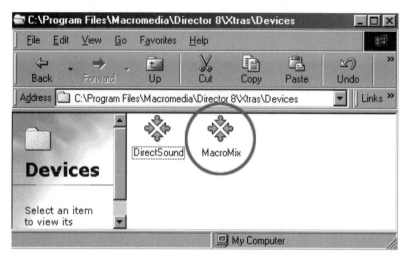

Figure 7–16 The Macromix.dll file must be installed on your Windows system to play multiple sound files at once.

If you have background music playing or other sounds and you want to add sound effects to rollovers, make sure to put the background sound file in Audio Channel 2. This way, both sound files will play, with only a slight pause on the puppeted rollover sound. Puppet sounds are automatically placed in Audio Channel 1. Therefore, if you leave the background music in Channel 1, Director will cut off that sound to play the rollover puppet sound.

Two-Channel Audio

There are a few things that you should know about how Director works with audio files that can potentially save you hours of aggravation and frustration. Macintosh and Windows systems have different architectural structures for handling sound. The Windows architecture has only one audio channel. Whichever program you are working in, Windows has to convert it down to one single track. Again, Windows requires the use of a Director Dynamic Link Library file (commonly referred to as a .DLL file) called Macromix.dll (found in the Xtras folder). This .DLL file basically acts as a mixer to combine multiple layers of sound files from Director down into one audio track that Windows can handle. Depending on the speed of the playback system, this usually causes some sort of noticeable delay.

MacroMix can combine AIFF and WAVE digital audio files. It cannot mix digital audio files and the audio from digital video files at the same time. Director will play whichever sound file reaches the sound channel first. The other file will not begin until the first file has completely played through.

The score in Director contains two sound channels. You can place your audio cast members into these channels to incorporate sound into your movie. As the playback head enters the frame of the sound sprite, Director begins to play that audio file as quickly as the system allows. More often on Windows platforms, when you start using both sound channels at the same time is when you might begin to experience some problems. Director for Windows has to mix the sound files for Channel 1 and Channel 2. The sounds will be able to play together as long as they are not both linked audio files (external files). The system is not capable of reading two large external files residing on the hard drive in two different locations at the same time. To hear both audio channels at the same time, at least one if not both of the files needs to be imported internally into Director. This way, the internal files are loaded completely into RAM and play from there.

The two audio channels in the score do not function as right channel/ left channel. Stereo audio files (if created that way) will play as one sprite, occupying only one audio channel in the score.

> **To avoid running into the problem of having two externally linked audio files attempt to play at the same time while developing your movie, you may choose to set up your score by putting only internal sound files on Channel 1 and external sound files on Channel 2.**

VIDEO

One thing about interactive applications that still seems to interest viewers is video. Although it has been a part of the multimedia world for years, because video has improved in quality, people are starting to use it more as a normal part of their presentations. However, due to the large file sizes of digital video clips, these files still need to be compressed to play them back on a computer.

Capture Video Content

Just like with audio, you need to capture, edit, and compress your digital movie files outside Director. These digital video workstations can range in price from a few hundred dollars to hundreds of thousands of dollars. Depending on the applications you are developing and the requirements of your programs, you may only need access to one of the basic packages. If you have the privilege of working on a high-powered editing system, you will be able to work with better quality source footage and have more editing features available. Your source footage can come from almost any type of video tape, depending on the type of equipment you have available. To capture video clips into your computer, you will need:

◆   A video capture card.

◆   Capture and editing software (e.g., Avid or Premiere).

◆   Multimedia-capable high-speed hard drive.

◆   Sound card (to record audio).

The most common formats that you may experience include:

◆ VHS.

◆ S-VHS.

◆ 8mm.

◆ Hi-8.

◆ 3/4" U-Matic.

◆ Beta SP.

◆ DVC Pro.

◆ DV.

Digital Video Applications

As a developer of multimedia products, you must be aware of the ever-changing formats that people are using to display and distribute the movies you design using Director. It is your responsibility to learn about the different requirements for your digital video files and which are the optimal formats to use. This type of information goes beyond the scope of this book, but nevertheless, will greatly impact your development capabilities using Director. Some common platforms today include:

◆ CD-ROM.

◆ DVD-ROM.

◆ Kiosks.

◆ Web sites.

◆ Intranet training sites.

Size and Frame Rates

Video frame rates are very similar to the frame rates of your Director movies with one exception. Whereas a certain frame rate may work fine for a Director movie, a digital video file may not be able to play back at that same rate. The cumbersome file size of digital video clips can cause some less powerful computer systems to hang up or skip frames. When you are capturing your video clips, the original source material (the video tape) is playing at approximately 30 frames per second (fps; 29.97 to be exact). Unless you have an extremely high-end computer with lots of RAM and high-speed hard drives, you will not be able to play back your video clips at 30 fps. Keep in mind, even if you are capable, the average end-user's system will not be able to handle such a high frame rate. Most multimedia projects use somewhere around 15 fps. If you are processing these files to be played over the Internet, slow modem connection speeds may even require fewer fps. The standard frame rates are:

◆   30 fps—Output to any video tape format.

◆   15 fps—CD-ROM quality.

◆   10 fps—CD-ROM quality.

◆   7.5 fps—Internet quality.

◆   5 fps—Internet quality.

The physical size of your video files will also affect the allowable frame rate. The larger the physical size of your video, the harder the computer will have to work to meet the demands of playing back the digital video file. You generally set the physical size of a video (how many pixels wide by how many pixels high) when you export your video out of your capture or editing program. Figure 7–17 shows you the setting controls that allow you to customize the exact configurations and optimize the performance of your video file. Programs like Movie Cleaner Pro allow you to recompress and resize the properties of your digital video files. This is a must-have program if you want to seriously work with digital media files.

The movieRate Command

Use the movieRate command to determine the playback property for a digital video file in a particular channel. Using this Lingo command, you can control which way the video plays. A value of 1 means the file will play at normal speed forward; a value of −1 means the file will play in reverse; and a value of 0 stops the movie. Altering the speed and direction of your digital video files can be very memory-intensive on your system. The configuration of each system will determine the quality and smoothness at which video clips play back. You can use other variables, such as 0.5 or 2.0, but the results will vary from system to system as to the playback capabilities of your files.

```
the movieRate of sprite (which sprite) to (value)
```

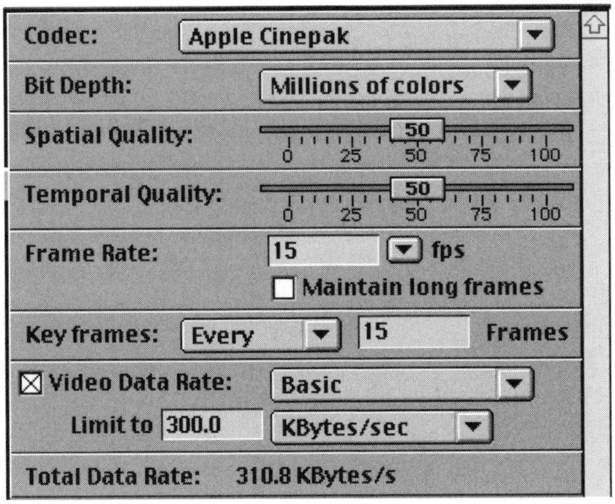

Figure 7–17 QuickTime export options.

If you attempt to apply these settings and the digital video sprite is not currently on the stage, you will get an error message:

```
Not a digital video sprite
```

Types of Files

When developing your Director movies, keep in mind the platform that they will be running on. This is especially important when using digital video files. Currently, QuickTime (.MOV) is the digital video standard for cross-platform multimedia development. When you create and compress your video to be a QuickTime file, there is generally an option to "flatten" your movie and make it cross-platform (Figure 7–18). Macintosh systems usually have the QuickTime extension loaded when you install the operating system, thus having the capability to play back QuickTime movies. QuickTime on Windows platforms, however, requires that QuickTime plug-in be installed on the system.

Many multimedia software products come with a version of QuickTime. If not, you can download any of the QuickTime plug-ins and extensions for free from www.apple.com/quicktime.

If you are developing your Director movie for PC-compatible systems only, you may opt for using the Video for Windows format (.AVI). This file format will play on any Windows system without the need for a plug-in. Whichever file format you choose, you will still need to compress your digital video file to make it playable on most computer systems.

If you need to convert a QuickTime movie into an .AVI file or vice versa, there are some free and shareware conversion programs available for download off the Web. SmartVid is extremely easy to use and will convert your files in either direction. You can download this application from www.intel.com/sg/support/technologies/multimedia/indeo/smartv.htm.

Codecs

As technologies have changed and the requirements to produce larger, cleaner video files have increased, many different companies have entered the world of digital video

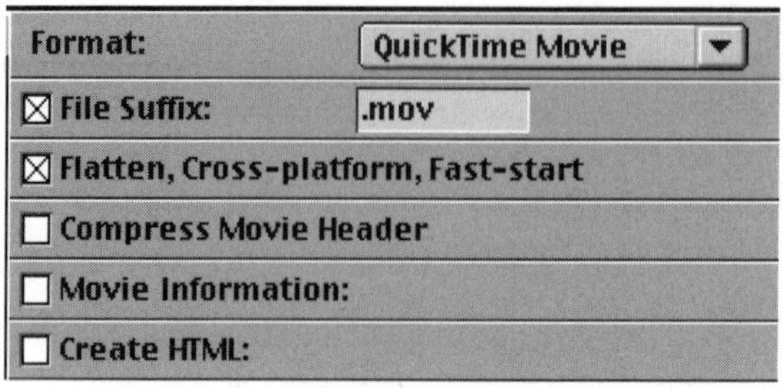

Format:	QuickTime Movie ▼
☒ File Suffix:	.mov
☒ Flatten, Cross-platform, Fast-start	
☐ Compress Movie Header	
☐ Movie Information:	
☐ Create HTML:	

Figure 7–18 Using the Flatten option allows digital video clips to be saved as cross-platform files.

compression for playback on your computer. The object: Get the best quality video playback while taking up the least amount of storage space. How is this possible? With the use of codecs.

A major innovation in the development of multimedia has been the development of codecs. Codecs have the ability to compress large files into the smallest possible components while conversely trying to preserve the best possible quality. Codec stands for compression/decompression. Basically, you use one of these compression applications to compress your original digital video file to reduce its file size and optimize it for playback on a computer. Then, using that same type of technology, you play that file back on your computer with the assistance of the decompression portion of that application. There are several different formats available for you to choose from when creating your digital video files depending on the specifications of your project:

◆ Cinepak.

◆ Animation.

◆ MPEG.

◆ Indeo.

◆ Video.

◆ Sorenson.

◆ None.

Some of these formats require the codec to be installed on the system to view the movies.

A program like Terran Interactive's Media Cleaner Pro is one of the best compression applications available. You can choose to repurpose just about any type of digital media file into any format and custom-set the quality that is required for your project. Generally, the settings used during compression determine the quality of the entire digital video file. The decompression portion of the codec is usually a very small file, in the form of some type of plug-in or system extension, used as a key to unlock and play back the video file.

If you are distributing Director movies that require a codec to play back the movie compressed with a specific codec, either distribute a copy of the codec with the application or let your users know where they can obtain a copy. To find out more detailed information about codecs, check out www.CodecCentral.com.

Check with each vendor for information concerning distribution of their codecs and licensing issues. Most companies allow you to distribute their codecs for free.

Work with MPEG

One of the file formats growing in popularity is MPEG. Although MPEG is not one of Director's standard cast members, it can be played with the assistance of MPEG Xtras. There are some companies providing Xtras that contain an MPEG decoder so that you can distribute your Director movies with MPEG-quality video. You then need to make sure the

Xtras folder is provided with the Projector and individual MPEG files. Companies like Visible Light and Tabuleiro have created Xtras with customizable parameter windows to optimize the performance of your digital video files (Figure 7–19). Check out Tabuleiro's MPEG XTRA 3.2 at http://xtras.tabuleiro.com for more information.

MPEG movies are not internal or linked to Director, but instead use a type of control referred to as an MCI call. You can set up MCI calls via Lingo commands as follows:

```
mci "play" && the pathname & "videofile.mpg"
```

QuickTime 3.0 for Windows does not support playing MPEG digital video files, unlike QuickTime 3.0 for Macintosh, which does support MPEG playback.

Although MPEG is a standard file format, the different brands of hardware and software decoders handle the playback of your digital video files differently. This can lead to problems in the implementation and testing phases of your project. Be sure to test your movie on a system that uses the same type of MPEG decoder software or hardware that will be used by the end-client.

Import Digital Video Files

Importing digital video files into Director is the same process as importing any other media element.

1. Choose Import from the File menu or click the Import icon on the toolbar.

2. Using the standard file hierarchy to locate the correct location, select the file you want to import (Figure 7–20).

3. Click the Add button to bring the selected file into the bottom window. Or, click the Add All button to move all of the files within that folder.

4. Click Import.

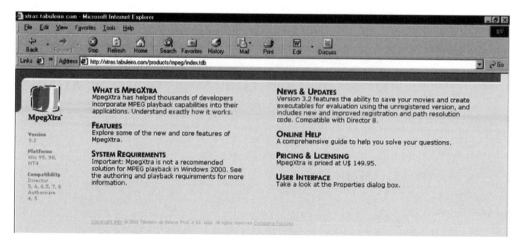

Figure 7–19 Tabuleiro's MPEG system.

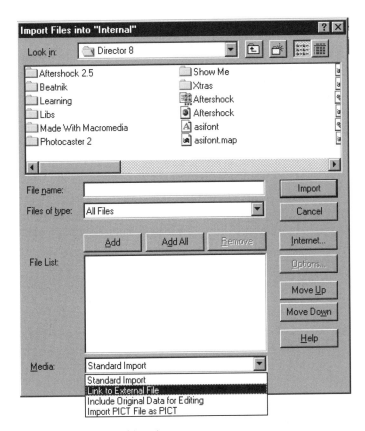

Figure 7–20 Select a file to import.

The only difference between importing still graphics and digital video files is that digital video files are imported as linked files and remain outside of the regular Director movie. Director indicates that these cast members are linked files by displaying an ellipsis in the Cast Member icon (Figure 7–21).

Because Director references a digital video clip as an external file and it is not stored inside the Director movie, any changes made to that file will be reflected inside your Director movie as it plays back that file, even after it has been imported.

Vital Statistics

The Property Inspector is very helpful in providing information about your video file that you can use to troubleshoot problems with any video playback errors. Properties for digital video cast members can be found in the Property Inspector. These properties cover basic information about your clip and display settings (Figure 7–22).

Figure 7–21 Linked External Cast Member icon.

Using a combination of these factors along with a general understanding of what variables affect the playback of digital video clips in Director, you will be able to troubleshoot common problems associated with the improper playback of your digital video files.

Separate Sound and Video from Digital Video Files

The playback properties include an option to independently choose whether you want to display the video or hear only the audio portion of a digital video file. Deselecting video is a great way to use the audio portion from a video clip without having to create a separate audio file. And, with the video file being external, it will not increase the size of your Director movie.

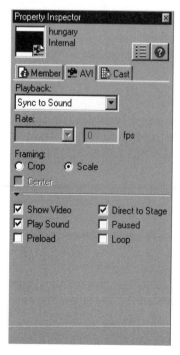

Figure 7–22 Digital video properties in the Property Inspector.

Loop Video Clips

One way to have a digital video file loop is to select the Loop option in the Property Inspector. But this will only loop if there is a command to keep the playback head in the current frames and not continue to other sections of your movie. Add a go to the frame command somewhere within the duration of the sprite to keep the video clip looping. Another way to get your video to keep looping is to loop the section of the score where your digital video sprite resides:

1. Place a digital video sprite into the score.
2. Add a marker at the first frame of the digital video sprite.
3. Set a Wait for Cue Point [End] command in the Tempo channel a frame before the last frame of the digital video sprite (Figure 7–23).
4. Put a Lingo command in the last frame of the digital video sprite to loop the section:

```
on exitFrame
        go loop
end
```

This script will loop the playback head back to the marker which indicates the start of the digital video sprite.

Pause Video

Director begins to play a digital video file once as the playback head enters into the frame containing the video sprite. Some situations may require having control over when the digital video file begins to play. To have the video start in pause mode and

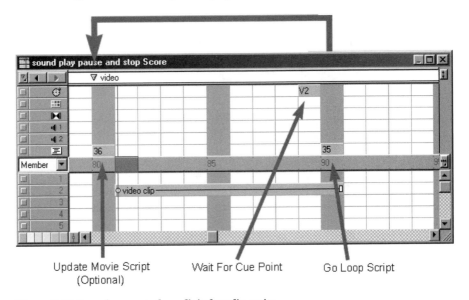

Figure 7–23 Sample score to loop digital media sprite.

not play until otherwise instructed, select the Paused option in the Property Inspector. With this option selected, the video display area will hold on the first frame until a play command is activated.

Show Controller

The Controller option determines whether to place a video control slider under the video display area in your movie. Some applications will find having this feature available on-screen very useful (Figure 7–24). Training programs and instructional design applications that have the video controller directly on-screen allow the user to pause the video at any point, rewind to review a section, or skip ahead to any point and play again.

Only QuickTime movies have the option to select and deselect the control slider in the Properties window. If you want to have a control slider available on video for Windows (.AVI) files, you need to design and implement custom Lingo scripts. You can also use the Widget Wizard Button Library, located in the Xtras menu, to put together some graphical navigation controls to combine them with video control behaviors to control your digital video clips.

Transitions and Digital Video Files

Digital video files are probably the most memory-intensive portion of any multimedia project. Adding transitions to the score greatly increases the strain on the system's playback capabilities. Depending on the throughput speed of your system and the amount of RAM installed, less powerful systems may experience some flickering with video clips if you try to play a transition and a digital video file at the same time.

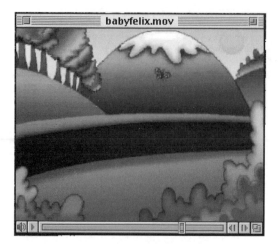

Figure 7–24 Digital video clip with control slider (see also color figure 22).

Wait for Digital Video Files to Finish

Playing back digital video files in Director can be as easy as dragging an imported cast member onto the stage or into the score and playing your movie. Make sure that the sprite spans enough frames to play back the entire duration of the digital video file. To check the total length of the file, open the Property Inspector. You may need to stretch the sprite to cover more frames in the channel. Using more score frames does not increase the file size or memory requirements of your Director movie. There are several ways to control the playback of your digital video files to ensure that the entire duration will be played:

1. Extend the length of the sprite to span more frames (Figure 7–25).
2. Slow down the tempo of your Director movie (a frame rate of 1 fps will require fewer frames).
3. Use a tempo control such as Wait for Cue Point…[End] (see the section "Wait for Cue Point" at the beginning of this chapter).
4. Use frame script Lingo commands.

Using the Wait for Cue Point…[END] option will not allow any interactive controls to be active while the digital video is playing. Director will record these events and perform them once the movie is completed. Instead, try using a Lingo command to allow the digital video to completely play while interactive controls still function.

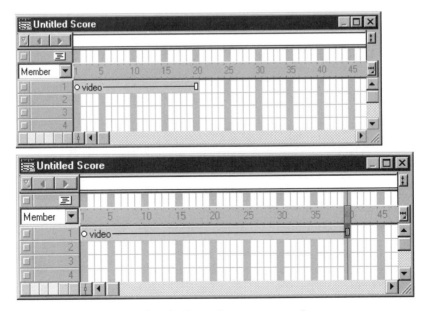

Figure 7–25 Extending a digital video sprite to span more frames.

Lingo Commands that Allow Digital Video Files to Finish

Up to this point, we have discussed several reasons why your digital video clips may not completely play for their full duration or even play at all. Advanced developers usually choose to control the flow of their movies using Lingo. To set your digital video sprites to play through completion:

1. Figure out the total duration of the digital video file.
2. Enter the following frame script command:

```
on exitFrame
  if the movieTime of sprite (sprite number) < (number of ticks)
then
    go to the frame
end
```

This Lingo script is instructing Director's playback head to determine whether the exact time (in increments of ticks, with one tick equaling 1/60th of a second) is less than the total duration of the sprite specified. If that value is less than the total duration entered (number of ticks), then go back and loop in that frame until the `movieTime` value equals or exceeds the total number of ticks set in the equation. When it reaches that number, the digital video file should be done playing and the playback head can continue on to the next frame.

Simultaneous Interactive Controls and Digital Video Playback

If you need to have access to the interactive buttons and navigational links on your screen while a digital video clip is playing, you will need to use a frame script that allows these events to occur. Enter the following frame script:

```
on exitFrame
   if the movieRate of sprite (sprite number) = 1 then
      go to the frame
end
```

This command allows the user to maintain control of the interactive buttons and links on the current screen while continuing to play the video until it is complete. When the video finishes playing (`movieRate` is reached, or True in this case), the script instructs the playback head to `go to the frame`, or continuously loop in the current frame, until the user selects one of the navigational choices available on the screen.

Interactive Scrolling through Digital Video Files

This command lets the user jump through the video clip either ahead or in reverse a few frames or a few seconds at a time (Figure 7–26).

1. Set the digital video playback to pause. You can do this either for the entire movie upon entering the frame by selecting Paused in the Property Inspector or you can use a Lingo script to pause the movie (movieRate of sprite [channel number] to 0).

2. Apply either sprites or cast scripts for the navigational buttons (e.g., forward and backward arrows).

3. Enter the following script to scroll forward through the digital movie by two-second intervals:

```
on mouseUp
    set the movieTime of sprite to 1 to (the movieTime of sprite 1) +
(60*2)
    updateStage
end
```

This script is telling Director to advance through the digital video sprite in Channel 1 to the current time/position of the video plus two seconds (60 ticks per second times 2 = 2 seconds). updateStage instructs Director to refresh the image on the screen and show the new frame of the digital video clip. To create the script for a Back button, simply change the plus sign to a minus sign. You can set the variable for how many seconds or frames you want the video to change from with the click of these buttons by entering a different value in the last part of the math equation:

◆ 60*2 = 2 seconds.

◆ 60*1 = 1 second.

◆ 60*5 = 5 seconds.

Figure 7–26 Digital video clip with virtual fast forward and rewind controls.

Resize and Reshape Video Files

Director allows you to alter the viewing size of your video display area. The Scale feature will take the entire size of the original video file and stretch it horizontally and vertically in any rectangular form while always showing the entire content area. Figure 7–27 shows three different clip sizes: original, 50%, and 150%. The Crop feature works in a different way. The actual size of the content inside the visible area never changes size, just the borders around the video clip. Cropping your video will actually alter the aspect ratio of the clip's visible area. You can crop out part of the image on the side of the screen or make a letterbox movie effect (Figure 7–28). You can crop the size of the original video file to make it smaller, eliminating portions of the visible area; however, you cannot crop a file to be larger than the full size of the original video file.

Scale a Digital Video File

1. Select the digital video sprite you wish to resize.
2. Open the Property Inspector.
3. Click the QuickTime or AVI tab (Figure 7–29).
4. Select Scale.
5. Drag the handles around the bounding box of the digital video sprite and resize the image as desired.

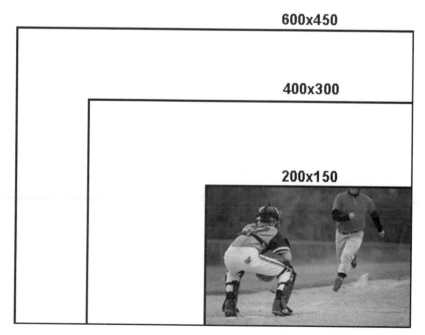

Figure 7–27 Comparison of resized video clips.

Figure 7–28 Use the Crop feature to remove unwanted portions of a video clip.

Crop a Digital Video File

1. Select the digital video sprite you wish to crop.
2. Open the Property Inspector.
3. Click the QuickTime or AVI tab.
4. Select Crop.

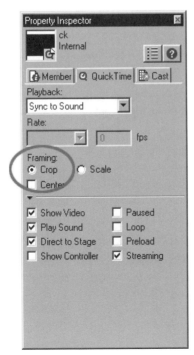

Figure 7–29 QuickTime or AVI settings in the Property Inspector.

5. Drag the anchor points around the bounding box of the digital video sprite and crop the image as desired. Check the Center box to crop equally from both sides of the image at the same time.

Director requires a lot of RAM to adjust digital video files. For best results, size and set video properties during the editing, exporting, or compression stage before you import the files into Director.

Reshape Video Files

As an AVID Certified Instructor, trying out new video editing tricks and techniques is a passion of mine. In a high-end video editing system, designing these interesting video special effects is easy. Most multimedia programs present their video clips in the standard rectangular shape that they come in when the digital video files are made. Director's unique layering capabilities and support of digital video files allow you to create some new ways to present your video clips. Figure 7–30 (also found in color section) shows video clips not in the standard rectangular form. Some are circular, while others actually have portions of other graphics covering an area of the video screen. These types of effects are relatively easy to create, and yet catch the attention of every viewer.

Mask your Videos

The trick to getting odd-shaped video files is achieved not by affecting the actual shape of the video, but instead by manipulating the images layered over the video file. If you experience the video display always on top of the other images, regardless of which channel you put your sprites in, deselect the Direct to Screen option in the Cast Member Properties window. This will give the digital video files the same layering capabilities as any other sprite (Figure 7–31). To mask your video files:

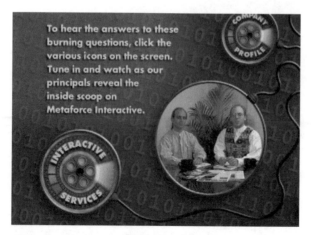

Figure 7–30 No more rectangular video displays. Video clips can be displayed in just about any shape.

1. Select the video cast member in your cast that you wish to manipulate.
2. Open the Property Inspector and select the QuickTime or AVI tab.
3. Deselect the Direct to Screen option.
4. Drag the video cast member to the proper position on the stage.
5. Create or import a new cast member to be used as a mask or overlay graphic. Make sure it is large enough to cover the entire video image. The shape of this image you create will determine which portions of the video clip will be visible and which parts will be covered.

    Deselecting the Direct to Screen option allows you to layer digital video files as you would other sprites in the score. Where the video is placed in the score in relation to sprites in the other channels will determine what is displayed above and below the video.

6. If you have not done so, create the area on the overlay graphic in white for which portion you want to cut out to display the video clip.
7. Place the overlay graphic cast member in the channel directly below the video sprite in your score (remember how layers work in the score; a sprite in Channel 3 will be displayed on the stage over a sprite in Channel 2).
8. Move the overlay graphic into the correct position on the stage, completely covering the rectangular video display area.

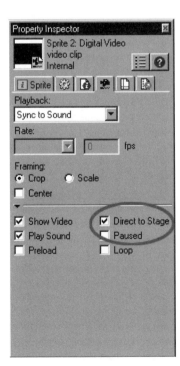

Figure 7–31 Direct to Screen option displays the digital video clip on top of all other images regardless of its layer in the score.

9. Apply a Background Transparent ink effect to the sprite. This will make the white portion of the overlay graphic transparent and the video will play in the shape of the cutout area.

10. Rewind and play back your movie. Only the portion of the video clip that was positioned underneath the transparent (white) area of the graphic should be visible.

To create a custom mask:

11. Double-click on the overlay graphic cast member to open it in Director's Paint window.

12. Choose Duplicate from the Edit menu. The Duplicate function automatically creates a new cast member and displays the cloned copy in the Paint window.

13. Select the Transform Bitmap option from the Modify menu.

14. Change the color depth to 1-bit. This will change the graphic into a black and white image.

15. Click the Transform button.

16. Use the paintbrush and other tools to clean up the image. Use black to paint the portion of the image you wish to leave opaque (visible). The areas that you leave white will become transparent.

    The more intricate the design of your object, the more careful you will have to be when filling in the areas to be masked to get a clean cutout shape.

17. Close the Paint window when you are finished.

18. For the mask effect to work, you must place the new black and white cast member immediately following the original in the cast (Figure 7–32, also found in color section). There cannot be any other cast members or empty frames between the original image and the black and white image.

19. Drag the original overlay graphic cast member and place it in the channel directly below the video sprite in your score.

20. Move the overlay graphic into the correct position on the stage, completely covering the rectangular video display area located directly below.

21. Apply the Mask ink effect to the sprite. This will make all of the white portions in the cloned overlay graphic transparent so you can see the video play in the shape of the custom cutout area.

22. Rewind and play back your movie. Only the portion of the video clip that was positioned underneath the transparent (white) area of the graphic should be visible.

Direct to Stage

Direct to Stage is a feature that Director uses to allow QuickTime and Video for Windows controls to drive the playback performance of your digital video files. Use

Figure 7–32 a, b, & c Mask cast member placed directly after original cast member.

Direct to Stage to get the best possible frame rate from your digital video files in Director. But with all good things come some bad things.

Disadvantages of using the Direct to Stage feature:

◆   Digital video files always appear on top of all other images, no matter on which channel of the score they exist.

◆   Ink effects are not applicable.

Turn off Direct to Stage in the Property Inspector to layer your digital video behind other sprites or apply ink effects (except matte ink) to the video file itself.

The Direct to Stage option needs to be turned on to use QuickTime digital video files in Director on the Windows platform. Video for Windows (.AVI) files on a PC platform and QuickTime on a Macintosh system do not require Direct to Stage to be active.

Export Digital Videos

Director is a great program in which to design and build your animations and interactive movies. When you are finished, you can export your entire Director movie out as a single digital video file. There are a few pitfalls to keep in mind, however. Chapter 10 covers some of the exporting options and limitations that Director has when outputting your movies as digital video files.

Package External Files for Distribution

Because Director only imports links to external audio and video files, you must remember to include these files when you distribute your Director project. See Chapter 10, "It's All Finished … Now Deliver It," for more details on packaging your external digital video and audio files.

Test, Test, Test

Time is generally everyone's biggest enemy. I have yet to meet a multimedia developer who works 9 to 5.

However, 2:00 AM, last-minute changes for the client are no excuse for not taking the proper time to go through and test your work, especially on other systems. If you have access to the actual system(s) that you will be running your movies on, then that is the true ideal testing situation. You will know right off the bat whether the hard work you have just killed yourself to complete has paid off.

Testing is especially important when you are working with digital audio and video files. These files tend to be the most notorious for causing headaches. They require more detail when creating them and even more detail when trying to play them back. Every system out there seems to be able to play basic Director animations of bitmapped images. Generally, color palettes or monitor display settings are to blame for more of the problems with graphics not playing correctly. But when it comes to audio and video media, the files are much larger, require more RAM and fast-access hard drives, and usually need some type of media player installed on the system. Depending on which codecs you choose to compress your files, you may need additional hardware or software applications to even open the media files.

SUMMARY

As computer and television technologies merge closer together, people want to see full-screen, full-motion video clips and hear the thunderous quality of surround-sound audio on their laptops. (And I'm not talking about little postage stamp-sized files.) What is more scary than these requests is that manufacturers are developing the technology so that soon you will be able to interactively see and hear any video or audio file you want, when you want, all with high quality. This video-on-demand concept is partially here today and will soon be the way everyone watches programming. There are millions of clients who want to use the features and capabilities of multiple audio channels and high-quality video. Now, through the use of Director 8, you can design your best applications using numerous audio and video files in your next production.

c h a p t e r 8

TIDBIT TOOLBOX

If there's one thing I have learned when working with programs as involved as Director, no matter how long you use them, there are always a few tips that you pickup that save you invaluable time (and avoid frustrating headaches) on your next project. Learning the basics of Director is not very hard, but to become an expert takes a great deal of hard work and dedication. The more effort you apply and hours you spend trying to develop new ideas, the more you will improve the quality and level of your applications. This chapter covers a wide variety of topics, explaining many of the little techniques that will save you time and greatly improve the functionality of the programs you develop.

MOVE AND STRETCH ONE- AND TWO-FRAME SPRITES

No matter how far you zoom into a score, it is hard to stretch a sprite that spans only one frame (Figure 8–1). If you go and click on it and try to drag it, the single-frame sprite will move from frame to frame instead of stretching to span over several frames. This can drive you crazy if you don't know what to do. To stretch a one-frame sprite:

1. Hold down the Alt key (Windows) or Option key (Macintosh).
2. Click and drag the sprite using your mouse. This will lengthen the span of your sprite more than one frame.

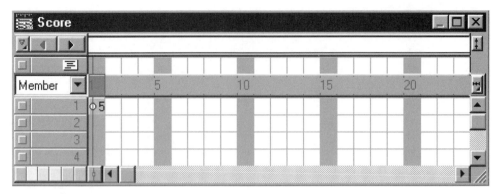

Figure 8–1 Sprite spanning one frame.

Conversely, trying to move a two-frame sprite without extending the span of the sprite is rather difficult itself. One of the features added back in Director 6 was the ability to alter the span of a sprite in the score simply by clicking on an endpoint and dragging it to its new length. The last frame (or second frame of this two-frame sprite) contains a handle that allows you to maneuver and manipulate the number of frames you want a sprite to span in your score (Figure 8–2). To move a two-frame sprite around in the score without changing the length of it:

1. Single-click on the sprite.
2. Hold down the Spacebar.
3. Drag the two-framed sprite around in the score to its new location.

EXCHANGE CAST MEMBERS

The Exchange Cast Members feature will come in handy when you want to swap cast members in the score for part of an existing sprite or an entire sprite (Figure 8–3). The

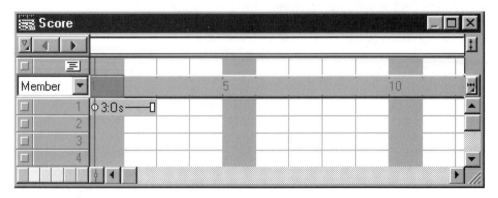

Figure 8–2 Sprite spanning two frames.

Exchange Cast Members function really adds benefit when you have already set keyframes and other animation characteristics for the initial sprite. If you delete portions of the existing sprite to place in another, the new sprite will not have any of the animation characteristics or paths that were previously set for the original sprite.

For example, if you place a cast member of an image (i.e., person running) on the stage and animate it around the screen using the tweening technique, you have set the keyframes for that sprite's position and motion path (Figure 8–4). Suppose you want to add other cast members into that animation to make the person actually move his legs (Figure 8–5). To replace the new sprite over portions of the existing frames, you would have to try to manually set the new sprite's position and motion to match that of the rest of the animation you previously created. This would be nearly impossible to match up for a complex animation. Instead, use the Exchange Cast Member feature to switch cast members and retain all of the keyframed positions and motion characteristics.

To implement this feature:

1. Add a cast member to the score.
2. Animate the sprite around on the stage using keyframes.
3. Select Edit Sprite Frames from the Edit menu.
4. Mark the region of the sprite for which you want to change cast members. To select a range of frames:

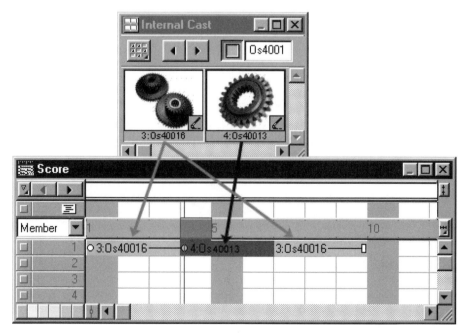

Figure 8–3 Use the Exchange Cast Member feature to replace part of a single sprite with another cast member.

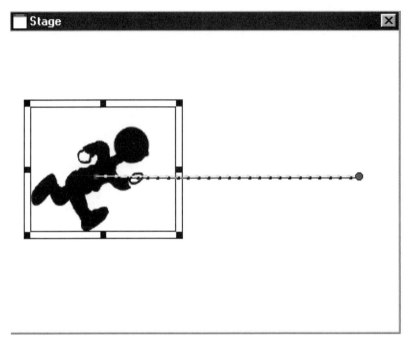

Figure 8–4 Single sprite moving across the stage.

A. Single-click on the beginning frame of the area you want to select.

B. Hold down the Shift key and click on the last frame of the area that you want to select. All of the frames between the first selected frame and the last selected frame should become highlighted (Figure 8–6).

5. Single-click on the cast member you want to add in place of the highlighted area.

6. Select Exchange Cast Members from the Edit menu or click on the Exchange Cast Members button in the toolbar at the top of the screen (Figure 8–7).

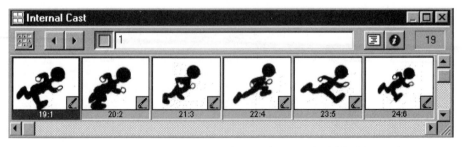

Figure 8–5 Cast of animated characters to make the character look like it's running.

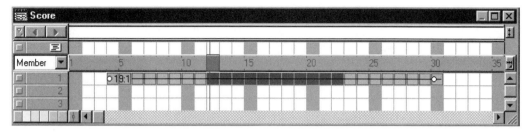

Figure 8–6 Highlight the frames in the score that you want to replace with a new cast member.

Figure 8–7 Exchange Cast Members buttons.

EMBED FONTS FOR ACCURATE TEXT DISPLAY

Typically, applications require that the end-users have the same fonts installed on their system as the ones used when creating the movie. If the same font is not present, the system will substitute a font close to the structure of the one required. Many times, it does not select a suitable font and the text in your movie is displayed incorrectly. Director allows you to embed fonts that you plan on using in your movie so that the fonts you used are properly displayed, even if they are not installed on the user's system. Embedded fonts are compressed to keep the overall file size of your movie down to a minimum, generally adding only 14 to 25K to the file.

By law, you cannot copy or distribute fonts. Distributing applications using embedded fonts is legal because the fonts are only available within the Director movie.

To embed fonts into a Director movie:

1. Select Media Element from the Insert menu.
2. Select Font from the popup menu. The Font Cast Member Properties window will appear.
3. Select one of the system fonts already installed on your computer from the Original Font pull-down menu.
4. Optional: You can include bitmapped versions of a font for smaller sized text that should look better than the standard anti-aliased, outlined fonts.
5. Enter the point size(s) that you want to include when embedding fonts (Figure 8–8).

Figure 8–8 Pre-determined bitmapped fonts can be included within your movie for better display.

Note Enter the font name followed by an asterisk when embedding fonts (Times*). This will use the embedded font for all text displayed in the movie, saving you the time and hassle of setting the font for all the text used throughout the entire movie. These fonts are now displayed as cast members and can be applied with the same parameters as other text cast members and sprites (Figure 8–9).

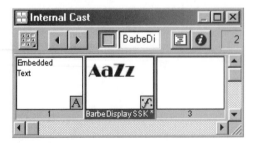

Figure 8–9 Embedded fonts displayed as cast members.

UPGRADE FROM POWERPOINT

To date, the majority of corporate presentations have been created in or derived from some type of PowerPoint presentation. PowerPoint has a very easy learning curve, allowing beginners to start right off and begin building a presentation in no time. Although it has taken major steps forward with the addition of some more interesting features, PowerPoint is really designed as an application for novice programmers who like to work with the program's generic screen templates (Figure 8–10). But with limited interactivity, minimal Web integration, and inadequate means of handling digital video, audio, and animations, PowerPoint leaves a lot to be desired for the more advanced programmer. The good news is that a typical PowerPoint presentation can be the building block for a more advanced Director movie. Director puts together the same types of presentations that PowerPoint does, but includes many more sophisticated features that PowerPoint just cannot touch.

There is no reason why you should throw out your old PowerPoint presentations. You can import your PowerPoint files into Director quickly and easily and begin to expand on them immediately. Director will create a new cast member for each screen of your presentation (Figure 8–11). Director will also auto-compile the score for you based on the order in which you built your presentation (Figure 8–12). This includes basic navigation and transitions. To bring your existing PowerPoint presentation into Director:

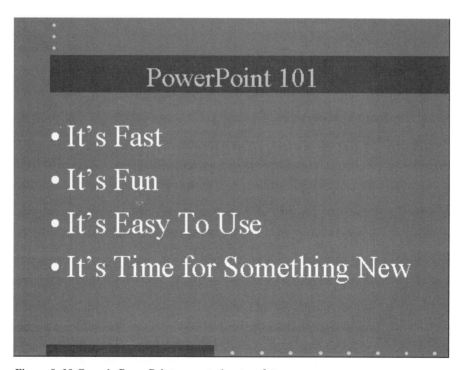

Figure 8–10 Generic PowerPoint presentation template.

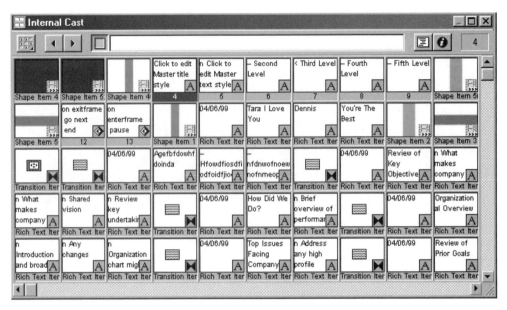

Figure 8–11 Director automatically creates a cast member for each element used in PowerPoint.

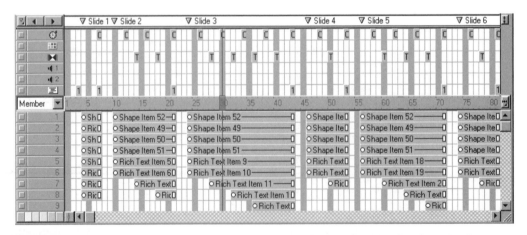

Figure 8–12 Director automatically builds a score to deliver the same functionality that exists in PowerPoint.

1. In PowerPoint, finish building your slide show.
2. Select Save As from the File menu.
3. Name the file.
4. Select PowerPoint 4.0 from the Save As Type pull-down menu (Figure 8–13).
5. Select a destination folder and click OK.

6. In Director, select the cast where you want Director to store your slides from PowerPoint.

7. Select Import PowerPoint File from the Xtras menu.

8. Select the PowerPoint file (.PPT) you saved in Step 5.

9. Enter the settings for optimizing the presentation in the PowerPoint Import Options window (Figure 8–14).

10. Click Import. A progress bar appears, indicating that the slides are being transferred into Director and the programming is being written to the score.

11. Click OK in the Import Results window when your presentation has been successfully imported into Director (Figure 8–15). Depending on the type of presentation you created, your cast will be filled with various types of graphics, text, navigation, and transition cast members. The score data will also be automatically constructed with all the properly layered sprites, transitions, and interactive commands.

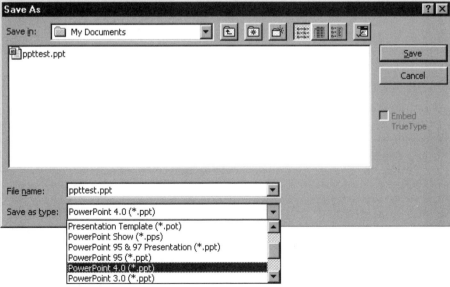

Figure 8–13 Director imports PowerPoint 4.0 presentations.

PowerPoint Import Options			
Slide Spacing:	2	Frames Between Slides	Import
Minimum Slide Duration:	4	Frames Per Slide	Cancel
Item Spacing:	4	Frames Between Items	
Fly Transition Item Spacing:	8	Frames Between Items	Help

Figure 8–14 PowerPoint Import Options window.

Test your presentation thoroughly after you import your PowerPoint file into Director. There are some features and commands that do not translate into Director's formatting. These inconsistencies are just stripped out by Director.

CREATE HYPERLINKS IN DIRECTOR

Just like on the Web, you can include hyperlink text in your Director movie, as shown at the bottom of Figure 8–16. This hypertext can provide just about any type of link or other interactive aspect normally associated with navigational commands. Use the hyperlink to navigate to a specific URL on the Web, or have it jump to another section of your movie.

To create hyperlink text:

1. Select Text from the Window menu or click the Text Window shortcut button on the toolbar (Figure 8–17).

2. Type in the desired word or phrase that you want to have hyperlink characteristics. If you only want a portion of the phrase to be hypertext, highlight only that text (Figure 8–18).

Figure 8–15 Import Results window.

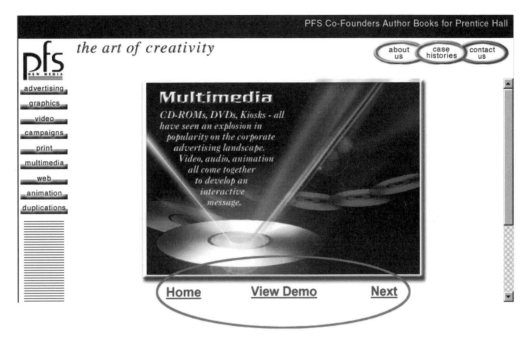

Figure 8–16 Hypertext links created in Director work the same as on the Web.

Figure 8–17 Click the Text Window shortcut button to open the text window.

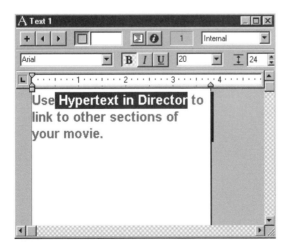

Figure 8–18 Highlight the text to be hyperlinked.

3. Select Inspector from the Window menu.

4. Select Text from the submenu. The Text Inspector window will appear.

5. Enter the URL in the Hyperlink box for where you want to link or any message you want to send to the `hyperlinkClicked` handler.

6. Close the Text window.

7. Select the text cast member in the cast.

8. Open a new script.

9. Enter the following script:

```
on hyperlinkedClicked
    go to frame "markerName"
    —enter any type of navigational or control command
end
```

10. Rewind and play your movie.

 Director's default hyperlink settings include displaying the hypertext in a blue underlined font that changes to purple once it has been selected.

REGISTRATION POINTS FOR AN EVEN EXCHANGE

Director uses the registration points of sprites to align images when using the Exchange Cast Members function. If similar images (altered versions of the same image) seem to shift during the animation or interactive action after using the Exchange Cast Members feature, check that the registration points of the two images are lined up exactly (Figure 8–19). If they are not in the same position, you will need to reset their registration points. To change the registration point of a cast member:

1. Double-click on the cast member to open it in Director Paint.

2. Select the Registration Point tool.

3. Click the area of the image where you want to set a new registration point (Figure 8–20).

4. Close Director Paint to apply the changes to the cast member.

 Graphical cast members default to having their registration point in the center of the image. If you accidentally move the registration point and want to reset it, double-click on the Registration Point tool.

Figure 8–19 Registration points properly align the images used for the animation.

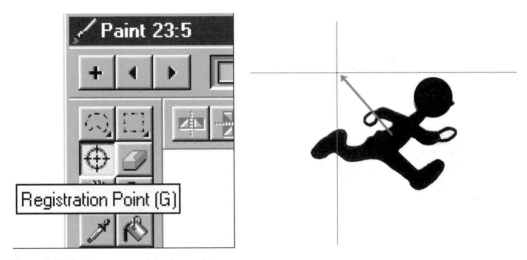

Figure 8–20 Setting new registration points.

You can use the Onion Skinning feature to display other cast members to help visually line up registration points.

If you have changed the default editor for your cast member to something other than Director Paint:

1. Right-click (Windows) or Option-click (Macintosh) the sprite or cast member you wish to alter.

2. Select Edit Cast Member from the popup menu (Figure 8–21). The Director Paint window appears.

3. Use the previously listed steps to reset or reposition the registration point of your image.

Once you apply an animation or interactive function (such as a rollover) to a sprite, the registration points are still used to evenly swap the cast members or sprites. If you move a sprite to another location on the stage, the registration points will move also and all adjustments will be made correctly when the animations or interactions take place.

REVERSE AN ANIMATION

A portion of your program may require one or more sprites to animate on-screen into a given position and then reverse themselves following the same path back to their initial starting point. Getting sprites to animate in the exact opposite direction by setting new keyframes to recreate the movements of how they came into position would be very difficult, if not impossible. Fortunately, Director has taken all the guesswork out. To have Director reproduce an exact movement pattern in reverse:

1. Animate the sprite(s) around the stage as desired.
2. Highlight the sprite(s) in the score that you want to reverse.
3. Select Copy Sprites from the Edit menu or use the keyboard shortcut Control-C (Windows) or Command-C (Macintosh).
4. Single-click in the score on the first frame where you want to place the copied sprites.

Figure 8–21 Edit Cast Member option from popup menu.

5. Select Paste from the Edit menu or use the keyboard shortcut Control-V (Windows) or Command-V (Macintosh).

6. With the sprite(s) still selected, choose Reverse Sequence from the Modify menu.

7. Rewind and play back your movie. The sprite(s) should animate into place and then move along the same path in reverse back into its original starting position (Figure 8–22).

ADD PRINT CAPABILITIES

Director allows you to print movie content to review and mark screen changes, create sign-off sheets for client approval, show changes made to the rest of the design/development team, or make handouts for presentations. There are several print options to use during the authoring stages of your movie:

◆ Print an image of the stage, score, cast art, cast thumbnails, or the contents of the text cast members.

◆ All scripts or a range of scripts (movie, cast, score, and sprite scripts).

◆ Comments in the Markers window.

◆ The entire Cast window.

Depending on the nature of your finished program, most applications do not require the ability to print a page from a Director movie. However, there may be times when having a print feature is beneficial. The following simple Lingo command will print a frame or series of frames of whatever is displayed on the stage during the specified frames:

```
printForm (fromFrame), (to frame)
```

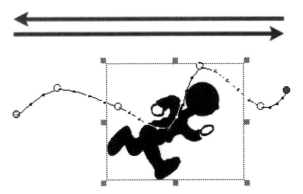

Figure 8–22 Reverse animation plays a sprite backward along the same path as it played forward.

All images are printed at 72 pixels per inch in the portrait (vertical) layout, regardless of the orientation of the Page Setup settings.

The command `printForm 1, 5` tells Director to print the images as they appear on the stage for Frames 1 through 5. You can also instruct it to change the percentage value of the image to one of three choices: 100%, 50%, or 25%. To reduce the print size of an image, add the percentage value at the end of the Lingo command:

```
printForm (fromFrame), (to frame), (reduction value)
```

The command `printForm 1,5, 50` tells Director to print what is displayed for Frames 1 through 5 at half of the original size of the image.

 There are a few third-party Xtras, including the PrintOMatic Xtra, which you can purchase to add more printing options to your Director movies. You can find the source for this and other Xtras at www.macromedia.com/software/xtras/director.

PLAY SELECTED FRAMES

During the authoring stage of your project, Director allows you to play back only a specific range of frames that you select. This feature comes in handy when you want to keep testing a certain area without having to play back your entire movie every time you click play. To select a region of the score to play back:

1. Open a Director movie.
2. Click on the first frame of the area you want to mark as the selected range of frames.
3. Hold the Shift key and select the last frame of the area you want to play. The marked region should become highlighted.
4. Open the Control Panel from the Window menu or press Control-2 (Windows) or Command-2 (Macintosh).
5. Click the Selected Frames Only button at the lower right corner of the Control Panel (Figure 8–23).

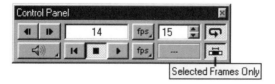

Figure 8–23 The Selected Frames Only button located in the Control Panel.

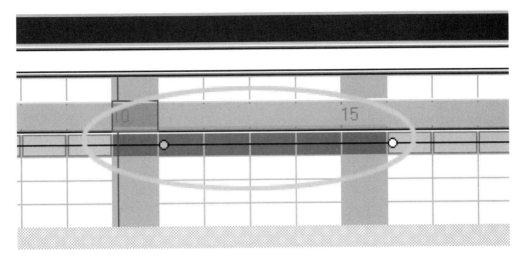

Figure 8–24 A green line indicates selected frames for playback.

Notice that a green line appears in the score, indicating the marked area for playback. When you click Play, the playback head starts playing your movie from the first selected frame and continues to the last frame of the selected region (unless it comes across any `wait` commands or Lingo scripts interrupting the playback of your movie). When the playback head reaches the last frame, it loops back to the first frame of the selected area, not the first frame of your movie (Figure 8–24).

WORK WITH EXTERNAL EXECUTABLE FILES

There are many advantages to creating separate Director movies and linking to them from the current movie you are working in. A common request is to develop a program that incorporates elements from existing programs. Usually, these programs have been authored in Director or Authorware. Instead of wasting the time trying to recreate these programs, use a Lingo command to open one of these movies and play it. You can also have it return back to your original Director movie when the external program is done playing. To set up this feature:

1. Open the main Director movie you are using to launch other movies and programs.
2. Add a sprite script or frame script in the appropriate location where you want to launch an external program.
3. Type in the Lingo code:

   ```
   play movie "name of movie"
   ```

4. Rewind and play back your movie.

Depending where in the file structure the new movie you are linking to is stored, you may have to add in the specific path for Director to locate the proper movie. The best solution is to keep all externally linked files in the same folder.

Director is able to open other executable files and applications, not just Director movies. Generally, any Windows application containing an .EXE file extension or Macintosh application program can be opened from a Director movie.

WORK IN THE SCORE

There are a number of things you can do as a programmer to make maneuvering around the score more efficient. The score is the main work area, or timeline, where you control the majority of elements used in your movie. These elements include all of your cast members (which become sprites in the score), scripts, layering hierarchy, ink effects, duration of sprites, and so on. The following points should provide a few methods for properly setting up and testing the sequence you constructed in the score.

Turn Sprite Channels On and Off

Because the score can contain upward of 1,000 channels, having the ability to turn some of these channels on and off could be a huge timesaver in troubleshooting multi-layered movies. The small gray buttons in the far-left side of each channel toggle the visibility and functionality of sprites located in that particular channel (Figure 8–25). This allows you to isolate whether a particular channel is causing a conflict with the playback of your movie (a sprite with a lingering script that is adversely affecting other sprites in the same channel). You may also want to hide certain channels for aesthetic purposes. Turning off a particular channel allows Director to play your movie without displaying the sprites in that channel. You can compare playback with and without the channel displaying the images, scripts, or effects contained in that channel. This technique is the easiest method for hiding channels without having to delete any of the sprites contained in those selected channels.

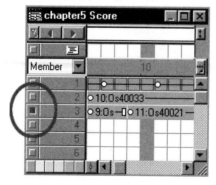

Figure 8–25 Toggle any channel in the score on and off.

Hiding channels is a good technique while you are still in the development stages of your program. However, the sprites in these hidden channels are still factored into the file size of your movie. Eliminate any unnecessary channels when you have finished building your movie and are ready to package the final project, either as a Projector or a Shockwave movie. This will reduce the overall size of your movie.

Turn Effect Channels On and Off

Turning channels on and off in the effects channels is essentially the same as turning channels on and off for the regular sprite channels. To toggle any channel on or off, click the button to the far-left side of the channel. The advantage for turning these channels on and off can help you troubleshoot your movie, especially when trying to find out whether a tempo setting or script is causing your movie to play incorrectly if at all. By turning a channel off using this technique, you can test to see if your movie plays back correctly when not activating the options selected in those particular channels of the score.

Example: If a playback or display error occurs between two screens, check the transition channel. Play back your movie with and without that channel selected. If the movie plays the same in both cases, the problem lies somewhere else in your movie. If hiding the Transition channel fixes the problem, then you may need to go back and recheck the settings for that troublesome transition or remove the transition altogether.

Alter the Display of your Score

For those of you who remember (or still work with) Director 5, you should recall what a tough time it was working in the score. Sprites were represented by their cast member numbers, which were displayed for each frame that the sprite spanned in the score (Figure 8–26). More important than just looks, you can now see and utilize more information pertaining to each sprite. The one obvious factor is that sprites are now displayed as single objects (Figure 8–27). This allows:

♦ Sprites to be stretched in either direction by simply dragging either endpoint to cover more or fewer frames.

♦ Sprites to be moved to a new channel or set of frames by clicking on any part of the sprite and dragging it as a unit to the new location.

♦ Sprites to display additional internal information directly in the score. Click on the sprite content pull-down menu (Figure 8–28). These various displays make reading and editing a complex score easier. You can select from:

   ♦ Member—Displays the name and/or number of the associated cast member.

   ♦ Behavior—Displays the associated cast member's name and/or number of any behaviors were applied to any sprites in the score. The sprite remains blank if no behavior was used.

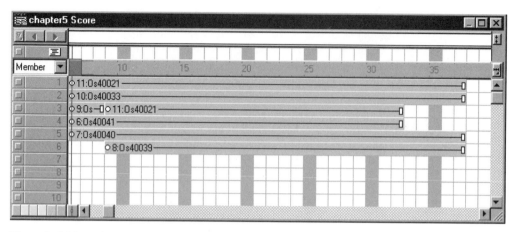

Figure 8–26 Reverting your score to look like a Director 5 display.

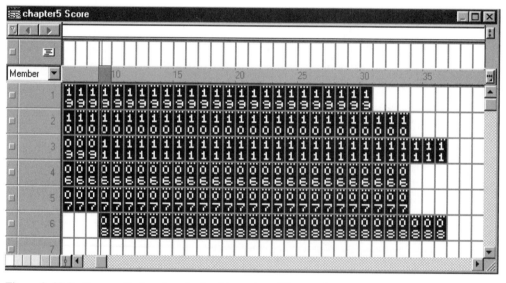

Figure 8–27 Sprites are displayed as single objects since Director 6.

◆ Location—Displays the location of the sprite (top left corner of bounding box) on the stage.

◆ Ink—Displays the type of ink effect applied to each sprite.

◆ Blend—Displays the transparency level for each sprite: 100% is opaque; 0% is completely invisible.

◆ Extended—A unique combination of all the sprite content choices (Figure 8–29).

Figure 8–28 Sprite content pull-down menu.

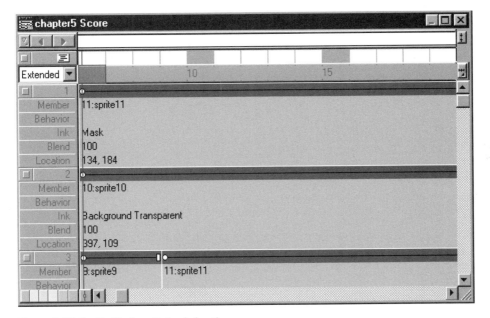

Figure 8–29 Sprite display: Extended option.

You can also change the information that is displayed for sprites in your score by choosing how and when sprite information is displayed within a sprite itself. This is referred to as sprite labeling. To select how and when the information selected in the sprite content menu is displayed:

1. Choose Sprite Labels from the View menu.

2. Choose from one of the following sprite label displays:

- Keyframes—Displays the information (selected in the sprite content menu) at every keyframe marked in the score for every channel.

- Changes Only—Displays the information in a sprite only when a new sprite is added to the score.

- Every Frame—Displays information for every frame of every sprite. Unless zoomed all the way into your score, it becomes very difficult to work with this setting and distinguish which sprite you want to work with.

- First Frame—Displays the information for each sprite only at the beginning of each sprite.

- None—Does not display any information for any sprites in the score.

Change the Focus of your Timeline

Depending on the size of your movie and the number of frames a sprite spans in the score, you may need to change the zoom factor of your timeline. To do this:

1. Click on the Zoom menu at the right side of the Score window.

2. Choose from one of the preselected zoom percentages listed in the popup menu (Figure 8–30).

   OR

   Use the shortcut keys Control-(+) (Windows) or Command-(+) (Macintosh) to zoom in closer to the timeline to see more detail and decrease the number of frames displayed. Use Control-(-) (Windows) or Command-(-) (Macintosh) to zoom back to a wider view of the timeline.

Being able to see more detail will come in handy when you need to add or change a single frame or small group of sprites (such as adding a keyframe). Displaying a wider view of the timeline will come in handy when you are trying to move a sprite or group of sprites to a section of the score much later in time (Figure 8–31).

Narrower	Ctrl+ -
Wider	Ctrl+ +
12 % (1)	
25 % (2)	
50 % (3)	
75 % (4)	
100 % (5)	
200 % (6)	
✓ 400 % (7)	
800 % (8)	
1600 % (9)	

Figure 8–30 Zoom menu for the score.

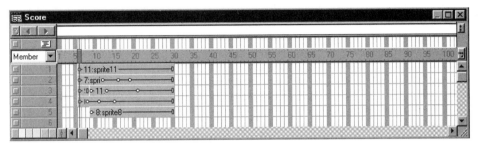

Figure 8–31 Comparing different views of the score (800% vs. 75%).

To assist in adding keyframes (single frames) or other subsets (portions) of a larger sprite, change the display under the Edit menu from Edit Entire Sprite to Edit Sprite Frames (Figure 8–32). This gives the score the look of Director 5, allowing you to break up and change any sprite frame by frame.

LOCATE THE PLAYBACK HEAD

When developing a program in Director, many times it is easy to lose sight of the playback head in the score. You might have clicked on a navigational link that has taken you to a frame much further down in your timeline than what is currently displayed in the score. Or you might be trying to troubleshoot a movie and want to stop the playback head at the precise moment of a problematic frame. You must be careful not to click anywhere in the score or you will move the playback head to the new location where you accidentally clicked. The other alternative is to scroll through your score to try and locate the position of the playback head. This can waste time and be quite cumbersome.

Instead, Director provides a quick-find locator that automatically finds the frame that your playback head is in and changes the view of your score so that the playback head and adjacent frames are displayed in the center of the screen. To perform this function, click on the Center Current Frame button located at the lower left corner of the score (Figure 8–33).

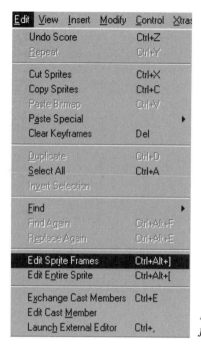

Figure 8–32 Changing the view of the score from Edit Entire Sprite to Edit Sprite Frames.

TROUBLESHOOT TECHNIQUES

Debug your Application

No matter how simple you may think your program is or how sure you are that every element you added to your movie works correctly, there's always room for errors when the gods of multimedia want to step in and have some fun. There is always the possibility that a typo occurred while you were typing in a Lingo script, sprites and cast members were rearranged while you were trying to test something and were not put back into their proper positions, or linked files were not able to be found or recognized by your Director movie.

Therefore, it is very important to go through, test, and debug your program thoroughly before considering it ready for distribution. Debugging basically means trying to maneuver through your program from start to finish, accessing every possible navigational combination, and trying to see if clicking something at the wrong time doesn't screw up the program or cause it to perform incorrectly. Many times, developers will go through their programs and click on all the right buttons. As expected, the program usually performs the way it was designed to play.

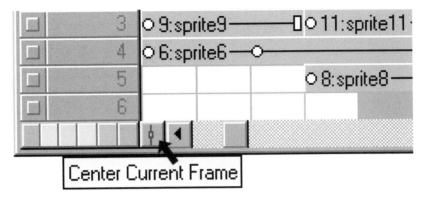

Figure 8–33 Center Current Frame button.

Sure enough, however, there will be times when items that were not supposed to be clicked cause the program to malfunction in unexpected ways. There is no way to prevent users from clicking around on the screens. Therefore, you must take the time to check all possible areas that may lead to an error in your program (as if you are trying to get it to fail). If you can get through the entire program several times without encountering a single error, then I would say your program is ready for distribution.

Have someone else, who has not had any involvement in the development of your program, go in and try to maneuver through the program. You should observe carefully to make sure that all of the buttons and links are navigating to the right sections.

Find a Problem, Figure It Out, and Fix It

While in the process of debugging your Director movie (or even just in the development stages), it is important to analyze a problem before rushing in to fix it. The first thing to do (after panicking that your movie doesn't work) is to write down exactly what went wrong. Be specific and document the details of what caused the error. If an error message appears, write it down. This message may be helpful in determining what needs to be fixed. This error message will also be helpful if you wind up calling Macromedia's Technical Support.

Create a developer's journal that you can use to keep notes on all of your multimedia projects. This can be useful to find out relevant information about project requirements, dates, and version numbers of phases presented to clients for approval, special or unique developing techniques used, and troubleshooting hold-ups and their appropriate fixes.

Once you have come across an error and have logged it in your developer's journal, begin to focus on the problem. Try to track down the cause of the problem. Can you easily identify what is causing the error to occur or is it more involved than that? Work your way backward through the steps that you performed to see if you can figure out precisely what caused the error. Use Director features, such as the Debugger window, Watcher window, and Message window with Trace, to check through your scripts to display the line that is causing the problem.

The last step is to eliminate all other potential factors or external variables that may be causing the problem. If you can isolate the error to a specific incidence every time it occurs, even under different circumstances (i.e., running your program on another system), then you should be able to go in and correct the problem or eliminate it altogether.

To double-check that a problem you have diagnosed is truly the correct reason for the error, try and recreate the error in a test movie. Make a simplified version of the real application and see whether or not the problem occurs. If you know the steps it takes to successfully reproduce the error, then you will know the steps to take to correct the problem.

Step-by-Step Commands with Trace

Turn on the Trace feature while playing your movie to see exactly how Director is functioning. The Message window will display all the commands and scripts as the playback head encounters them. Scroll back through the trace list to find out where any errors in your application are originating. To activate the Trace feature:

1. Select Message from the Window menu. The Message window appears.
2. Click the Trace button at the top of the Message window (Figure 8–34).
3. Run your movie with the Message window visible. All Lingo scripts and behavior commands will be displayed every time the playback head encounters a command. You can stop the movie after experiencing an error in your application to check the code that is causing the problem.

Playing your Director movie with the Message window open and running Trace can slow down the playback performance of your application.

CREATE A LIMITED-TIME DEMO

There are many reasons why you should consider adding a feature to prevent your application from running after a certain date:

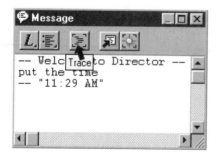

Figure 8–34 Trace button located in Message window.

◆   You do not want an incomplete version (an alpha or beta version made for evaluation only) of your software floating around forever. Clients and end-users are likely to think it's the final version, when in essence, there may be several changes that need to be implemented.

◆   You want to get approval from your client, but want to make sure you get paid before releasing the final version.

◆   You are sending out a trial version for people to examine before they purchase your program.

Whatever the reason may be, all you need to do is program Director to compare the current date of the system that is running your program to a date you set for it to cease running. To add this feature to your movie, type in the following Lingo script:

```
on startMovie
    expirationDate = date("20010101")
    - where January 1, 2001 is the desired Expiration Date
    if the systemDate > expirationDate
    alert "The Trial Period for this application has expired!"
    - add in your own message
    halt
    end if
end
```

This script will be executed when you play the original Director movie or a Projector file created from it. An alert window will appear, displaying the message you input in the `alert` line of the script (Figure 8–35). When the user clicks the OK button, the program will automatically quit. The Projector file will quit and will no longer be accessible. The Director movie will just stop playing, not allowing the application to run any more. However, you still have full control of the program and can go back in to alter the script for further development.

TOP SECRET: ADD A PASSWORD

Director's ability to interact with the user via Lingo scripts and behavior commands allows developers to include features in applications that are not accessible to the general public.

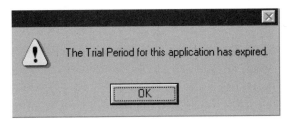

Figure 8–35 An alert window indicating the trial period for the application has expired.

In these cases, the user would be required to type in a pre-determined password that is created during the development of the program. This does not give the user the ability to enter her own password or change the existing password. Director contains a Password behavior to make adding a password into your program easy. To implement a password in your Director movie:

1. Open the Tool Palette from the Window menu or press Control-7 (Windows) or Command-7 (Macintosh) on the keyboard.
2. Create a Field Text window on the stage using the Field button.
3. Open the Library Palette from the Window menu.
4. Select Text from the Library List pull-down menu (Figure 8–36).
5. Click and drag the Password Entry behavior onto the Field Text box. The Parameters for "Password Entry" window appears.
6. Enter the desired password in the Password field (Figure 8–37).
7. Enter a command or handler in the Valid password message field.
   (e.g., `myHandler`).
8. Enter a command or handler in the invalid password message field
   (e.g., `quit`).
9. Click OK.
10. Create a new movie script and set the following global variables:

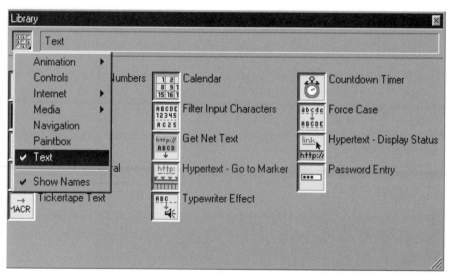

Figure 8–36 Display the Text behaviors accessed from the Library List menu.

Figure 8–37 Enter the desired password in the Parameters for "Password Entry" window.

```
global gFlag

on exitFrame
    if gFlag = 1 then
        go to frame (frameNumber or markerName)
    else
        go the frame
    end if
end
```

11. Create a new movie script. This can be done by clicking the plus sign.

```
global gFlag

on startMovie
    set gFlag = 0
end



on myHandler
    set gFlag = 1
end
```

12. Rewind and play your movie.

13. Click on the stage to make it the active window. Use the keyboard to type in a password.

For the aforementioned example, if the password is entered correctly, the playback head will navigate to the frame number or marker name set in the script, allowing the user to begin the program (Figure 8–38). If the user enters an incorrect password, you can set the program to either stay in the frame or quit on the user.

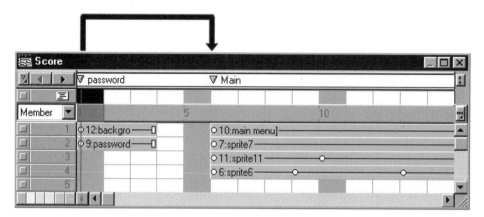

Figure 8–38 The playback head navigates to the Main section of the movie upon entering the correct password.

 Do not use editable text for the Password field text. This will cause the password feature to not function properly.

You cannot enter a `go to` command for the Valid or invalid password message field. (Thanks to Dave at Macromedia Technical Support for figuring this one out.)

Make sure to add a `loop on frame` command (or similar) in the score so that the playback head does not continue playing past the password section of your movie until the user enters the correct password.

Password-protected applications can be used for programs distributed over the Internet via Shockwave that you want to make available only to selected individuals. This can be useful for posting projects to key clients around the world before releasing them to the public. This application now functions more like an intranet site accessible over the pipelines of the World Wide Web.

 Password entry requires a system-specific font to function properly. Set up your field text to use the Arial font for Windows and Helvetica for Macintosh systems. Bullet points appear in the Field window to hide the actual password being entered.

HELP USERS WITH TOOLTIPS

Just like the majority of programs on the market, Director allows you to add popup labels identifying the name of a button or link when the cursor is left sitting over one of these functions for a short period of time (Figure 8–39). This type of feature is very helpful to the user when trying to learn where each link is located on an unfamiliar interface. To add this feature to your application:

1. Build a Director movie as you would normally or open an existing movie.
2. Open the Tool Palette window from the Window menu or press Control-7 (Windows) or Command-7 (Macintosh) on the keyboard.
3. Select the Field text box and drag a new Field window onto the stage.
4. Open the Library Palette from the Window menu.
5. Select Controls from the Library List pull-down menu (Figure 8–40).

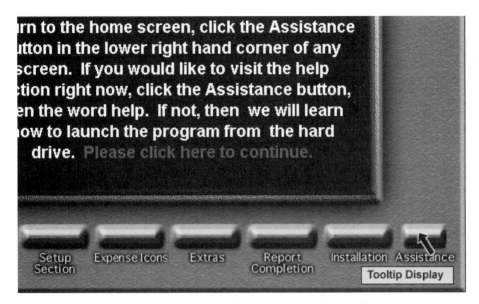

Figure 8–39 Standard popup message window called a tooltip.

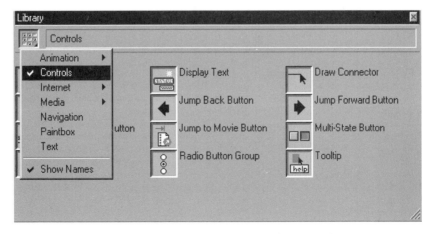

Figure 8–40 Display the Controls behaviors accessed from the Library List menu.

6. Click the Display Text behavior and apply it to the Field sprite. The Parameters for "Display Text" window appears.

7. Select Tooltip from the pull-down menu (Figure 8–41).

8. Click OK.

9. Select Tooltip from the Library List menu and apply it to the sprite that you want to have the Tooltip feature. The Parameters for "Tooltip" window appears.

10. Type in the text you want displayed as the "tip" in the Text of tool tip field (Figure 8–42).

11. Set the timing and position options as desired.

12. Important: Select the cast member number of the Field text box that you added in Step 3 by dragging the slider bar located at the bottom of the Parameters window.

13. Click OK.

14. Rewind and play your movie. The tooltip is displayed when you park your cursor over the sprite.

Leave the Field window empty when you add it to your stage (see Step 3). This window will not be displayed when you play the movie.

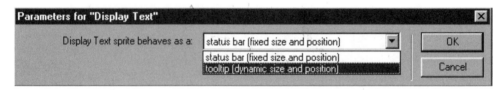

Figure 8–41 Select Tooltip from the Parameters For "Display Text" window.

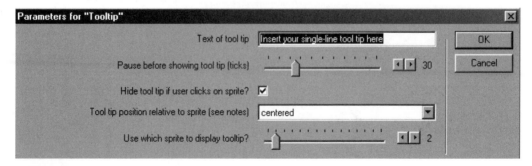

Figure 8–42 Parameters for "Tooltip" window.

IMPROVE TEXT: SUBSCRIPTS AND SUPERSCRIPTS

Director is always making major improvements in version after version, but it's the little details that they add that seem to be the things most often needed in a project. This one I have to credit to Joe, my senior multimedia developer at PFS. We were recently working on a project where we needed to add a registered trademark® in the body of some text. Trying to get it to look right at first was tough. Then he remembered that Director text has the ability to use subscripts and superscripts. This is not a new feature in Director, but one that might be forgotten if you don't use it from time to time. To change text to a subscript or superscript:

1. Open the Text window by selecting Text from the Window menu or by using the keyboard shortcut Control-6 (Windows) or Command-6 (Macintosh).
2. Type new text or highlight the existing text that you want to change.
3. Right-click (Windows) or Option-click (Macintosh) on the highlighted text.
4. Select Style from the popup menu.
5. Select Subscript or Superscript from the secondary popup menu.

   OR

   Open the Font window (Figure 8–43).

MAKE MOVIES SPECIAL WITH XTRAS

Xtras are software plug-ins or extension modules that increase the functionality and capabilities of Director in a variety of ways. These modules come in all shapes and sizes. Some appear in a separate Cast window and others are accessed through their own user interface to allow for customized settings. Director comes bundled with a number of Xtras, yet it allows you to install third-party Xtras as well. Depending on which Xtras are used in your program, make sure that the user has the required Xtras installed on his system or is provided with a copy of these Xtras with the final version of your movie. Director has the ability to embed most of the commonly used Xtras into a Projector file. Therefore, you may not be required to distribute a separate Xtras folder with your movie (see Chapter 10 for more information regarding packaging and distributing your movies).

To install Xtras, place them in the Xtras folder found in the Director application folder located on your hard drive.

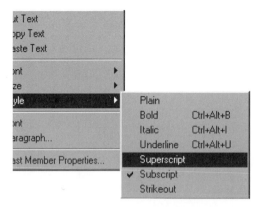

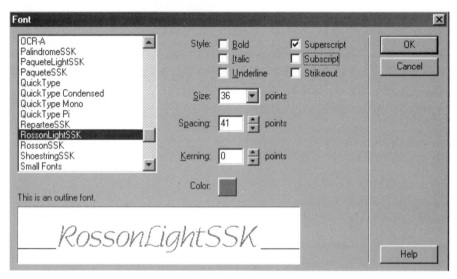

Figure 8–43 Use the Text Style menu or the Font window to alter the layout of text.

There are five general types of Xtras:

◆ Image filters—Consist of third-party filters, such as Adobe Photoshop and Premiere filters, which alter the way your images appear on-stage.

◆ Transition Xtras—Consist of third-party plug-ins that add new transitions to the standard ones that come with Director.

◆ Xtra cast members—Consist of a variety of items, including images, digital media, databases, and utility applications, which add different functionality to your movie. All Xtra cast members are accessed from the Insert menu and place a copy of the Xtra into the cast.

◆ Lingo Xtras—Consist of added scripts and commands to add more control and flexibility to your interactive movies.

◆ Tools Xtras—Consist of small applications that assist you in developing certain aspects of your movie, including simple animations and effects.

Director projector files and Shockwave movies can be designed to automatically download required Xtras, if available, from a specific URL address. To implement this option:

1. Select Movie from the Modify menu.
2. Select Xtras from the submenu.
3. Click Xtras in the list to be downloaded from the Movie Xtras window (Figure 8–44).
4. Click the Download if Needed checkbox at the lower left corner.

FIND MOVIE XTRAS

Director can display a list of all the Xtras used in a movie to assist you in making sure that you have either bundled all the right Xtras internally with the movie or provided a separate folder containing the required Xtras. Enter the following command in the Message window:

```
put movieXtraList
```

This command will return a linear list of all the Xtras used in the current movie (Figure 8–45). Each of these Xtras will contain one of two possible properties, which are also displayed in the list:

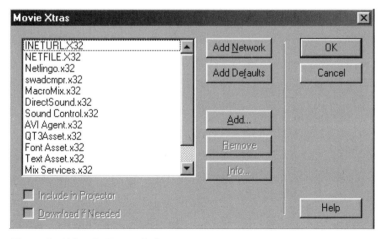

Figure 8–44 Movie Xtras window.

- ◆   #name
- ◆   #packagefiles

The #name property describes the name of the Xtra used on the current platform. If a #name description does not appear, it means that the Xtra listed is only available on the current platform. The #packagefiles property describes an Xtra marked for downloading. This property contains a sublist of the #name and #version. Having this information is useful when gathering and making sure all of the required Xtras are available for packaging and distribution.

SUMMARY

This chapter included a mixture of features to include to improve the capabilities of your Director programs. Obviously, there are millions of tips, tricks, and other techniques that I would love to put into this book, but I focused on just a select few to keep this book down to a short, quick reference guide. The features listed here are techniques that I seem to find myself using on a wider number of projects. I hope they save you time and come in handy.

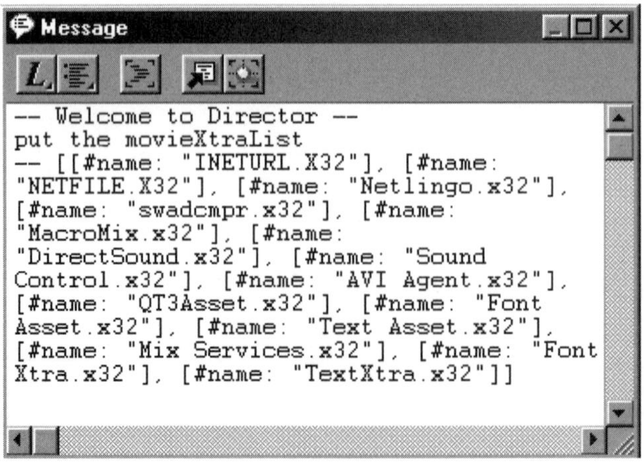

```
 Message                                   _ □ ✕

  L ≣    ≣    ≣    ⊡ ⊙

-- Welcome to Director --
put the movieXtraList
-- [[#name: "INETURL.X32"], [#name:
"NETFILE.X32"], [#name: "Netlingo.x32"],
[#name: "swadcmpr.x32"], [#name:
"MacroMix.x32"], [#name:
"DirectSound.x32"], [#name: "Sound
Control.x32"], [#name: "AVI Agent.x32"],
[#name: "QT3Asset.x32"], [#name: "Font
Asset.x32"], [#name: "Text Asset.x32"],
[#name: "Mix Services.x32"], [#name: "Font
Xtra.x32"], [#name: "TextXtra.x32"]]
```

Figure 8–45 List of Xtras necessary for current movie.

chapter 9

ADVANCING
TECHNIQUES WITH
BEHAVIORS AND
LINGO

It would take volumes of books to describe all the different applications for which you can use behaviors and Lingo, covering every type of project imaginable. Since the scope of most individual Lingo commands gets case-specific, depending on the number of variables you have set in your movie, I don't want to make you believe that Lingo commands can be summed up in a few pages. Rather, my goal in this chapter is to introduce you to a variety of ways behaviors and Lingo commands can be applied for various uses. I think you will find the topics covered in this chapter helpful, but use it more as a concept chapter to challenge yourself on how and when to use the power of Director's programming capabilities. Don't get frustrated. Even the best programmers experiment with multiple commands to get the desired results. Keep plugging away and watch the quality level of your movies skyrocket when you start harnessing the power of behaviors and Lingo.

TIME FOR BEHAVIORS

Here's a neat application you can build in no time (excuse the pun). It's building a real, working clock that you can run on your computer or (with the help of additional software) turn into a custom-designed screen saver. Personalize it and e-mail it to your friends for a holiday gift. The point is, I want to demonstrate how powerful Director's behaviors are and how simple they are to use. By dragging a simple behavior onto some vector graphics you create, the coding already written inside of these behaviors pulls the resources from your computer's internal clock to actually allow the hands of your analog clock to move accurately.

To build this timeless treasure:

1. Create any type of graphic(s) to be used as the face of the clock.
2. Create vector images inside Director or import Flash elements to be used as the hands of the clock. Create an hour hand, minute hand, and second hand.
3. Place the registration point at the back end of each hand, opposite the "pointer." This will allow the hands to rotate, or pivot, from that point.
4. Place each hand on the stage over the image of the face of the clock.
5. Open the Library Palette from the Windows menu.
6. Select Controls from the Library List.
7. Apply the Analog Clock behavior to each hand sprite individually. The Parameters for "Analog Clock" window will appear (Figure 9–1).
8. Apply the appropriate setting for each hand.

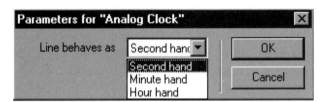

Figure 9–1 The Parameters for "Analog Clock" window.

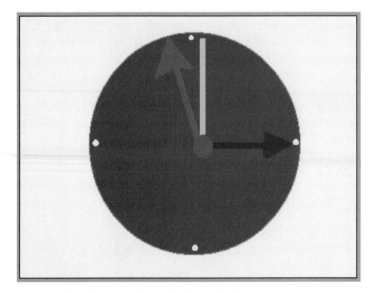

Figure 9–2 Build an analog clock that really keeps time.

When you play your movie, the hands should automatically adjust to the correct time. These behaviors read from your computer's internal clock to display the current time (Figure 9–2). You will actually see the second hand tick accurately around the clock. This is a very simple application to build with almost zero programming skills necessary. Be creative with the hands and the look of the clock.

 Tip **Building a custom clock makes for a great screen saver.**

CREATE POPUP MENUS/ DROP-DOWN LISTS

Two very common features to implement into your interactive applications are popup menus and drop-down lists. These have been very popular on the Web and can add to the amount of interactive choices available to the user. Director's behaviors allow you to add these features into your movies very quickly and easily. You can use these menus and lists as navigational tools with content from a text field, marker name, or movie name. Director will automatically navigate to those markers or movies if selected from a popup menu. To build a menu/list:

1. Open the Field Text window from the Window menu (Figure 9–3).

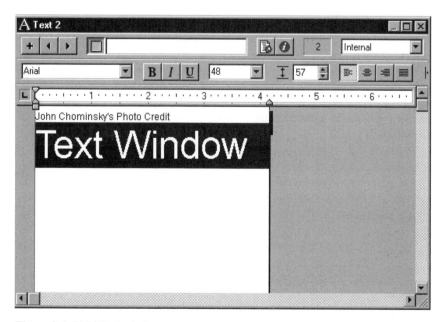

Figure 9–3 Field Text window.

2. Type in the text to be used in the drop-down menu.

3. Close the window when you are finished entering all of the desired text.

4. Place the Field Text cast member onto the stage (Figure 9–4).

5. Open the Library Palette from the Windows menu.

6. Select Control from the Library List popup menu.

7. Apply the Dropdown List behavior onto the Field Text sprite (Figure 9–5).

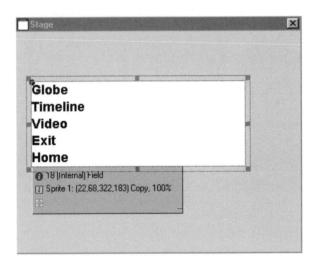

Figure 9–4 Field Text list on-stage.

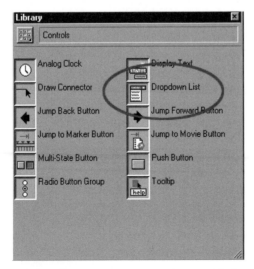

Figure 9–5 Dropdown List behavior is applied to Field Text sprite from Library List menu.

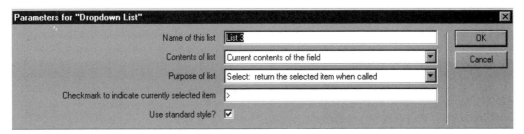

Figure 9–6 The Parameters for "Dropdown List" window.

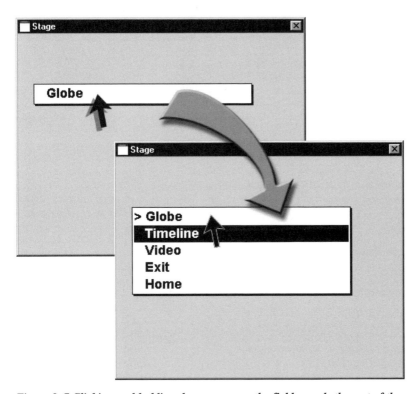

Figure 9–7 Clicking and holding the mouse over the field reveals the rest of the words in the drop-down menu.

8. Select the appropriate settings in the Parameters for "Dropdown List" window based on the functionality you would like to add to the choices in the menu (Figure 9–6).

9. Rewind and play the movie. Only the first entry should be visible.

10. Click and hold the mouse key on the text field to display the entire list (Figure 9–7).

You can use the items in a popup menu as navigational choices that link to different sections of a movie (Figure 9–8).

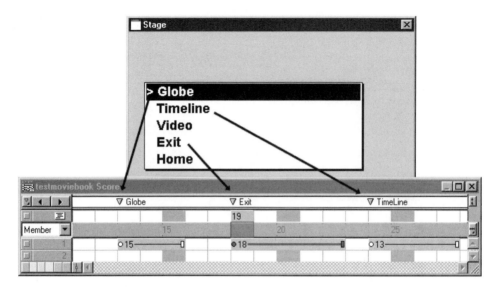

Figure 9–8 Names in drop-down menu coincide with marker names for navigational purposes.

To implement this feature:

1. Add all the necessary sprites to your score for each section of your movie.
2. Add markers to the first frame of each new section and name them.
3. Create a list using the Field Text option.
4. Drag the Field Text cast member to the score.
5. Open the Library Palette from the Window menu.
6. Select Controls from the Library List.
7. Drag the Dropdown behavior onto the Field Text sprite. The Parameters for "Dropdown List" window appears.
8. Name the list.
9. Set the Content of the list to "Markers in this movie."
10. Set the Purpose of the list to "Execute: go movie/go marker/do selectedLine" (Figure 9–9).
11. Click OK.
12. Rewind and play back your movie. Only the first field item should be displayed on your stage.
13. Click on that field to display the contents of the entire list.
14. Click and hold the mouse to highlight a selection.
15. Release the mouse over the selected item to navigate to that section of your movie.

Parameters for "Dropdown List"

Name of this list:	List 1
Contents of list:	Markers in this movie
Purpose of list:	Execute: go movie | go marker | do selectedLine
Checkmark to indicate currently selected item:	>
Use standard style?	✔

OK

Cancel

Figure 9–9 "go marker" selected as navigational command for drop-down text.

EDITABLE TEXT

Many interactive applications require the ability to enter text. The ability to have user-defined entry of text information is common on forms for Web sites, training programs, and player profiles for games (Figure 9–10).

To set up editing properties for a Text cast member:

1. Create a Field cast member.
2. Select the Property Inspector.
3. To make the cast member editable, click the Editable box (Figure 9–11).

Standard Text cast members can only be edited in the authoring mode. Once you create a Projector file, standard Text cast members become bitmaps. Field cast members, however, can be edited and interpreted by Lingo in both the authoring mode and as Projector files.

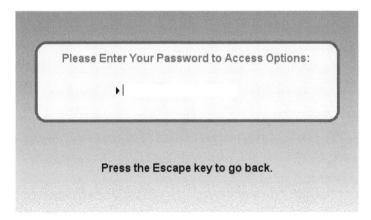

Please Enter Your Password to Access Options:

▶|

Press the Escape key to go back.

Figure 9–10 Text field can be used to enter user information.

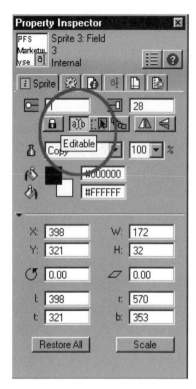

Figure 9–11 Editable text button selected in Property Inspector.

Lingo can check the text entered in a field by a user. The Lingo element `contains` or an equals sign (=) is typically used to check the string of a field entry. The `contains` command works by comparing whether one string contains the same information as the other string. The equals sign works by seeing if the contents of the Field cast member match exactly to the string command. This method is commonly used for question-and-answer-type applications. If you want your user to enter an answer and submit it by pressing the Enter key (Windows) or the Return key (Macintosh), set up the following function:

1. Create the required Field cast members and name them (Figure 9–12).

2. Enter the script (sprite script or cast member script):

```
on keyDown
    if the key = RETURN then
        checkAnswer
end

on checkAnswer
    if field "question1" contains "(theCorrectAnswer)" then
        go to frame "Correct"
    else
        go to frame "Wrong"
    end if
end
```

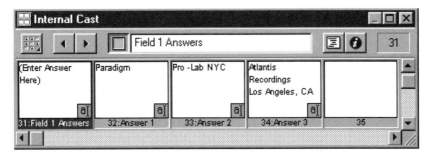

Figure 9–12 Cast members of Field text answers.

The structure of this command can be applied to each question in your program. If the user enters the right answer (the characters entered match the string set for that particular field), then the playback head is sent to the section of the movie labeled "Correct". Otherwise, if an incorrect answer is submitted, the playback head goes to a section of the movie labeled "Wrong" (Figure 9–13).

You can also use the contains command to have Director see if the character string entered is part of the Field cast member. If the answer contains several correct responses, use the following format:

1. Create the required Field cast member and name it.

2. Enter the script:

```
on testAnswer
    if the field "NameofField" contains "possibleAnswer" then
        go to frame "Correct"
    else
        go to frame "Wrong"
    end if
end
```

Capitalization does not matter, but spelling does count.

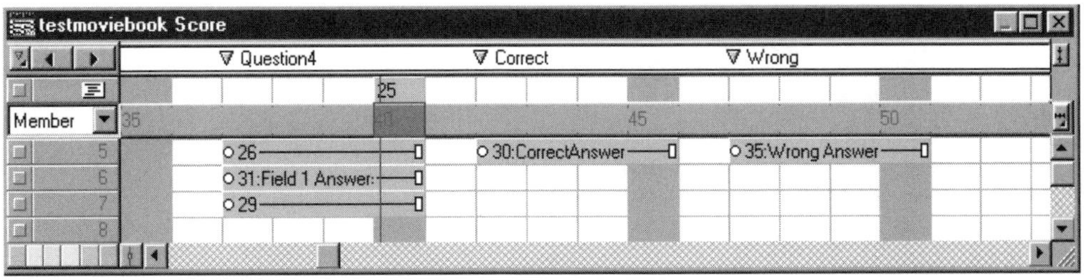

Figure 9–13 Sample score for quiz section (user input links to either "Correct" or "Wrong" marker).

SET CONSTRAINTS FOR MOVEABLE SPRITES

A common element added to interactive applications is to allow the users to move a sprite along the screen. Usually, you would not want them to place the sprite just anywhere, but rather limit it to a particular path or area of the screen. In the example in Figure 9–14, the users have the ability to drag the decoder window up and down the screen to the section that they wish to select. This function would not work properly if the users were able to drag the sprite over to the other side of the screen. It is important to set limits and constrain the horizontal positioning of this particular moveable sprite.

To set up this feature:

1. Create and import all necessary images.
2. Build the interface as desired.
3. Add all the required navigational links to the buttons to jump to each one's associated section of the movie.
4. Place the decoder window sprite in the highest channel of the score (Figure 9–15).
5. With that sprite selected, click on the Moveable button in the Property Inspector (Figure 9–16).

Figure 9–14 Setting moveable sprite's horizontal or vertical constraints.

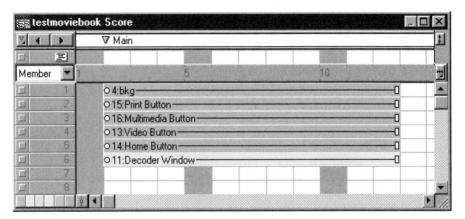

Figure 9–15 Setting a moveable sprite in the highest sprite channel.

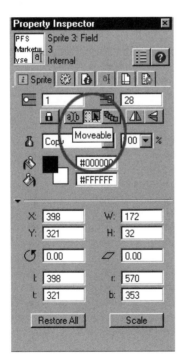

Figure 9–16 The Moveable button allows the sprite to be repositioned outside the authoring mode.

6. Open a script window for this sprite and type:

```
on mouseUp
    set boundary = 500
        — where number is pixel position of sprite on stage
        if the locH of sprite 3 >= boundary then
```

```
            puppetSprite (channel number), TRUE
    set the locH of sprite (channel number) = boundary
        updateStage
    end if
end
```

This command checks the horizontal position of the sprite as soon as the user releases the mouse button. If the sprite's registration point is set for 500, Director positions the sprite 500 pixels from the left-hand side of the screen. If the user moves the sprite to a position less than 500 pixels from the side, Director automatically places the sprite at 500.

You may also want to set a vertical constraint stating that the sprite can go no lower than a particular position. Use the same script, substituting locV for the locH command.

For Lingo users, you can set a sprite to be moveable on-screen while the movie is playing by setting the moveableSprite property to be True.

SET A TIME LIMIT

I'm sure most of you have taken a test at least once in your life where you were given a certain amount of time to complete a task. A proctor whose only job was to announce "pencils down" at the end of the session sat in the front of the room. Why not continue this tradition in the Computer-Based Training (CBT) applications you create in Director. This can be a very useful feature for training programs where speed and/or reaction time are important factors in the training process. You can develop your application to display a countdown clock on which you can set a specific time interval from which it will begin counting down. This can run in units of days, hours, minutes, seconds, and hundredths of a second (Figure 9–17).

A typical example of how to utilize a countdown in a program is to provide a link that navigates to the next section of the program if the user responds correctly to the situation within the allotted time. If the time expires, the user is sent to another location, either to review the materials or try the question again.

When developing any movie that involves complex interactive navigational aspects, be sure to map out your links on paper before you begin to program the movie in Director. See Chapter 2, "Planning a Project from the Start."

To add a countdown clock to your application:

1. Add a text or field box on the stage.
2. Select Library Palette from the Window menu.
3. Select Text from the Library List pull-down menu.
4. Drag the Countdown Timer behavior from the Library window and apply it to the text or field box. The Parameters for "Countdown Timer" window appears (Figure 9–18).
5. Use the menus and sliders to customize how you would like the timer displayed and from what starting point.

Figure 9–17 Countdown clock created from the countdown timer behavior being applied to a Field text box.

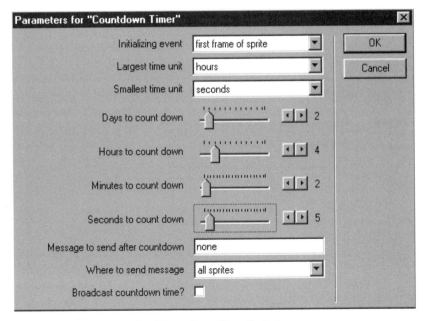

Figure 9–18 Parameters for "Countdown Timer" window.

6. Enter the message (function to take place) in the Message To Send After Countdown field for what the program should do once the countdown reaches zero.

You must remember to define your message with the proper handlers and commands (such as a `keyDownScript`) for the function to operate or else the countdown will reach zero and do nothing.

ACCESS MEDIA ON CD-ROM FROM DESKTOP PROJECTOR

One of the more complex features in Director allows you to access external media files from a CD-ROM while running the projector from the hard drive of the computer. One reason for going through this process is to allow yourself the opportunity of updating movie files and just redistributing a new disk. Also, if your system's hard disk space does not have a lot of available storage space on it, keeping all of the linked media on a CD-ROM frees up that amount of drive space on the system. Although you might not think about it, software theft does happen quite frequently. Keeping media on a CD-ROM is a good way to deter people from stealing unauthorized copies of the program off your computer. By storing all the media files on a separate disk, no one can take a fully functioning copy of your work. This is especially valuable if you are selling your programs or demonstrating a prototype application.

To set up this option:

◆ Use a movie script to determine the drive letter of the CD-ROM on a Windows system (see the section below "Determine CD-ROM Drive Letters for Windows Systems").

◆ Use the `searchPaths` command to have Lingo track down the appropriate file paths and destinations. This allows Director to follow the system file's hierarchy where the movie was saved.

```
set the searchPaths = ["c:\mainDirectory\folder\ &
  d:\cdrom\source\"]
```

OR

```
set the searchPaths, 1, myCDROM & "\myFiles"
  —where the number represents the sprite, myCDROM
  represents the CD-ROM drive, and myFiles represent the
  exact location of the required media files.
```

If you know that all the external files are coming off the CD-ROM, there is no reason to have your system check through the folder from where your Projector file is launching.

```
set the searchCurrentFolder = False
```

When redistributing updated movie files, remember to use the same filenames and directory structure or the paths will not be able to correctly identify the linked media.

DETERMINE CD-ROM DRIVE LETTERS FOR WINDOWS SYSTEMS

The previous section discussed running a Projector file from the hard drive of a system while accessing media stored on a CD-ROM. If you are distributing your applications to different users, their CD-ROM drive letters might vary from system to system. For this to work properly on the Windows platform, your application must be able to reference the letter of the CD-ROM drive on a system (Figure 9–19). If you or the end-user receives an error message stating that the linked media cannot be found on the CD-ROM, it was probably assigned to a different drive letter than the drive letter used during authoring.

Make the following changes to your program:

◆ Install a version of FileIO Xtra on your hard drive.

◆ Use the `searchPath` command described in the previous section.

◆ Use the following movie scripts:

```
on startMovie
    put CheckDrive ("fileName.mov") into myCD
    —type in the correct file name and extension here
    append the searchPath, myCD & "\folderName"
end
```

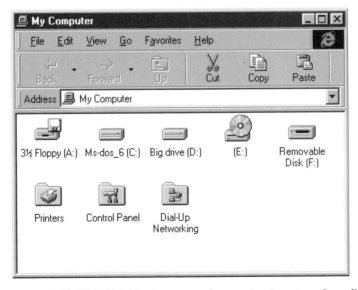

Figure 9–19 CD-ROM drive letters vary from system to system, depending on the number of devices and partitions dedicated to a particular system.

```
on CheckDrive findFile
   —where findFind is defined as a local variable
   repeat with I = 67 to 90
   set drive = numToChar ( i )
   set thisPath = string(drive & ":\"&findFile)
   set myFile = new(xtra "fileio")
   openFile (myFile, thisPath, 1)
      if status(myFile) = 0 then
   set myFile = 0
   return drive & ":"
   exit
      end if
   end repeat
   set myFile = 0
   alert "Please check the file "fileName" is on your CD-ROM"
end
```

This combination of software and settings will search for the file by the name specified in the `searchPath` command on the root level for each drive and device mounted on the system. The call will return the letter name for the CD-ROM drive it finds containing that specific filename.

This technique for determining the drive letter only applies to Windows systems. Use the following path example for Macintosh systems: "`MyCD:Folder:MovieName`". Any Macintosh-mounted drive with that name and path will recognize and play that file automatically.

There are other third-party Xtras and applications that can also be used to determine the drive letter of your CD-ROM drive. Check out MasterApp from UpdateStage at www.updatestage.com.

SCORE FOR GAMES

This section will come in handy if you ever have to create a scoring mechanism for a game. The concepts apply to most typical video games, where you score points as certain events occur. The premise in scoring with these and other similar style games is that points are earned (or deleted) when two objects intersect. For this example, we created an ever-popular boardwalk-style Frog Bog game. The scoring principles are the same—the intersection of two objects. Here, when the user launches the frog, if it lands in the same proximity of a floating lily pad, the user scores a point (Figure 9–20, also found in color section).

The best way to set this up is to create a global for the scoring. Here's a shell for how to construct the Lingo for scoring a gaming application:

Figure 9–20 Joe G's Famous Frog Bog Game, developed for OnlineBoardwalk.com.

```
global gpos,gscore,gfrogslanded,gmiss

on beginsprite me
  set the loch of sprite  21 = gpos
  put the loc of sprite 21 into gmiss
  set the loc of sprite 23 to gmiss
end

on exitframe me
  froghit(me)
  putscore(me)
end


on froghit me
  if sprite 21 intersects sprite 10 then
    set gscore = gscore + 10
    set gfrogslanded = gfrogslanded + 1
    set the visible of sprite 30 = 1
  else if sprite 21  intersects sprite 11 then
```

```
      set gscore = gscore + 10
      set gfrogslanded = gfrogslanded + 1
      set the visible of sprite 31 = 1
  else if sprite 21 intersects sprite 12 then
      set gscore = gscore + 10
      set gfrogslanded = gfrogslanded + 1
      set the visible of sprite 32 = 1
  else if sprite 21 intersects sprite 13 then
      set gscore = gscore + 10
      set gfrogslanded = gfrogslanded + 1
      set the visible of sprite 33 = 1
  else
      frogmiss(me)
  end if
end


on frogmiss me
  set the visible of sprite 23 = 1
end


on putscore me
  put gscore into member "score field"
  put gfrogslanded into member "frogs landed field"
end
```

To explain what is going on, break it down into sections. First, four globals are created, one each for position. The global position determines where the sprite is located.
Next, a custom handler (global `froghit me`) tells the program that if one sprite
intersects with the another sprite, add a value of 10 points to the score. Therefore,
through the use of global commands, every time object A intersects with object B, 10
more points are added to the value in the score. You can add optional features, such
as the handler on `frogmiss`, to display an image indicating that the user did not
score any points (in this case, we displayed a "splash" animation showing the frog
missed the lily pad and fell into the water). The last portion of this script gives the
command to change the Score Field cast member and display the current points
earned on-stage.

**Building a fully functional game takes more creativity than just
having two sprites intersect. You will need to create custom scripts
and behaviors to get your games to work the way you intend them
to function (Figure 9–21).**

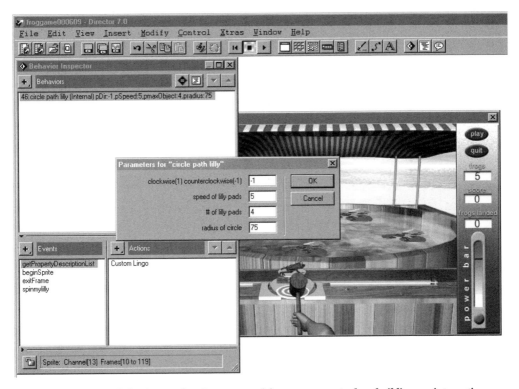

Figure 9–21 Custom behaviors and scripts are used for every aspect when building an interactive game.

BUILD A CHAT ROOM WITH MULTIUSER SERVER

Since more developers are using Director and other Macromedia products to build applications for use on the Internet, Director incorporated a whole new level of functionality that allows you to have more than one person accessing the same movie at a time. This is done with the Multiuser Server feature. Shockwave Multiuser Server comes with your Director application CD. Follow the on-screen instructions to install it on your computer.

 To find out the IP address of a server, select Server from the Status menu (Figure 9–22).

Creating a chat room is simple with the use of some new Director behaviors. To set up a basic application to be used as a chat room:

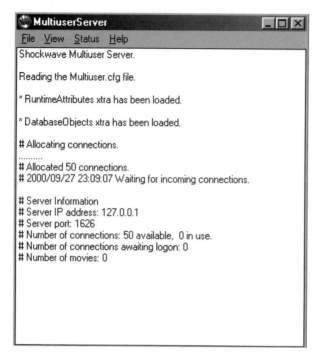

Figure 9–22 Use the Shockwave Multiuser Server to open up your movies for more than one user at a time, such as in a chat room.

1. Design any desired graphics for the screens and buttons and add them to your score (as necessary).

2. Set up your score with Login and Chat markers. Other sections can be added, including a loading screen.

3. Add a field text box to the Login section of your score (over any images that you might have used for that page) for the user to enter her username.

4. Enter the following script for the Text Field sprite:

```
on keyDown

    if the key = RETURN then
            sendAllSprites(#returnKeyPressed)
            dontPassEvent
            else
                pass
            end if

end
```

5. Create a button to be used to connect to the server and position it on the stage.

6. Open the Library Palette from the Window menu.

7. Select Internet from the Library List.

8. Select Multiuser from the popup menu (Figure 9–23).

9. Apply the Connect to Server behavior to this button. The Parameters for "Connect to Server" window appears (Figure 9–24).

10. Enter the Server Name, IP Address information, and where you want your playback head to navigate to based on the results of the connection to the server (e.g., the Chat marker or Error marker). This will allow communication through the server to and from your movie.

11. Under the Chat marker, add a text field for the user's comments/input (i.e., what he wants to post), a large text field where each person's input is posted, and a text field to display all of the users currently logged into the chat room.

12. Apply the Chat Input behavior to the user's input field. Do not change the default settings.

13. Apply the Chat Output behavior to the text field that will display all the user's comments. Do not change the default settings.

14. Apply the Send Chat Button behavior to the Submit button. This will communicate with the multiuser server and post the user's input text into the "all user message display area."

15. Add an Exit feature so a user can log off of the chat room. Apply the Disconnect from Server behavior to a Quit or Exit button.

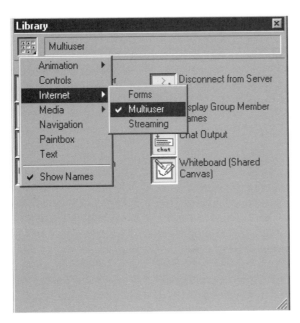

Figure 9–23 Director includes Multiuser Server behaviors, allowing easy integration of users across the Internet with minimal programming.

Parameters for "Connect to Server"		☒
Which member holds the user name?	member 2 of castLib 1 ▼	OK
Which member holds the user's password?	<no password required> ▼	Cancel
Which marker to go to while connecting?	loop ▼	
Which marker to go to when connected?	loop ▼	
Which marker to go to if connection fails?	loop ▼	
server address	trialserver.macromedia.com	
Port number:	1626	
Movie ID string	Movie ID string 4428776	
Text mode (for IRC, POP or SMTP servers)?	☐	
Encryption key (leave blank for no encryption):		
Save user profile in which file:	profile.txt	
Time out connection attempt after:	◼ ◀ ▶ 30	
	seconds ▼	
Which member will display errors?	<Show alert> ▼	

Figure 9–24 The Parameters for "Connect to Server" window.

 Be aware of any legal guidelines that may apply to chat room accessibility, especially when it comes to public chat rooms that children can access.

Creating a chat room environment can have more uses than your standard open user chat. Use it on your site for market research information, or to run informal surveys to learn more about the people visiting your site. Offer users more personalized information. If you work in a large office environment or in separate locations, set up a multiuser chat room to keep in touch with people via an Internet connection. Use your imagination and think when and where having multiple user communication would come in handy.

CLEAR DIRECTOR'S CACHE

Here's a last little tip that seems to help out when a project just doesn't seem to be running correctly even when you think you programmed everything correctly. Sometimes it's best to clear Director's cache to help optimize the way your movie performs. Try adding this to the beginning of your movies to give them the best opportunity to run correctly:

```
on startMovie
        clearCache
end
```

 This feature is different than clearing your browser's cache.

You never know why certain errors occur. This simple code gives your movie the best possible chance at playing back correctly since it is starting with a clean slate.

SUMMARY

There is so much you can do with the power of Lingo and Lingo-loaded behaviors. There are people who can build almost anything with Lingo. It's all a matter of understanding the principles of the language and applying the correct commands to get your Director or Shockwave movie to perform the way you want it to work. This chapter showed you some advanced concepts from a functionality perspective. Remember, even if you use behaviors, there's usually a great deal of Lingo coding running in the background. Someone just took the time to write it all for you. Build your own behaviors. Write your own Lingo commands. Have fun with it and truly add life to your movies.

chapter 10

IT'S ALL
FINISHED ...
NOW DELIVER IT

Once you have finished creating all of your images, importing your files, and animating your sprites, it's time to show the world your movie ... well, almost. There are a few things that you should be aware of to get your Director movie to the end-user in the best way. Right now, your raw Director movie (.DIR file) is inherently cross-platform-compatible (that is, with Director). This means you can take any Director movie you have created and open it on any system that has Director installed on it. Whether you built your movie on a Windows-based platform or a Macintosh-based system, Director movies can open on either platform. Be aware, however, that movies that link to files that are platform-specific (such as .AVI digital video files) will not be able to play on the opposite system.

You can open movies created on the same version automatically. Movies created in a lower version (6 or 7) should be updated and saved when bringing them into Director 8 (Figure 10–1).

PREPARE YOUR MOVIE
FOR DISTRIBUTION

Distributing your Director movie "as-is" requires the end-user to have a compatible version of Director installed on his system. Obviously, the majority of your viewing audience will not have a copy of Director on their systems. Distributing your original Director movie in this format is also not recommended. People who do not have

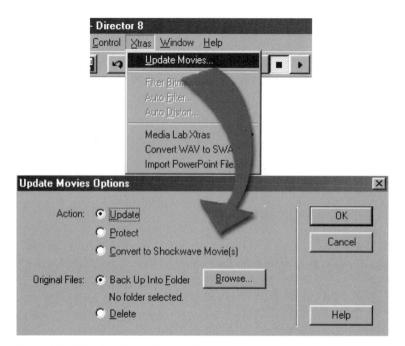

Figure 10–1 Use the Update Movies feature found under the Xtras menu to bring older Director movies into the latest version.

Director will not be able to play your movie. People who do have Director will be able to open your files and make changes to them. This can lead to many serious problems down the road. This chapter describes the best solutions for finalizing and distributing your movie to end-users.

Most of the concepts covered in this chapter discuss the options you have with your finished movie. These concepts should be considered during the developmental phase of your project, not just when your movie is complete. Pre-planning some of these steps will ensure the best results with the fewest headaches in the end.

TEST YOUR MOVIE

Do not wait until your movie is complete before deciding to test your application to make sure everything is functioning properly. One of the worst feelings you can experience while authoring a program is to have it not work when you think you are done. Testing is immensely important if you are designing applications to run on both Windows and Macintosh platforms. Throughout the process of your development, continually check that the files and functions work properly on both systems. As you import files, make sure graphic images appear correctly and that digital media files play the same way inside Director as they do outside Director (Figure 10–2). If not, bring your files back into their respective editing applications and see if they look or play correctly there. It's possible to have files corrupted while being compressed, converted, or transferred between locations. Another reason to test your movies often is to make sure external files do not lose their links with their associated cast members. Many times, externally linked files are moved to different locations on your system and Director is unable to match up the proper links. If you move external files, you must relink or re-import these files back into your Director movie. If you do not recreate these links before you play the movie, a window will appear, prompting you to manually select the location of the unlinked file (Figure 10–3).

Figure 10–2 Cast member image will show whether or not a graphic file has been imported properly.

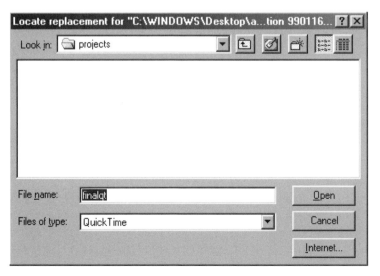

Figure 10–3 A "Where is…" dialog box appears if Director has lost its link with an external file.

Testing your movies regularly can be very crucial when you begin to develop applications that will be delivered via the Internet. Here you will not have the same control over knowing which platform the end-user will be viewing your program on, let alone the performance level of that system. That is why it is so important to test frequently on multiple types of machines and keep track of how your movie performs on each system. For more information about creating your movies for the Internet, check out Chapter 11, "Shock It for the Web."

SYSTEM REQUIREMENTS FOR PLAYBACK

Every movie you create and distribute should contain some basic information (either on the packaging or as a readme file) for the end-user to review before trying to start your application. This information will probably vary for each project you create based on the size of the program and the type of media it contains. If you are using simple graphics and text created inside Director, you will be able to run this application on a low-end computer containing at least the following minimum requirements:

For Windows:

◆ 386/33MHz processor.

◆ 8MB RAM.

◆ Windows 95, 98, or NT 4.0 operating system.

◆ Enough hard drive space required to fit your project.

For Macintosh:

◆ 68030 processor.

◆ OS 7.0.

◆ 8MB RAM.

◆ Enough hard drive space required to fit your project.

These system requirements will hardly do any movie justice. I highly recommend increasing the specifications in all areas to the highest degree possible while still maintaining the system's lowest common denominator required by the end-user. Director is a memory-intensive program and functions much better with more RAM, faster processors, and more supportive peripherals. Advanced applications will probably require:

◆ Pentium (Windows) or PowerPC / G-series (Macintosh) processors.

◆ 16MB RAM or more.

◆ CD-ROM drive.

◆   High-resolution monitor.

◆   Graphics accelerator card with extra video RAM.

◆   Sound card and multimedia speakers.

◆   Any required software, plug-ins, or extensions (i.e., QuickTime).

The faster the system, the better performance you will experience when playing back movies that contain multiple animations of large-sized sprites and digital video movie clips.

DIFFERENT WAYS TO SAVE YOUR WORK

Saving your work is something that I do not believe I have to explain. I do, however, want to explain the different ways Director allows you to save your movies.

◆   Save.

◆   Save As.

◆   Save and Compact.

◆   Save All.

Each method provides a slightly different purpose when saving your Director movies. The Save feature works by adding new information to the end of an existing file from the last time it was saved, never actually deleting the placeholders of the unwanted information as new changes are made to your movie. This process takes very little time, but can actually increase the file size of your movie. This method is fine to use during the developmental stages of your movie (and I highly recommend doing this often), but use the Save As or Save and Compact command when saving the final version. Both of these methods rewrite a completely new file. The Save As command optimizes your file while allowing you to save the movie under a different name, replace the existing file, or move it to a new location. The Save and Compact command allows you to only replace the existing file, but goes inside to clean out any unwanted information. To optimize your movie:

1. Open your Director movie.
2. Select Save and Compact from the File menu. A progress bar will appear on your screen, indicating the clean-up process of your file. The smaller the file, the less time this process takes.

The Save All command allows you to save a copy of all of your files at once. This is a time-saving feature so that you do not have to select each window and save each cast singly.

Because Director only has limited undo capabilities, use the Save As function to make back-up copies of your movie before trying out a new feature. If you change your movie beyond a quick repair, delete the current file that got messed up and open one of the backup copies you saved to pick up where you left off before making the alterations (Figure 10–4).

CLEAN UP DIRECTOR MOVIES

Updating a Director movie is one way to optimize it to be used in the correct format and have the most up-to-date files. The Update Movies option allows you to convert older versions of Director movies and casts to the latest version you have on your system (e.g., from Director 6 and 7 to Director 8). It also cleans up your files to keep only the necessary files used in your movie, removing all unwanted information. Consolidating your movies using the Update Movies function also reduces the overall file size of your movies by eliminating any garbage information still lingering around in your fragmented movie files. To update a movie:

1. Select Update Movies from the Xtras menu.
2. Select Actions: Update from the Update Movies Option window.
3. Choose either to Backup Original File or Delete.
4. Click OK.

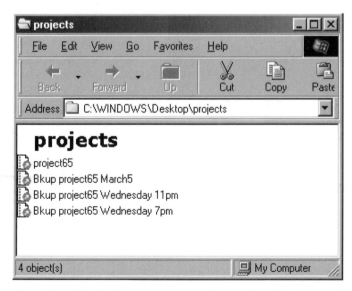

Figure 10–4 Use the date, time, or a version number when naming files to help identify the correct version.

5. Select the Director movie you want to update.

6. If you chose to back up original files, select a folder where you want to save the original files.

7. Click Continue to update and compact your Director movie.

You cannot save original movie files in the same folder as where you are saving the updated file. Director puts the updated file in the folder where the original movie was in order to keep all links to other files functioning properly.

CREATE A PROJECTOR FILE

A Projector file is a very small stand-alone application that you create from an original Director movie. The Projector file contains enough of the run-time codes to play your Director movie in a play-only environment without the need for Director to be installed on the end-user's system. Depending on the complexity of your movie, the Projector file may be the only file required for distributing your application to end-users. To create a Projector file:

1. Select Create Projector from the File menu. The Create Projector window appears.

2. Select the Director movie(s) and external cast(s) (if applicable) that you want to add to Projector file (Figure 10–5).

3. Click the Add button to transfer a filename to the File List window below.

4. If selecting multiple movies, use the Move Up and Move Down buttons to rearrange the order of the movies.

5. Optional: Click the Options button to further customize your movie. (See "Customize Projector Options" later.)

6. Click the Create button to make the Projector file.

7. Name the Projector file and save it to a location on your system.

When you open that folder, notice that a new Projector icon has been created with the name that you saved it as in Step 7 (Figure 10–6). Double-click on this file to view the play-only version of your movie. This is the packaged file of your application that you will distribute to the end-user.

Although Director movies are platform-independent, Projector files are not. To create a Macintosh Projector, you need to perform the previous steps using the Macintosh version of Director. To create a Projector capable of playing on a Windows system, you need to perform the same steps using a version of Director for Windows.

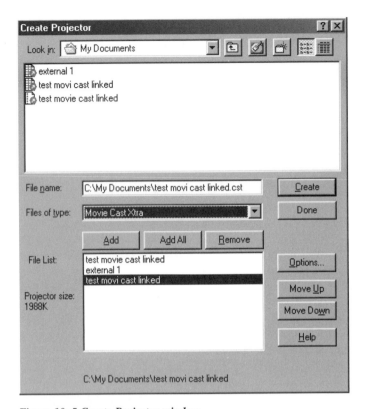

Figure 10–5 Create Projector window.

Figure 10–6 Projector icon.

CUSTOMIZE PROJECTOR OPTIONS

The Projector Options window contains the basic settings for determining how your movie will play back on the end-user's system (Figure 10–7). In this window, you have several different choices for optimizing your movie and determining how it will be displayed when the user launches the Projector application.

Director keeps the option settings from the previous project that you created with your last Director movie. Therefore, if you distribute your movies under the same general guidelines, you will only need to make these settings once.

Playback

Playback Every Movie is an option that tells the Projector to play every movie that was added to the play list (Figure 10–8). If you do not select this option when adding multiple Director movies to the list while creating a Projector file, only the first movie in the list will play. The only way to get the other movies to run is to have them launch from within the first Director movie via the playMovie Lingo command, which can navigate to each individual movie.

Rearrange your movies in the Playback List window to select the proper playback order. Place the movie you want to play first at the top of the list. The order that is displayed from top to bottom indicates the order in which the movies will play back.

Animate in Background is a feature that allows your movie to continue running even if the user switches to another application. If the option is deselected when creating a

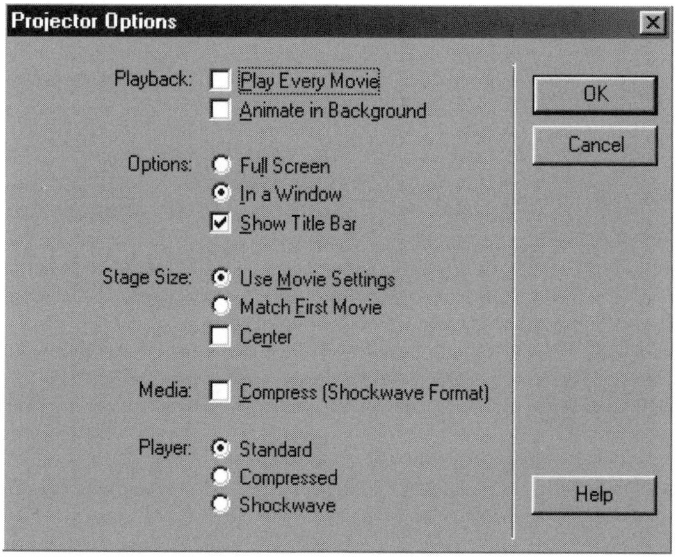

Figure 10–7 The Projector Options window.

Projector file, your movie will go into a pause mode when you select another application as the active window. The movie will continue to play when it is selected as the active window (Figure 10–9).

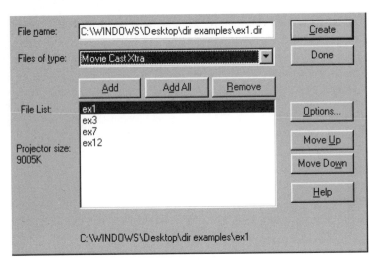

Figure 10–8 Add multiple movies to play back in the play list.

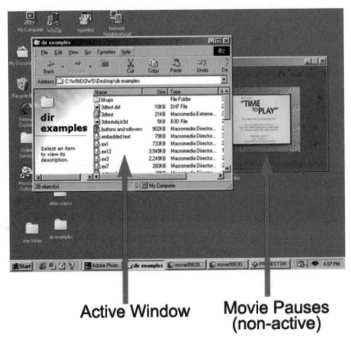

Active Window   **Movie Pauses (non-active)**

Figure 10–9 Director movie pauses if it is not the active window on the desktop.

The Reset Monitor to Match Movie's Color Depth is a Macintosh-only feature that allows your computer display to automatically adjust to match the color depth settings of the current movie. This function will adjust the color depth for each movie independently if you have added several Director movies to the play list. This ensures that the playback of all your movies and their images is displayed correctly.

Options

Full Screen is a very important feature to select. Most applications run covering the entire screen. If you set your monitor's resolution to be higher than the stage size of your movie, the user will wind up seeing parts of her desktop around the outside of the movie display (Figure 10–10). By selecting the Full Screen option, the Projector file fills the remaining visible portions of the screen outside the area used to display your movie with the color selected for the stage color. This will mask out and cover up any signs of the desktop display around the outskirts of your movie (Figure 10–11, also found in color section). If this option is not selected, your movie will play in a box with the desktop visible on all sides. This feature is referred to as In a Window.

 Displaying movies set to play In a Window will only play at the size of the original movie settings. These windows cannot be sized.

The Show Title Bar option is only available if In a Window is the current display setting for the movie. With this option selected, your movie will play back in a window that has a title bar attached to the top of the window (Figure 10–12). Use this title bar to reposition the playback window to a new location anywhere on your screen.

Figure 10–10 The desktop is usually visible around Projector files saved with the "In a Window" feature selected.

Figure 10–11 Full-screen display projectors cover the entire screen, regardless of resolution.

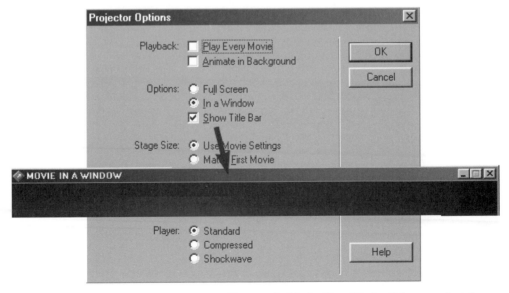

Figure 10–12 Adding a title bar to Projector files saved with the "In a Window" feature selected.

Stage Size

The next group of settings in the Projector Options window determines how to best display the size and position of your movies when you add multiple files to the playback list. Use Movie Settings adjusts how to display the stage size of your movie. This allows you to set whether a movie will take on the size of the current movie or whether it will use the size from the new movie.

The Match First Movie option affects the appearance of movies used in a multiple-movie play list. This function resizes and repositions all of the other movies listed in accordance with the settings from the first movie.

If you have problems with the appearance of all of the movies in your play list, double-check this setting. This can cause all of your movies to conform to the dimensions of your first movie's settings.

If the user of your application has his screen set to a higher resolution than the size of your movie, the Center option will automatically position your movie in the center of the screen (Figure 10–13). Otherwise, your movie may default to an undesirable position on the screen that cannot be changed once the Projector file has been created.

Media

The next section in the Projector Options window deals with compressing your movie and how best to play the compressed movie back. Select Compress (Shockwave Format) to compress the file size and movie data into a Shockwave format. For anyone to view this movie, they would need to have the Shockwave plug-in installed on their system. You can choose to include a player within the Projector file or reduce the file size by selecting Use System Player to use the Shockwave player.

Compressing your movie with Shockwave will reduce the size of the Projector file, but may increase the time required to open your movie as it decompresses.

You can also set the Player Type under the Projector Options window. The three choices include Standard, Compressed, and Shockwave. Selecting Standard will include the uncompressed player code in the Projector file. Since there is no compression, this will begin playing the movie the quickest out of the three options, but will conversely create the largest file size. The Compressed option will create a compacted version of the player, reducing its file size, but ultimately increasing the time it takes to start playing the movie. Selecting Shockwave creates the smallest file. This is because no player is included in the Projector file. For the end-user to view this movie, he will have to have the Shockwave player installed on his system.

If the user does not have an updated Shockwave player, she will be prompted to download the latest version.

Once you have selected all of the options for the movie:

1. Click Create in the Create Projector window.
2. Enter a new name for the Projector file.

3. Select the location where you want to save the Projector file.
4. Click Save.

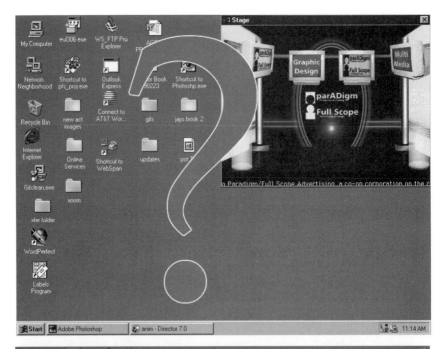

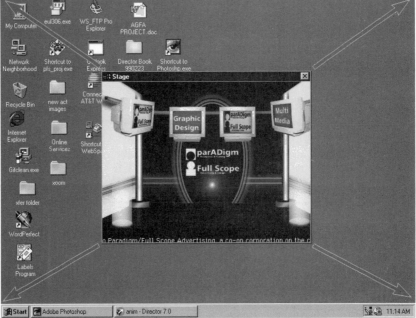

Figure 10–13 Comparison of movie playback positions on-screen.

Director will package the movie(s) that you added to the play list, the associated casts, and required Xtras and will create one Projector file.

 Moving Projector files to a folder that is different from where they were originally created can cause linked files not to be recognized. When the user goes to play the movie, they will be prompted to select the location of each external file.

CREATE SMALL MOVIES

A good technique to incorporate into your development skill set is to design several small movies instead of working with one large file. For example, create the main interface of your application as one movie. Have each button or link on the interface open a new Director movie via a Lingo command. Therefore, each subtopic would be reliant on its own independent movie (Figure 10–14). There are several advantages to packaging your movie in this fashion:

◆ Smaller files are easier to work with. The score for each smaller movie will be less cluttered than trying to work with all of your sprites in one giant score.

◆ Smaller files are easier to troubleshoot. You can make changes in your score more accurately without having to worry about altering another section of the movie. If something is not functioning properly, you can quickly narrow down the location of your errors.

◆ Smaller files will perform better, especially on low-end systems. The system's RAM will not be bogged down with unnecessary files. It will only need to load up the required information for the current movie.

◆ Smaller movies allow you to build your own library of Director movies. You can use these movies as templates if you ever need to reproduce the same functionality for another application without having to recreate it from scratch or wade through a lot of unwanted information contained in a single larger movie.

Director movies do not have a maximum file size. However, the larger you make a movie, the more potential there is for running into playback problems.

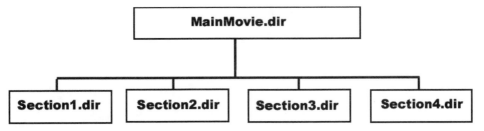

Figure 10–14 Schematic layout for individual subtopic movies.

THE BENEFITS OF CREATING TEST PROJECTOR FILES

One technique that will save you time when testing your movie during the entire development process is to create a stub or test Projector file to be used over and over again. This process will allow one Projector file to activate each movie you create, saving you the hassle of constantly creating new Projector files every time you want to test your movie. To create a test Projector file:

1. Name the movie you are currently developing "Movie1.dir."

2. Create a new Director movie.

3. Add the following Lingo command to Frame 1 of the Script channel (Figure 10–15):

```
on exitFrame
    go to movie "Movie1.dir"
end
```

4. Choose Save from the File menu.

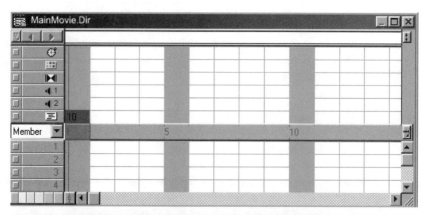

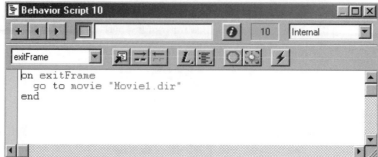

Figure 10–15 Creating a test Projector file.

5. Name the movie "Test.dir."

6. Save it in the same folder as Movie1.dir (Figure 10–16).

7. Choose Create Projector from the File menu.

8. Add the Test.dir movie to the playback list window (Figure 10–17).

9. Click Create.

10. Save the Projector file as "TestProj."

Now you have a Projector file that can be used for each movie you create and initially name Movie1.dir. As you keep saving your movie, this useful tip allows you to continually use this test Projector file (TestProj) to launch your application at any stage of the authoring process. Testing this way will ensure that your movie functions properly every step of the way. When you finish your movie, save your final Director movie under a new name using the Save As command and create a final Projector file for the movie.

PROTECT EXTERNAL MOVIES FOR DISTRIBUTION

If you are sending out movies that are external to the main movie contained in the Projector file, you probably do not want end-users to have the ability to open up your existing .DIR files and make changes to your movie, steal your images, or copy your custom Lingo codes. Protected Director movies play back exactly the same as the original movies but do not allow you to open them back up in Director to edit the files. Once you create a protected movie, it is displayed with a new extension (.DXR). To protect a movie:

Figure 10–16 Place Test.dir and Movie1.dir in the same folder.

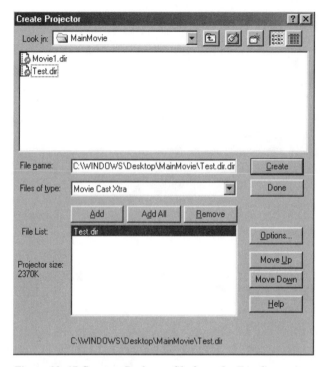

Figure 10–17 Create a Projector file from the Test.dir movie.

1. Open Director.
2. Select Update Movie from the Xtras menu.
3. Select Protect from the Update Movies Options window (Figure 10–18).
4. Select the Director movie you want to protect (original .DIR files only).
5. Click the Proceed button.
6. Select the folder where you want to save and back up the original raw file. You must select a different folder than the one containing the protected file. An error message will prompt you if you try to save the backup and the protected files to the same location (Figure 10–19).

You can choose to delete the original file and save only the protected file by selecting Delete from the Movies Options window. I strongly recommend saving a backup copy of your original file just in case you need to add anything to it or make any changes. Otherwise, you will need to start over from scratch.

Open up the folder to verify the location of the protected file. Launch the file to make sure it was saved correctly. The .DXR files are displayed differently in the folder than regular .DIR files (by icon). These files cannot be opened by Director and can only be played by a projector. All of the information required to open and edit these files is stripped away.

You can also protect externally stored casts using the same process. These protected cast files are saved with a .CXT extension (Figure 10–20).

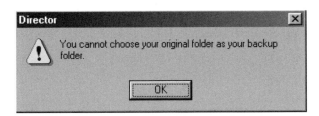

Figure 10–18 Update Movies Options window.

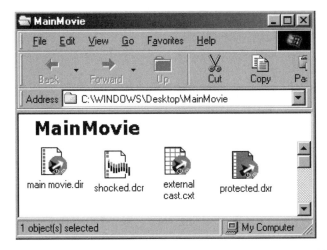

Figure 10–19 Error message warning you that you cannot save the original file in the same place as the protected file.

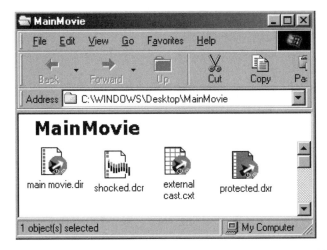

Figure 10–20 Protected files are saved with their own unique file extension.

When using a Lingo call to open up another movie after you have protected it, be sure to specify the exact filename and extension. Director will not differentiate if you want to open a .DIR, but only have a .DCR file saved.

Protected files are uncompressed and therefore open faster than files saved as Shockwave movies.

SAVE AS SHOCKWAVE MOVIES

One way to distribute your movie is to save it as a Shockwave file. Shockwave movies are saved with a .DCR extension. There are both advantages and disadvantages associated with saving your movie this way. One reason to save a movie as a Shockwave file, commonly referred to as "shocking" the movie, is to compress the overall file size of the movie for distribution over the Internet or on floppy disk (Figure 10–21). Another reason is to protect the movie so that end-users cannot open it up and make any alterations to your original files. The downside is that Shockwave movies are compressed to reduce the overall size of the file and will take a bit longer to initially open the file. To learn more about working with movies using Shockwave, see Chapter 11, "Shock It for the Web."

WHICH FILES TO INCLUDE

When you begin to distribute your movies, depending on how you created them, you will probably need to include more than just the Projector file. Distributing a series of files is typical, especially when your movies become more complex (Figure 10–22).

When you go to package your finished movie, you must be aware of which files are necessary to distribute to the end-user. Some projects require that you only provide a Projector file, while other projects require a whole slew of files in addition to the Projector. If you are creating applications for stand-alone purposes (CD-ROMs and kiosks), one thing that you will almost always need to include is a Projector file, the executable application that runs your program. You must also include any linked media files. This includes all files that were stored externally from your Director movie, like graphics, audio files, and digital video files. All external movies should be kept in the same folder as the Projector

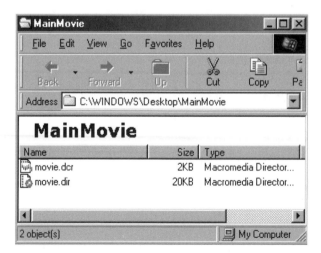

Figure 10–21 Shockwave movies are much smaller in file size compared to the original Director movies from which they were created.

Figure 10–22 Complex Director applications will require many supporting files to be distributed in order to run properly on the user's system.

file or in a folder inside the folder that the Projector file is in (Figure 10–23). If any one of these external links is changed or broken, the users will be prompted with a "Where is...," the particular file dialog window that appears when they go to play the movie for the first time and try to recreate the link (Figure 10–24). If your project includes external casts, these files must also be included in the packaged version.

Depending on the complex features used during the development of your movie, the Xtras folder is automatically bundled internally into each Projector file. If you use any third-party Xtras, you will need to include a copy of the Xtras folder with the rest of the movie's files to have the movie play back properly. One of the main things to include is any external Director movie that is being called from the main Director movie.

Another file to include for Windows platform Projector files is the Lingo.ini file. The Lingo.ini file is a text file that contains information about which Xtras, XObjects, and .DLL files need to be loaded to play back this Projector file on a Windows system. Therefore, it is important to include this file in the same folder with your Projector file.

Including externally linked files is crucial, whether they have been compressed, protected, or left in their original state.

Figure 10–23 All external movies should be saved in the same folder as the Projector file.

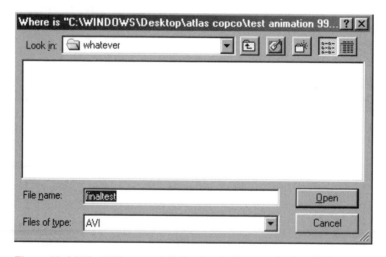

Figure 10–24 The "Where is..." dialog box indicates a broken link to an external file.

TRAS

Every time you create a sprite that requires the use of an Xtra, Director automatically adds it to the list of necessary Xtras in the Movie Dialog window. If you use any Xtras during the development of your movie, it is important to include the Xtras with your

Projector file. The end-user must have these Xtras present on her system to view the movie properly, if at all. If you do not distribute a copy of the Xtras along with the Projector file, your movie will not play back the way you intended it to play. To see which Xtras you used during the development of your movie:

1. Open a Director movie.
2. Select Movie from the Modify menu.
3. Select Xtras.

The Movie Xtras dialog box appears (Figure 10–25). This window shows a listing of all the Xtras that are used by Director movies. The easiest thing to do is to automatically have Director create an Xtras folder for you that includes these Xtras. Having all of these files assures that your movie will play back without any problems. On the other hand, having all of these Xtras available increases the size of your Projector file. Obviously, you may not need all of these Xtras for your movie. To minimize the Projector file's size:

1. Select the unnecessary Xtras from the Movie Xtras dialog box (Xtras not being used in the current movie).
2. Click the Remove button to remove these from the list of Xtras you want to distribute.

To have Director analyze your movie for required Xtras when you are finished building your program:

1. Choose Create Projector from the File menu.
2. Open up the Projector Options window.
3. Select Check Movie for Xtras.

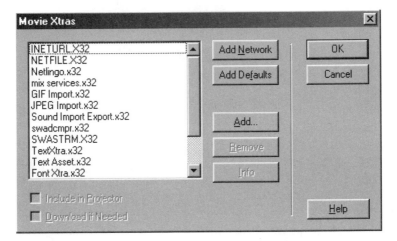

Figure 10–25 The Movie Xtras dialog box lists all the Xtras used in a Director movie.

When creating Shockwave movies, choose to have the required movie's Xtras downloaded when decompressing the application from the Web.

INSTALLATION PROGRAMS

When you are finished creating your Director movie, Projector file, and protected files, it's time to distribute the program to your end-users. Generally, you will not want to send out a CD-ROM containing a folder of the files and make the user copy it onto her system. Like most CD-ROMs you purchase, the program should contain some type of setup or installation application. Director does not have the capability to create one. You must use a third-party program to create this setup file that will automatically install all of the required files onto the end-user's system. One program that I use to create installation programs for Windows-based applications is Setup Factory 4.0 by Indigo Rose Corporation. To find out more information about this product, check out their Web site at www.indigorose.com.

Most third-party installation programs can create a guided wizard that will help the end-user properly install your program on her system with just a few clicks of the mouse. You can set up the wizard's screens to give your program a customized look and feel (Figure 10–26).

To create an installation program for your Director project:

1. Open Setup Factory or an equivalent program.

2. Select the name for your program.

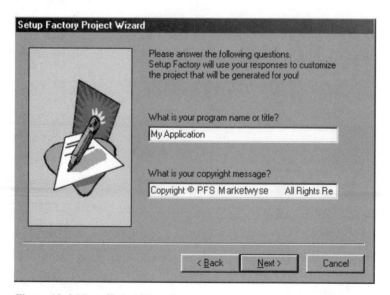

Figure 10–26 Installation Wizard screen.

3. Choose the file or folder you want to add to the installation program (Figure 10–27).

4. Select the destination where you want the application to be installed on the end-user's system.

5. Customize the appearance of the wizard by choosing which screens appear during the installation process and how they look.

6. Compile all of the selected files to create the actual installation file (setup.exe; Figure 10–28).

AUTOSTART FOR AUTO LAUNCH

Another popular feature to include when distributing the final version of your movie is to have the executable file automatically launch once the computer recognizes the file from the media disc it is on. That is, once the computer scans the disc, the autostart program quickly launches the application. This allows the program to be launched with fewer errors by the end-user and adds to the likelihood that the application will be viewed. I personally have used another Indigo Rose Corporation product called Autostart to implement this. It takes only a few seconds to walk through the setup screens to save your movie with the autostart feature.

CREATE SCREEN SAVERS

One of the more creative and interesting ways in which to distribute a Director movie is in the form of a screen saver. There are third-party programs that allow you to convert your normal Director movie into a screen saver format. Programs such as CineMac Screen Saver Factory by MacSourcery take your movie and convert the files into the

Name	Source	Destination	Package	Size	Icon
movie990307.dir	c:\windows\desktop\dir ex...	%AppDir%	None	1253128	No
Projector.exe	c:\windows\desktop\dir ex...	%AppDir%	None	3634408	Yes

Ready   Files = 2   Bytes = 4887536

Figure 10–27 Select the files that will be included in the installation program.

Figure 10–28 Double-click the Setup icon to install the program.

proper structure necessary for creating a screen saver application. Director comes with a demo version of CineMac on its CD-ROM. For more information about this program, check out the MacSourcery Web site at www.macsourcery.com. CineMac does all the work for you behind the scenes. Use its wizard to walk you step by step through the process of turning your movie into a screen saver file (Figure 10–29).

Figure 10–29 CineMac Screen Saver Wizard.

Note To create a screen saver to run on a Windows platform, just like Director, you need to use the CineMac version for Windows. To create a version to run on a Macintosh system, you need to convert your file using the CineMac version for Macintosh.

To create a screen saver version of your movie:

1. Launch the program.
2. Select Convert Projector from the File menu.
3. Select which Projector file you want to make into a screen saver program.
4. Click OK. A window will appear, indicating that the screen saver file has been created successfully.

There are several options to consider when designing an application to be used as a screen saver. The most common screen savers play a non-interactive movie that animates on your screen when the computer is not being used for a period of time. The screen saver is disabled when the user moves his mouse or presses any key on the keyboard. To create this option, you need to set a few script commands back in your Director movie.

Enter the following movie script to have the program quit when the mouse is activated or a key is pressed:

```
Global gMouseH, gMouseV - position of mouse at
        —movie start
on startmovie
    put the mouseH into gMouseH
    put the mouseV into gMouseV
    set the keyDownScript to "quit"
    set the mouseDownScript to "quit"
end startMovie

on enterframe
    if (the mouseH <> gMouseH or the mouseV <> gMouseV) then
    quit
    end if
end enterframe
```

To have your cursor disappear while the screen saver is running, use the following Lingo command to hide a cursor:

```
on startMovie
    set cursor = 200
end
```

This Lingo code will make your Director movie quit any time you move your mouse or press any key on the keyboard. It is very hard to develop programs when they are set up to keep quitting on you as you are playing your movie. Therefore, do not add these Lingo scripts until after you have designed the content of your movie. When you are satisfied, add the script just before creating a Projector file.

Follow the specific instructions that come with the screen saver conversion software you choose on how and where to install your screen saver application. Keep the file size of your screen saver movies small so that any system will be able to play the application smoothly. Small file sizes will also help with distribution methods, particularly from floppy disk or downloadable from a Web site.

Interactive Screen Savers

You can add interactivity to your screen saver, but then you will also need to add a Quit or Exit button for the user to leave the screen saver and return to her regular program. To create a screen saver with interactive options:

1. Create an interactive movie as normal.

2. Add a Quit or Exit feature using either a behavior or Lingo script (Figure 10–30, also found in color section).

   To use a behavior:

   A. Select a sprite.

   B. Open the Behavior Inspector.

   C. Create a new behavior.

   D. Select on mouseUp from in the Events column.

   E. Select Exit from the Action column.

OR

Figure 10–30 Add a Quit button to any screen saver that allows user interactivity.

To use a Lingo script:

A. Create a movie script.

B. Type in the following command:

```
on mouseUp
    quit
end
```

C. Create a Projector file.

D. Use CineMac or another application to convert your movie into the screen saver format.

Web Page Links From Screen Savers

Another screen saver option becoming popular as a tool for promotional and advertising applications is for a company to create and distribute a screen saver that links to their Web site when a certain action takes place (e.g., the logo on the screen is clicked; Figure 10–31). To add this feature to your screen saver:

1. Create an interactive movie as normal.

2. Add the following Lingo script:

Figure 10–31 Use any object or image on the screen, such as a logo, to link to the Web.

```
on mouseUp
   go to netPage "URL"
   — example: "http://www.pfsnewmedia.com"
end
```

3. Create a Projector file.

4. Use CineMac or another screen saver application to convert your movie into the screen saver format.

EXPORT DIRECTOR MOVIES AS QUICKTIME MOVIES

When you choose QuickTime as your format from the Export window, you have a number of choices to select from to customize the playback quality and other characteristics of your movie file. To access these parameters, click the Options button from the main Export window (Figure 10–32).

The Tempo setting exports your movie using the frame rate you set in the Tempo channel as a QuickTime movie setting. The Tempo setting determines the number of fps in the QuickTime movie. The faster the tempo, the more fps, and vice versa. Therefore, the final size of the QuickTime movie is ultimately determined by the:

1. Tempo settings.

2. Transition speeds.

3. Palette transitions.

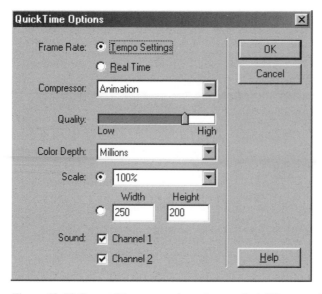

Figure 10–32 Export Director movie options as QuickTime movies.

The Real Time setting exports your movie as a QuickTime file at a rate that matches the performance of your Director movie. Each frame in your Director movie becomes one frame in the QuickTime movie. Playback problems can occur with how your movie was initially intended to look due to Lingo scripts, however. Test your movie with all Lingo scripts off to see how your movie performs before choosing the Real Time option.

Whichever setting you choose, you will still want to select a compression format to help reduce the file size of your movie. The compression format you choose will determine the playback quality of the movie. Use one of the standard compressors to set the different playback options, including size, sound track, and image quality of your movie. See Chapter 8 to get a more detailed explanation of digital video compressors and decompressors (codecs).

 Externally linked files are not included in the exporting process to QuickTime. Sound files set to loop will not loop when exporting to QuickTime.

EXPORT YOUR MOVIE AS A DIGITAL VIDEO FILE OR BITMAPPED FILE

Director allows you to export your movie, in whole or in part, as a digital video file. If you are working on a Macintosh system, you can export your Director movie as a QuickTime movie (.MOV). If you are working on a Windows system, you can export your movie as a QuickTime movie (.MOV) or a Video for Windows file (.AVI). This way, you can import your current digital video movie into other applications or back into Director as a single cast member. There are, however, several drawbacks to this feature:

◆   You lose all interactivity.

◆   You lose all sound when exporting as a Video for Windows file.

◆   You cannot control the frame rate for playback anymore.

◆   Any sprites animated by Lingo commands are lost.

You can also choose to export a series of frames or an individual frame from your Director movie. Director will output a BMP file on a Windows system and a PICS, PICT, or Scrapbook file on a Macintosh system.

Director takes snapshots of the stage, frame by frame, and puts them together to form the video file. This is why Lingo-activated sprites are not exported.

To export a Director movie as a digital video file or as a series of bitmapped files:

1.   Open a movie in Director.

2.   Select Export from the File menu. The Export window appears (Figure 10–33).

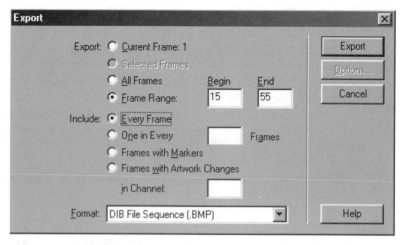

Figure 10–33 Export window.

3. Choose one of the export options:

   A. Current Frame—Exports the current frame displayed on the stage.

   B. Selected Frames—Exports a series of frames selected in the score (Figure 10–34).

   C. All Frames—Exports the entire movie.

   D. Frame Range—Exports a series of frames between a beginning frame number and ending frame number that you enter.

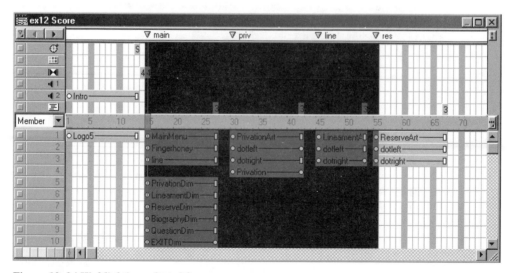

Figure 10–34 Highlighting selected frames to export.

4. Select one of the following options if you chose Selected Frames, All Frames, or Frame Range as your export choice. (Note: These options do not apply to digital video files):

A. Every Frame—Exports all the frames in a selected area.

B. One in Every ___ Frames—Exports only one frame per interval that you set (for example, One in Every 5 Frames).

C. Frames with Markers—Exports only the frames indicated with a marker (Figure 10–35).

D. Frames with Artwork Changes in Channel—Exports a frame each time a sprite changes in a given channel (Figure 10–36).

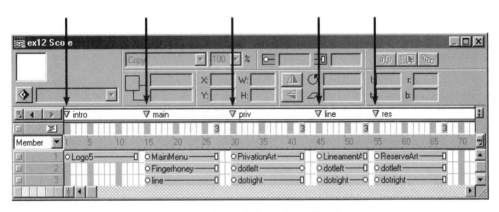

Figure 10–35 Export a bitmapped image for each frame identified by a marker.

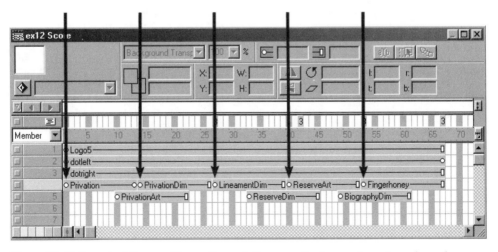

Figure 10–36 Export a bitmapped image for each time a sprite changes in a given channel.

5. Select a file format type from the popup menu located at the bottom of the Export window. The choices depend on which platform you are working on: BMP (Windows), Video for Window (Windows), QuickTime (Windows and Macintosh), PICT (Macintosh), PICS (Macintosh), and Scrapbook (Macintosh).

6. If you are exporting QuickTime digital video files, click the Options button to set the parameters for the video file.

7. Once everything is set, click Export. If you have not previously saved the movie, a dialog box will appear, prompting you to name and save the file.

When exporting BMP or PICT file formats, Director automatically adds the corresponding frame number as it creates a new file for each frame being exported. For example, the first frame would have 0001 attached to the end of the filename, and so on (Figure 10–37).

MADE WITH MACROMEDIA LOGO

Macromedia's licensing agreement allows you to freely distribute a Projector file (a file that allows a movie to run without Director) to the end-user as long as you are not selling your applications. If you begin charging a fee for your programs, then you must follow the terms and conditions listed in the Macromedia licensing agreement:

◆ Every project you create and distribute must contain the Made with Macromedia logo somewhere in your movie and on the exterior packaging (Figure 10–38).

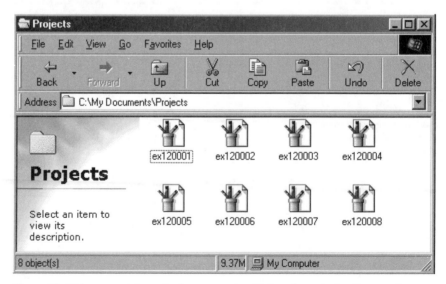

Figure 10–37 A sequential numbering system is added at the end of a filename for images exported from Director.

Figure 10–38 Made with Macromedia logo.

◆ You must sign a Macromedia licensing agreement for distribution.

◆ You must send two copies of your final project (packaging and all) to Macromedia.

If you have any questions regarding the Made with Macromedia distribution requirements, check out their Web site for the latest information at www.macromedia.com.

SUMMARY

This chapter pointed out the many different alternatives available to you as a developer preparing Director movies. As new technologies emerge, I'm quite sure Director will change to meet the distribution needs of new platforms and formats. Macromedia has come a long way with improvements for developing your movies, especially in the areas for Internet distribution. Check out Chapter 11 for more information on using and distributing your movies over the Internet. Be patient when finalizing your project. Trying to rush through it can lead to disaster. Failing to set one or two options can cause your movie to play incorrectly on the end-user's system. Good luck and take pride in your finished masterpiece.

SHOCK IT

FOR THE WEB

The overwhelming growth of the World Wide Web has created new ways for companies (and individuals) to advertise, educate, and entertain people on a global level. Today, Web addresses are more prevalent than street addresses. This new way of doing business has given birth to a whole new breed of programmers. Multimedia is not just being used by the radical companies out there, but by every type of organization imaginable. Capable of reaching millions of people around the world, the Internet has changed the way we communicate. Programs like Director allow you to build not just static Web pages, but highly interactive applications complete with layered graphics and animations that blow simple 3D frame-animated GIFs out of the water. The latest version of Director allows you to publish your work as a Shockwave movie and automatically write the necessary HTML documents directly from inside Director. Director 8 Shockwave Studio comes with all the tools you need to develop fully loaded applications geared for the Web.

Use the Publish option to turn your movie into a Shockwave movie. There is no need to compress your movies outside Director.

MULTIMEDIA'S EVOLUTION ON THE WEB

In the early days of the Internet (oh, some five or six years ago), multimedia applications were not able to run within a Web site browser as they do today. At best, most browsers supported animated .GIF files as a means of impressing viewers. As the limits of the Web were expanded, external applications and media-type players allowed you to download a file and view it in a separate window. Movie Player was used to display digital video files. Today, the boundaries of the Web have been once again broadened almost to an explosive state. The latest browsers come bundled with many of the most popular plug-ins and extensions, allowing you to incorporate interactive multimedia as the entire site or as part of the rest of the content of the page (Figure 11–1, also found in color section).

PREPARE A MOVIE FOR THE WEB

When starting from scratch, you should consider a different developmental process when designing an interactive movie for the Internet as opposed to your standard stand-alone media formats. This depends greatly on your target audience. Are you developing for Business-to-Business (B-to-B) applications or focusing on hitting a consumer market (B-to-C). Especially on the consumer side, keep in mind that the bandwidth, or speed at which information travels over the Internet to your computer, is typically much slower than any other platform you currently use to store or distribute interactive applications. The biggest complaint from viewers trying to access a Web site is the extremely slow connection speeds and long download times. There are a number of techniques you can incorporate into your development techniques to improve the way your movie looks and functions and decrease the time it takes to download your program.

Figure 11–1 Shockwave movie running inside a web browser.

◆ Stage size—The physical dimensions of your stage greatly affect the overall size of your movie. Try to keep the stage size down as much as possible for applications that will be accessible from the Web.

◆ Cast members—Delete any unused cast members from your movie. These files only add to the overall file size and increase the time it takes to download your movie.

◆ Vector images—When possible, use vector-based images over bitmapped graphics to reduce the size of the file. Vector images are computer-calculated images, not a series of pixels, which can be resized and reshaped without changing the quality of the image.

Having vector shapes animate in Director can actually slow down the playback of your movie. Use vector shapes created in Director for static images. Macromedia Flash is designed to animate vector images quickly, maintaining their small file size.

◆ Reduce color depth—There is very little reason to use 24-bit images on the Web. The sheer lack of widely available high-speed Internet connections means that most users have to wait inordinate amounts of extra time to see a higher quality image. There are a number of techniques, including transforming bitmaps and applying custom palettes, that can be used to get lower bit depth images to look exactly like their higher file-sized counterparts.

◆ Audio quality—Audio is a growing part of the Internet and intranet sites today. However, using lower sample rates for basic narration and musical pieces without a wide range of frequencies can dramatically reduce the file size of a clip without sacrificing too much quality.

◆ Video compression—Currently, Shockwave movies do not run digital video files. You must work with externally linked files. Due to the increasing demand for video on the Web, this drawback will quickly be changing, allowing you to include digital video files in your Shockwave movies. Digital video files for the Web require more compression and formatting than what is normally applied for CD-ROMs and kiosks.

◆ Streaming media—With the demand for faster access time to files, new technologies are emerging, allowing the user to either begin listening or viewing the content immediately or have it start playing before the entire file is downloaded.

WHAT IS SHOCKWAVE?

Shockwave is a technology that allows you to view Director and other applications in your Web browser (usually the format choice for distribution through the Internet due to the reduced file sizes). The ability to create Shockwave movies is commonly referred to as "shocking" a movie. Once the movie is shocked and posted on-line, Web users can then interact with the movie the same way as you would off a CD-ROM. Shockwave technology started off as an independent player that allowed you to view Director movies in a separate window. Like most things, Shockwave has become even more powerful. All you need is a simple plug-in that allows you to run a "shocked" Director movie in your browser. This is the same basic type of compression formerly used by the AfterBurner Xtra in early versions of Director, which has been incorporated as a part of Director's internal features for the past several releases. Shockwave is a type of application that allows you to play compressed movies (created by the Publish option under the File menu) from both stand-alone media formats or through the Internet. Shockwave technology is so powerful it is being incorporated into other programs for content distribution on the Web, including Freehand, Flash, Authorware, and xRes.

 Compressed Shockwave movies and uncompressed Director movies are cross-platform. Uncompressed Projectors file are platform-specific. Windows Projector files can only be played on a Windows system, and vice versa for Macintosh systems.

CREATE A SHOCKWAVE MOVIE

This will probably be the shortest section of this book. Director has made saving and creating Shockwave movies extremely simple. To create a Shockwave movie:

1. Open a Director movie.
2. Save the movie. Director will prompt you if you try to save a movie as a Shockwave movie without saving any changes made to your original movie (Figure 11–2).
3. Once the Director movie has been saved, select Publish from the File menu.
4. Name the Shockwave movie and click OK. Director will compress and compact the movie into the proper format and display it on your system as a Shocked icon instead of a regular Movie icon (Figure 11–3).

DIRECTOR ON THE WEB: THE PROS AND CONS

As you begin to develop a project, it is important to consider a number of factors that will make a difference as to whether or not you should develop your Director application for distribution via the Internet. Depending on the type of project you are working on, some of the following factors might affect your decision to develop a Web-based multimedia project.
    Advantages:

◆   Movies are accessible 24 hours a day.
◆   Cross-platform-compatible.

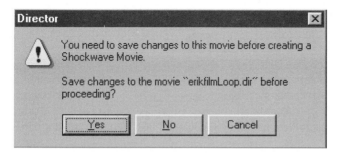

Figure 11–2 Warning to save the original director movie before being able to publish the movie.

Figure 11–3 Shockwave icon.

◆ Easy access from around the world (provided you are connected to the Internet).

◆ More interactivity capabilities and animated content than regular-style Web sites.

◆ Easy to update on a regular basis (at a fraction of the cost of re-burning new CD-ROMs for each time changes are made).

◆ Multiple, simultaneous user accessibility.

Disadvantages:

◆ Slow connection and access speeds.

◆ Bottlenecking and other bandwidth limitations.

◆ Interactivity and multimedia support limited compared to other types of media, such as CD-ROM and kiosks.

◆ File sizes need to be kept as small as possible by limiting physical movie dimensions, digital media, color issues (palettes), and quality of images.

◆ End-user may need to download plug-ins for browser.

SET YOUR SYSTEM'S DEFAULT BROWSER

Most computers today have at least one browser installed. Whether you prefer to use Netscape Navigator, Microsoft Internet Explorer, or another browser, check with each manufacturer to find out about any limitations that may exist with viewing Shockwave movies, especially with older versions of the browser software. If you have multiple browsers installed on your system, the first thing you should do is check to see which one Director recognizes as the system's registered browser. To check the path and application Director tries to open:

1. Select Message from the Window menu.
2. Type the command:

```
put browserName()
```

Director should return a new line, indicating the drive, path, and filename that it will use when it encounters a Net Lingo command (Figure 11–4).

To change the default browser or set a new path:

1. Select Preferences from the File menu.
2. Choose Network from the popup menu. The Network Preferences window appears (Figure 11–5).
3. Enter a path string in the Preferred Browser field.

   Windows example:

   ```
   C:\programs\netscape\navigator.exe
   ```

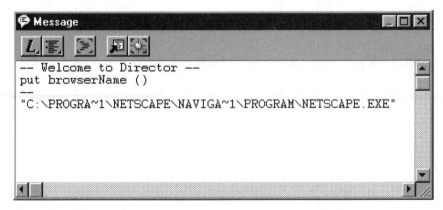

Figure 11–4 When you type put browsername *in a message window, it displays the drive and pathname to the default browser.*

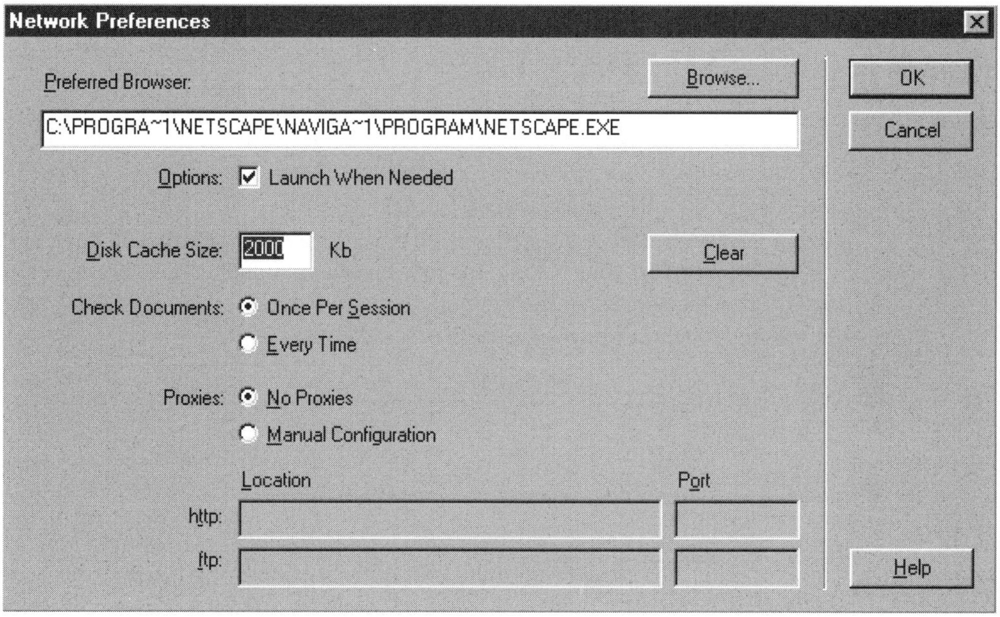

Figure 11–5 Network Preferences window.

Macintosh example:

```
Macintosh HD:Programs Folder:Netscape:Navigator
```

By setting the exact path for Director to follow from the drive name or partition to the exact executable application, Director can access that program as the default browser.

Be sure to check the Launch When Needed option for Director to effortlessly locate a Web browser.

EMBED MOVIES WITH HTML

Publish your movie as a Shockwave movie to run your application in a browser. The shocked file must first be embedded into an HTML document that is used to run the particular page being displayed. Director can even create the HTML page for you if you are unfamiliar with how to create an HTML document (Figure 11–6). To create a Shockwave movie and the HTML document in complete form:

1. Open the Director movie you want to compress into a Shockwave movie.
2. Select Publish Settings from the File menu. The Publish Settings window appears (Figure 11–7).

Director keeps the same name as your original movie because Director automatically adds the .DCR extension to the Shockwave version and an .HTM extension onto the file needed to display your movie in a browser.

If you are familiar with HTML coding and want to write your own HTML script, all you need to include is the following line to have your Shockwave movie appear in your browser when you launch a specific URL address:

```
<embed src="NameOf Movie.dcr"
```

Save your Shockwave movie in the same location as the original .DIR movie. This will help if you are linking to any external files.

NAVIGATE TO A WEB SITE

Just like Director can navigate to different sections within the same movie or open up a completely separate application, you can also give your movie the capability of linking to specific Web sites. You can add this functionality to any Director movie,

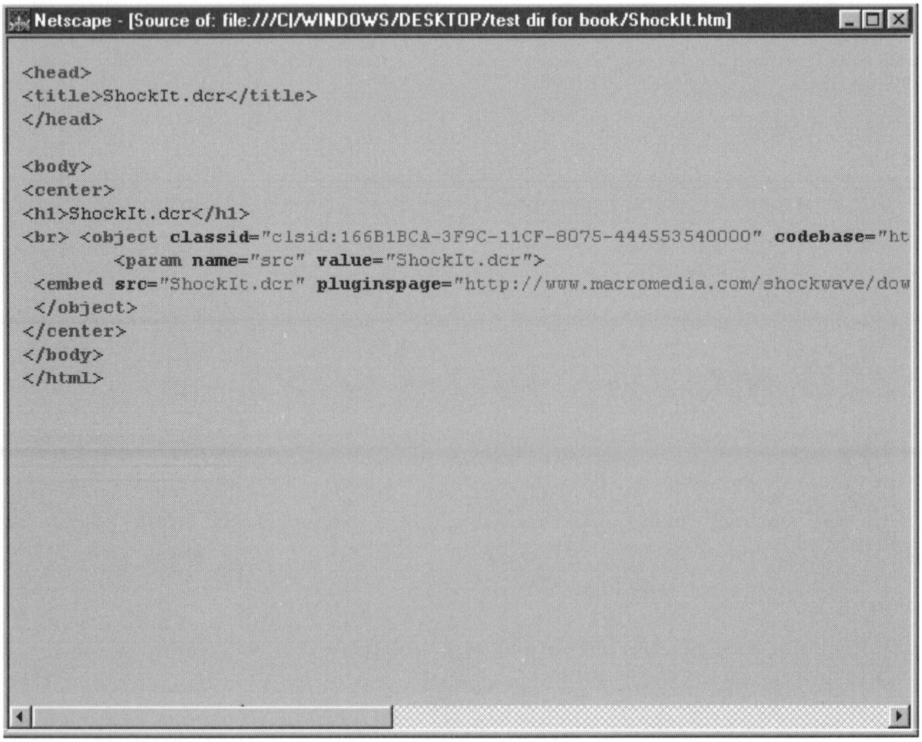

```
Netscape - [Source of: file:///C|/WINDOWS/DESKTOP/test dir for book/ShockIt.htm]

<head>
<title>ShockIt.dcr</title>
</head>

<body>
<center>
<h1>ShockIt.dcr</h1>
<br> <object classid="clsid:166B1BCA-3F9C-11CF-8075-444553540000" codebase="ht
        <param name="src" value="ShockIt.dcr">
 <embed src="ShockIt.dcr" pluginspage="http://www.macromedia.com/shockwave/dow
 </object>
</center>
</body>
</html>
```

Figure 11–6 HTML document created by Director.

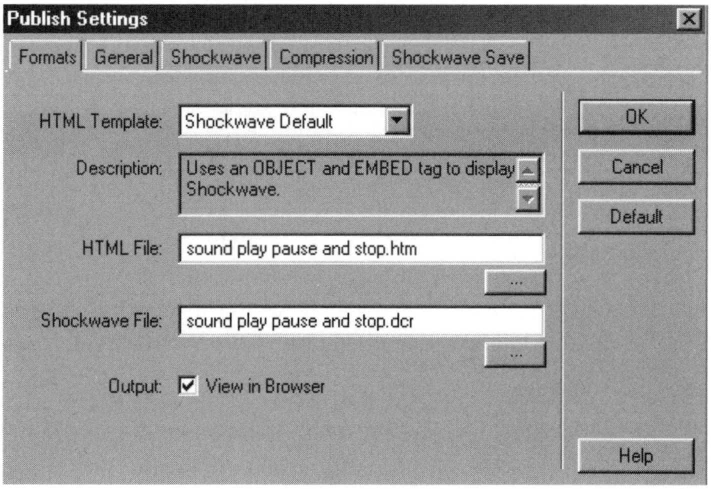

Figure 11–7 The Publish Settings window.

Projector file, or Shockwave movie. Through some simple Lingo commands or the use of behaviors, linking to a Web site is as easy as typing in the URL. For this feature to work, you must be on-line and connected to the Internet. Setting up this command will automatically open the browser that is installed on your system. If you are accessing the browser from a stand-alone application, you will automatically return to your Director movie once you close the browser.

To open a URL in the user's browser:

1. Using Lingo, enter the following sprite or frame script:

```
on mouseUp
    —enter any appropriate handler to activate the command
    gotoNetPage "URL address"
end
```

Using behaviors:

1. Select Library Palette from the Windows menu.

2. Select Navigation from the Library List menu.

3. Select the Go to URL behavior.

4. Enter the appropriate URL in the popup menu in the Parameters window (Figure 11–8).

Note If you have more than one browser installed on your computer, you can define which browser will become the system-preferred default browser (see the earlier section "Set Your System's Default Browser").

Figure 11–8 Use the Go to URL behavior to select a specific URL address to link to and from.

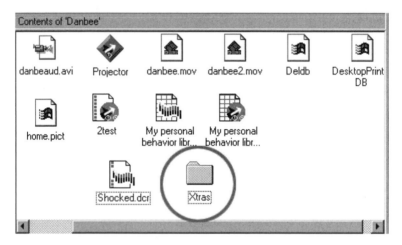

Figure 11–9 Include a folder containing any Xtras used in your project.

You will also need to include the Director Net Support Xtras if you are using Net Lingo in your movie. To make the appropriate Xtras available to your end-users:

1. Create a new folder in the same folder as your project.
2. Name it "Xtras" (Figure 11–9).
3. Copy any Xtras in your movie into this folder.

Do not use the Projector options Include Network Xtras and Check Movie for Xtras. They will not perform the same function and may not allow the user to view your movie.

Linking to a Web site can be of great use for many situations. One common feature is to have users access up-to-date help from the Web site. From the site, there might even be an e-mail link to contact someone for further assistance.

RETRIEVE SHOCKWAVE MOVIES FROM THE INTERNET

While playing a Director movie, you may want to open up and play a new Shockwave movie from the Internet. Using the `goToNetMovie` command allows you to play a new Shockwave movie in the same display area as the initial movie. You can use this command to access movies from either an HTTP or FTP server. To retrieve a Shockwave movie from a URL address, enter the following Lingo sprite or frame script:

```
on exitFrame
    —enter any appropriate handler to activate the command
    gotoNetMovie "http://www.thePageName.com/movies/movie1.dcr"
end
```

You can even choose to locate a marker within a given movie:

```
gotoNetMovie"http://www. PageName.com¬
/movies/movieName.dcr#markerName"
```

You must be connected through an ISP (Internet Service Provider) or have movies saved in a directory named DSWMedia on your local hard drive for testing purposes.

AUDIO ON THE WEB

In addition to adding interactive programs with animated scenes, you can also include audio in your Shockwave movies to give them more flare. For entertainment purposes, music and sound effects bring a silent screen to life. Narrative instructions make any training application that much easier to learn and the material more comprehensive. Shockwave audio is used to compress sound files, especially ones that will be transmitted over the Internet. Shockwave audio has become very popular as a streaming format, meaning it can start playing the beginning of the file before the entire file has been completely downloaded or decompressed. Director uses the Shockwave Audio Xtra to compress internal sound files. As with all types of compression, the higher the ratio, the lower the quality. Shockwave Audio (SWA) compression technology makes audio files smaller to access them faster from both stand-alone media or off the Internet. To have internal shocked audio in your movie:

1. Select Publish Settings from the File menu.
2. Select the Compression tab at the top of the Publish Settings window (Figure 11–10).
3. Select the checkbox for Shockwave Audio: Compression Enabled.
4. Select one of the Kbits/second choices (amount of compression) from the pull-down menu. This is based on the end-user's Internet connection speed.

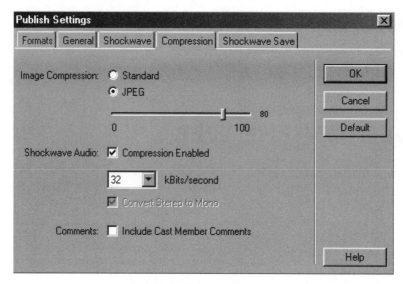

Figure 11–10 Shockwave Publish settings window.

5. Click OK.

To create external Shockwave files:

◆ Select Convert .WAV to .SWA from the Xtras menu (Windows).

◆ Use third-party applications like Peak LE 2 or Sound Edit 16 to export Shockwave audio files (Macintosh).

  Shockwave audio cannot compress the ever-popular MP3 file format.

Setting a bit rate of 48 Kbits/sec and lower automatically converts your sound file into mono.

You cannot test Shockwave audio inside your original Director movie. Audio clips are not actually compressed until a Projector file or Shockwave movie is made.

SHORTER WAIT TIMES WITH STREAMING MEDIA

Two topics that are sure to come up during a discussion of throughput on the Web are the limitations and lag times that accompany trying to move larger media files, such as digital video and audio files, over the Internet. The solution to this problem (besides everyone getting DSL or T1 lines in their homes) is to use the technology known as streaming.

Streaming media basically works by playing the beginning of a file before the entire file has been downloaded. Streaming gives the user the impression of instantaneous downloads by either displaying the first frames of a file or using a placeholder image. In other words, the media will start playing when the file has downloaded enough of the information to begin playing in an uninterrupted manner while the remainder of the file downloads. Director allows you to incorporate streaming audio files into your movie.

VIDEO ON THE WEB

Unlike audio files, downloading digital video files from the Web can take a good deal of time due to the size of the files. That's not to say that there are not ways of reducing file sizes to be optimized for Web distribution. Whichever compression settings you pick for your videos, streaming them can greatly reduce the long download times. To set up streaming digital video file options with your Shockwave movies:

1. Select Movie from the Modify menu.
2. Select Playback from the popup menu. The Movie Playback Properties window appears.
3. Click Play While Downloading Movie in the Streaming options (Figure 11–11).
4. Enter in the number of frames to download before displaying those images and begin playing your movie in the Download __ Frames Before Playing field.
5. Click OK.

Deselecting Play While Downloading Movie disables streaming and forces your movie to be completely downloaded before the digital video clip is started.

This will now cause your movie to be displayed almost instantly and begin to play while the remainder of the file downloads from the hosting server. The length and complexity of the movie and the speed of the modem to which you are connected will determine what percentage of the movie needs to be downloaded to play without getting hung up during the download.

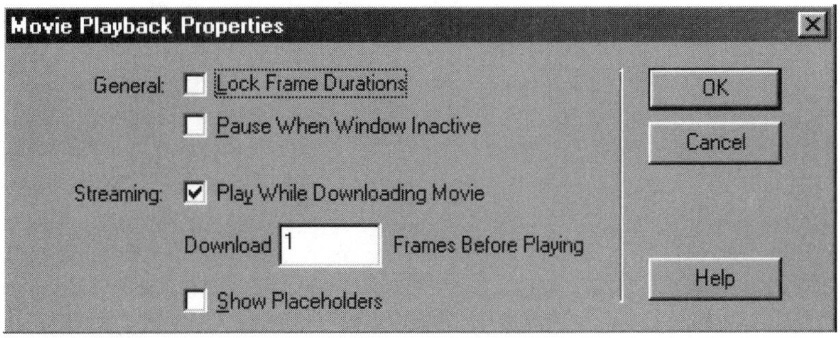

Figure 11–11 Movie Playback Properties window.

Currently, QuickTime 4 movies are supported through Shockwave for streaming. QuickTime 4 must be installed on your system to enable streaming for digital video media.

Due to slow download times with the Web, digital video files should be compressed as much as possible. You will not be able to get video playback at 15 fps unless the physical size of the file is smaller than a postage stamp. Programs such as Media Cleaner Pro by Terran Interactive are great tools to have if you plan to incorporate digital media in your Web site. Some tips to remember when working with digital video files for the Internet:

◆ Determine the average access rate of your user. Keep in mind that video will not look great coming over a 28.8k modem. A 56k modem is really the minimal speed at which to view a digital video file and still have it look like a digital video file (not a slide show).

◆ Reduce the number of fps in your clip. Standard video in the U.S. plays at a rate of 30 fps. Most CD-ROMs work at 15 fps. Web-based video clips probably run best at 5 to 10 fps.

◆ Reduce the physical size of your movie. Instead of working with a dimension of 320 pixels wide by 240 pixels high, drop down to 160x120 or smaller for better performance.

◆ Keep your clips short. Use only 10 to 15 seconds' worth of footage to keep download time to a minimum. If you really want to show more footage, provide a quick sample version (10 seconds long in a 120x90 pixel window) to view and then offer a larger version (30 seconds long in a 200x150 pixel window) to run as well.

◆ Have all of your videos set for QuickStart or Streaming options. This will display the first several images much more quickly than letting the user wait for the entire file to be downloaded.

DON'T FORGET THE PLUG-INS

You are probably already familiar with the term "plug-in" from working with Director's Xtras or other programs like Photoshop. Plug-ins are a group of players (or similar type application) required to be installed on the user's system to take advantage of viewing certain types of files in a Web browser. In essence, they add more functionality to a program, allowing a developer to expand the features available beyond the scope of the original program's capabilities. Plug-ins are also used for the Web to allow more complex applications and files to be accessible and functional. These types of plug-ins allow the viewer to experience QuickTime movies, VRML, Director movies, Authorware applications, Flash animations, Acrobat files, and more from the Internet. Some plug-ins now come standard with the latest browsers, while others need to be downloaded and installed on the user's system before being able to view these types of files. If you are adding a Shockwave Director movie to your Web site, you might want to provide a link to the Macromedia Web site (www.macromedia.com) so the user can quickly and easily download the latest version of the plug-in. The following are a few suggestions to help the user get the proper plug-ins and view your sight without any problems:

1. Create your Web page with a hypertext link to the plug-ins page for each company's Web site (Figure 11–12).

2. Provide instructions on your site about the steps the user should follow to download and install the proper plug-in.

3. Provide a copy of a plug-in if you are distributing a copy of your application on a CD-ROM or other stand-alone media. (Check the licensing agreements for permission before distributing copies of plug-ins.)

Because Shockwave has become such a popular and heavily used tool on the Internet, Shockwave plug-ins come as a standard feature when you install Netscape Communicator 4 or higher and Microsoft Internet Explorer 4.0 and higher on your system.

Figure 11–12 Hypertext links to other Web sites to download the necessary plug-ins.

If you provide a link to another company's site, I recommend you have it open in a new browser window. The advantage of this is that if the user begins hunting around or venturing off into new sites, no matter where they go, your browser window will still be open in a separate window when they close out of the second browser window.

ADD A LITTLE FLASH TO YOUR WEB SITE

Director allows you to incorporate vector-based Flash animations into your movies, whether you package them as stand-alone Projector files or Shockwave movies. The advantage to using Flash for movies geared toward Web site applications is that you can include some elaborate animations and some of Flash's programming capabilities while keeping the overall file size down to a minimum. This way, you do not have to sacrifice imagery to save on download time. Here are two ways to import a Flash animation into Director:

1. Build your animation in Flash and save it.
2. Open Director.
3. Select Import from the File menu. Import the Flash movie as you would any other file.
4. Select Cast Member from the Modify menu.
5. Select Properties from the popup menu.
6. Set the property values for the Flash movie.

   OR

1. Build your animation in Flash and save it.
2. Open Director.
3. Select Media Element from the Insert menu.
4. Select Flash Movie from the popup menu (Figure 11–13).
5. Click the Browse button in the Flash Asset Properties window to select the Flash movie you want to import from a fixed disk or click Internet to type in the URL address of the site to which you want to link (Figure 11–14).
6. Set the other parameters in the Flash Asset Properties window.
7. Click OK.

The variables that appear in the Flash Asset Properties window perform the following functions:

♦ The Linked media option stores the actual Flash movie as an external file. Deselecting this checkbox tells Director to make a copy of the movie and add it to the movie as an internal cast member.

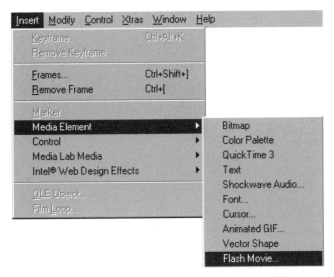

Figure 11–13 Incorporating Flash movies into your Director movies.

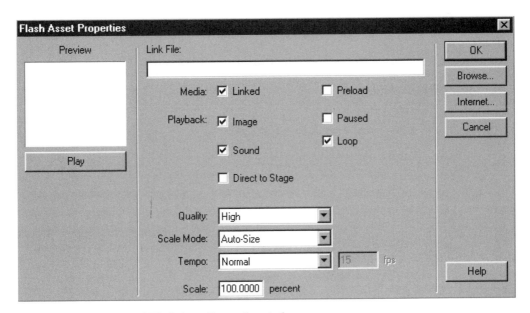

Figure 11–14 Flash Asset Properties window.

◆ Preload tells Director to load the entire movie into memory before beginning to
   play it. Otherwise, Director will begin playing the Flash animations as it is
   streaming the rest of the file.

- ◆ Image determines whether or not the movie is visible on-stage.

- ◆ Pause determines whether the movie starts out paused on the first frame or automatically begins playing when the playback head reaches the first frame of the sprite.

- ◆ Sound toggles any sound that was added in Flash on and off.

- ◆ Loop makes the movie start again from Frame 1 after it reaches the last frame. Deselecting Loop makes the movie play only once.

- ◆ Direct to Stage makes the Flash movie function like a digital video clip. If Direct to Stage is selected, your Flash animation will be displayed on top of all other images, regardless of which channel is placed in the score. If Direct to Stage is deselected, your Flash animation will have the same type of layering capabilities as any other sprite.

- ◆ Quality determines the appearance of your images. Setting the value to High will turn anti-aliasing on; setting the value to Low will turn anti-aliasing off. Using one of the auto settings will try to present the best quality image, but automatically switch to the other setting if Director cannot handle the frame rate at that quality.

- ◆ Scale Mode sub-menu choices determine how the movie is displayed on the stage.

  - – Show All keeps the aspect ratio of the movie and fills in any gaps with the movie's background color.

  - – No Border keeps the aspect ratio of the movie, but crops the image as necessary so as not to leave any borders.

  - – Exact Fit stretches the image to fill the dimensions of the sprite.

  - – Auto Size alters the sprite's bounding box to always fit the movie if the sprite is rotated or skewed.

  - – No Scale does not allow you to resize the sprite.

- ◆ Rate allows you to control the frame rate or speed at which your Flash movie plays back in correlation to your Director movie.

- ◆ Scale displays the size of the movie in percentages of its original size.

The Preload feature is only available if you select the Linked media option. Flash animations only play for as long as the sprite is in the score. This is similar to how digital video files work. Stretch the sprite to span more frames or use Wait for Cue Point to have Director play through the entire Flash animation before continuing to play the rest of the movie.

TIPS FOR OPTIMIZING YOUR WEB-BOUND MOVIES

There are always a few techniques that you can use to get faster download times, crisper images, and optimal results with your Shockwave movies. I encourage you to tell others about the tips you have discovered that make programming a lot smoother. (After all, we are all part of the same big happy family of Director developers.) The following is a brief list of suggestions, but there are many more:

◆ Reduce the color depth of your movie to 8-bit or lower.

◆ Design one optimal color palette or use as few palettes as possible.

◆ Reduce the size of your stage. Most Web-based movies do not need to run at 640x480.

◆ Keep the number of cast members down to a minimum. (Delete unused cast members from the movie.)

◆ For streaming movies, put your cast members in the order in which they appear so the Shockwave movie can download the cast members it needs to display first.

◆ Use short audio clips that loop (when possible) instead of long musical selections. Larger audio files lead to longer download times.

TEST YOUR "INTERNET" MOVIE

The most important process you can complete before advertising your site to the public is to test that the Shockwave movie functions correctly. To test the movie before going online:

1. Save your movie.
2. Select Preview in a Browser from the File menu.

Director compiles your movie and automatically opens your default browser, displaying your movie as a Shockwave file (Figure 11–15). This is done by creating a temporary Shockwave movie (stored in the RAM of your computer). When you are comfortable with the way your movie looks and operates in a browser, follow the simple procedures for publishing your movie for the Internet (outlined earlier in this chapter).

The next real test, once everything works well from your desktop computer, is to post it up on a server and view it off the Internet. From here, you will be able to tell whether all of your files are present and have been uploaded onto the server correctly.

Test downloading your movie from different modems to see the actual download times at the different data rates.

Frog Bog Beta Version 1.0

This game is for testing only. It is not fully functional.

You will need Macromedia Shockwave 8 to play this game.

Return to Main Index

Figure 11–15 Sample Shockwave movie displayed in a browser.

SUMMARY

There's no question that the Internet will be a major contender in the way information and entertainment will be channeled to millions of people worldwide. Its surge of popularity leads me to believe that people developing applications using Director will be able to transition into Web-based programming without any problems. Each version of Director that has been released has added more features and controls for developing for the Web. I'll bet that the next version of Director includes even more features geared for seamless Web integration. There's no reason why you can't have your movies up on the Internet today. Director 8 makes it possible.

INDEX